CISTERCIAN STUDIES SERIES: NUMBER TWO-HUNDRED FIFTEEN

THE BLESSING OF BLESSINGS

*Gregory of Narek's Commentary
on the Song of Songs*

CW01496193

CISTERCIAN STUDIES SERIES: NUMBER TWO-HUNDRED FIFTEEN

The Blessing of Blessings

*Gregory of Narek's Commentary
on the Song of Songs*

Translation, introduction and notes by
Roberta R. Ervine

Cistercian Publications
Kalamazoo, Michigan

First edition: *Srboy hōrn meroy Grigori Narekacwoy meknuĭun
Ergoc ergoyn Solovmoni*, Venice: i tparani srboyn Łazaru
(= San Lazzaro). 1789.

*The work of Cistercian Publications is made possible in part
by support from Western Michigan University to
The Institute of Cistercian Studies.*

ISBN 0 87907 215 5

Library of Congress Cataloging-in-Publication Data

Grigor, Narekats'i, Saint, 951–1003.
    The Blessing of blessings : Gregory of Narek's commentary on the
Song of Songs / translation, introduction, and notes by Roberta R.
Ervine.
        p.   cm. — (Cistercian studies) (Two-hundred fifteen)
    Includes bibliographical references and index.
    ISBN 978-0-87907-215-5
    1. Bible. O.T. Song of Solomon—Commentaries—Early works to
1800.   I. Ervine, Roberta R.   II. Title.   III. Series.

BS1485.53.G75   2007
223'907—dc22
                                                        2007038922

For Ruth

Truly, God's is a maternal love

Contents

Acknowledgments

I wish to take this opportunity to thank several people who have helped to make this volume possible.

To Robert W. Thomson, first of all, I owe many thanks, not only for the unassuming excellence of his scholarly example and the great work he has done in the field of Armenian patristics, but also for his encouragement in the publication of this particular translation.

I am especially grateful to His Beatitude Archbishop Mesrop II Mutafyan, Armenian Patriarch of Istanbul, for the wonderful gift of several secluded days on the island of Kinalada, during which the initial draft of the translation was produced.

And it must be said that without the curiosity and attention to detail of the students in a recent seminar on the Song of Songs at Saint Nersess Armenian Seminary, this volume would have lacked much.

Finally, the loving support of my husband Stephen has taught me more about the mystery of this text than any written source ever could.

Roberta R. Ervine

Saint Nersess Armenian Seminary
New Rochelle, New York

Abbreviations Used in the Notes

Agathangelos   Agathangelos, *History of the Armenians*, trans. Robert W. Thomson. Albany: SUNY Press, 1976.

Aristakēs   Aristakēs Lastiverts'i, *Patmut'iwn* [History]. Tiflis, 1912.

Asoghik   Step'anos Asoghik, *Patmut'iwn Tiezerakan* [Universal History]. Saint Petersburg, 1885.

Discourses   Gregory the Illuminator, *Girk' or koch'i Yajakhapatum* [The Writings Referred to as 'Frequently Related']. Istanbul, 1737.

Elishē   Elishē, *History of Vardan and the Armenian War*, trans. Robert W. Thomson. Harvard Armenian Texts and Studies 5. Cambridge: Harvard University Press, 1982.

Euringer   Sebastian Euringer, 'Ein unkanonischer Text des Hohenliedes (Cnt 8 15-20) in der armenischen Bibel', *Zeitschrift für alttestamentliche Wissenschaft* 33 (1913) 272–294.

Ghazar   *The History of Ghazar P'arpets'i*, trans. Robert W. Thomson. Columbia University Program in Armenian Studies: Suren D. Fesjian Academic Publications 4. Atlanta: Scholars Press, 1991.

Matean	Grigor Narekats'i, *Matean Oghbergut'ean* [Book of Lamentations], introduction by James R. Russell. Delmar, New York: Caravan Books, 1981.
Mkryan	M. Mkryan, 'Hay zhoghovrdi kazmavorman ev hay grakanut'ean skzbnavorman harts'ě" [The question of the Armenian people's formation and the beginning of Armenian literature], *Banber Erevani Hamalsarani* 1967/1, 29–56.
P'awstos	*The Epic Histories Attributed to P'awstos Buzand* (Biwzandaran Patmut'iwnk'), tr. Nina G. Garsoïan, Harvard Armenian Texts and Studies 8. Cambridge: Harvard University Press, 1989.
Tagher ev Gandzer	Armine K'yoshkeryan (ed.), *Grigor Narekats'i Tagher ev Gandzer* [Gregory of Narek, Taghs and Gandzes], Erevan, 1981.
Teaching of Saint Gregory	*The Teaching of Saint Gregory.* Edited Robert W. Thomson. Avant: Treasures of the Armenian Christian Tradition 1. New Rochelle, New York: St. Nersess Armenian Seminary, 2001.
Thomson, 'Number Symbolism'	Robert W. Thomson, 'Number Symbolism and Patristic Exegesis in Some Early Armenian Writers', *Handēs Amsōreay* 90 (1976) 117–138.
Thomson, 'Song'	Robert W. Thomson, 'Grigor of Narek's Commentary on The Song of Songs', *Journal of Theological Studies* 34 (1983) 453–496; rpt. in Robert W. Thomson, Studies in Armenian Literature and Christianity. London: Variorum, 1994.

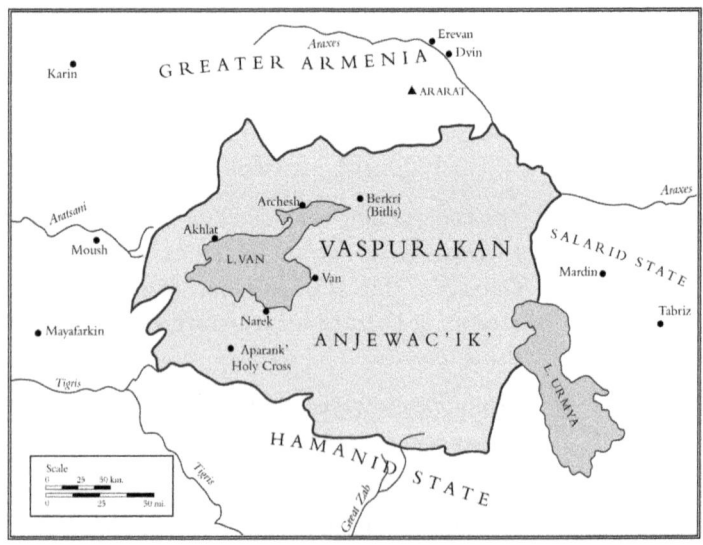

The Kingdom of Vaspurakan, 509-1021
Adapted from Robert H. Hewsen, *Armenia: A Historical Atlas.*
Chicago: The University of Chicago Press, 2001, 117.

Introduction

The Armenian tradition of *Song of Songs* interpretation is not extensive. Thus the work introduced here is all the more interesting for its rarity. Though universally acclaimed as being the work of the great Solomon, the problematic *Song of Songs* does not seem to have inspired among Armenians the same outpouring of monastic spirituality that it did in the West. But those who attained entrance to the inner sanctum of that Holiest of holies felt that they had indeed been made partakers in the *Blessing of blessings*.[1]

Gregory of Narek, to whose *Commentary on the Song of Songs* this volume is devoted, was the only one of the Armenian commentators, as far as we know, intentionally to share the *Blessing of blessings* with a secular audience. His own experience of 'our Mother . . . the Father Begetter, the omnipotent God' was a lifelong deepening in awareness of the ultimate intimacy and ultimate distance of the Parent who is at the same time also the soul's Spouse and Judge. The incarnation of the Word in Christ and of Christ in the Church, he felt, brought all humanity into the divine tension of that descending and ascending love, and Gregory experienced that tension both personally and on behalf

---

[1] As will be seen in the text, the phrase *Blessing of blessings* derives from the verses which are unique to the Armenian version of the Song of Songs; Gregory comments on these verses at the outset of his work. For more on these verses, see the section of our Introduction entitled "The Text of the Song of Songs employed by Gregory".

of the human race. He was rooted as firmly in the vast expanse of salvation history as he was in the soil of his own tenth-century life in an Armenian kingdom around Lake Van.

Fewer have read his *Commentary on the Song of Songs* than have read Saint Gregory's more famous poetic works, but a reading of the former does much to illuminate one's understanding of the latter. The spirituality whose basic lines are first drawn in the *Commentary* is the forerunner of the mature, complex spiritual expression in verse which has made Gregory of Narek one of the most revered figures in the Armenian Church's pantheon of saints. Poet, priest, monastic, and mystic as well as commentator, he was both a seer of visions and the inventor of a vocabulary in which to express them. In his poetic prayers, he showed that it is possible to speak with God both frankly and beautifully at the same time. His conviction that words are healing as well as expressive has been borne out in the medicinal uses to which his writings have been put across the millennium since they were written. His prayers are incorporated into the liturgy; his visions have inspired great music. Of his poetic work there are more copies and editions—manuscript and printed alike—than of any other original text in Armenian.

Although Gregory has proved to be a saint for all times and for several cultures, he was nonetheless very much a part of his own tradition, and a product of his own times and his own physical setting. Before turning to a consideration of his *Commentary on the Song of Songs*, therefore, something must be said concerning the context out of which the work and its author grew.

A Word on the General Background

As the first nation to have undergone, as a state, an official conversion to Christianity in the early years of the fourth century, Armenia has always felt a special connection to its Christian faith. Christianity became Armenia's official religion through the agency of people whose relationships were, initially, purely political. Persia and Armenia shared a common dynasty, that of the Arsacids. The backdrop for Armenia's christianization is the Sasanian overthrow of the ruling Arsacid dynasty in Persia. Armenia's greatest saint and the man responsible for its official conversion, Gregory the Illuminator, was the son of a Parthian who, acting on behalf of the Sasanian government, assassinated the Arsacid king of Armenia, Khosrov, and was himself killed shortly thereafter. King and assassin each left behind a young son. After certain vicissitudes of fortune, Khosrov's son Trdat succeeded to his father's throne. The assassin's son was raised in Cappadocia as a Christian. The story of how the two men's paths crossed—the one a convert to Christianity and the former a loyal client of the Roman Empire and persecutor of Christians—has become a national Armenian epic of mythological proportions. Gregory's return to Armenia, Trdat's discovery of Gregory's identity, Gregory's imprisonment by Trdat, and his subsequent emergence from an isolated pit to cure the king of mental illness (a story reminiscent of Nebuchadnezzar's humiliation in Daniel 4) set the stage for Armenia's state Christianity, and helped to determine that Christianity's orientation towards Cappadocia and thus towards the Roman/Byzantine Empire.[2]

---

[2] The state adoption of Christianity may have been earlier than was politic—Armenians have traditionally set the date of their christianization at 301, a time when the Roman policy of Christian persecution was still in force. This date has been debated, on various grounds. For an overview of the debate, see the foreword and introduction to Agathangelos. *History of the Armenians*, translation and commentary by R.W. Thomson. (Albany: State University of New York Press, 1976), and the introduction to Movsēs Khorenats'i, *History of the Armenians*, translated by Robert W. Thomson (Cambridge, Massachusetts: Harvard University Press, 1978). Comprehensive bibliography of the debates surrounding Movsēs, as well as of the literature on Agat'angeghos is to be found in Robert W. Thomson, *A Bibliography of Classical Armenian Literature to 1500 AD*, (Turnhout: Brepols, 1995). A recent, simple summary of Gregory the Illuminator's story is given in Michael B. Papazian, *Light from Light: an Introduction to the History and Theology of the Armenian Church*, (New York: SIS Publications, 2006), ch. 3. On the blend

Faith and politics were never far apart in pre-modern Armenia. Not surprisingly, then, faith has helped to precipitate many political events throughout Armenian history. Through all the vicissitudes of the national Church's more than 1700 years of existence, faith and ethnicity have traveled hand in hand, producing a unique, organic blend that comes near to being a seamless, if sometimes uneasy, whole.[3]

Classical Armenian literature—which covers everything written in the classical idiom from the fifth through the fifteenth centuries, and even beyond—is almost entirely clerical literature, and the overwhelming majority of it was produced in monastic settings. Study of this literature is still in its infancy, for a number of reasons, not least because of the lack of well-translated texts that would make these writings more readily available to people in other traditions

---

of Persian and Byzantine elements in Armenian thought and culture, see Nina G. Garsoïan, *Armenia between Byzantium and the Sasanians.* Variorum Reprints, Collected Series 218 (London: Variorum, 1985); eadem, *Church and Culture in Early Medieval Armenia,* Variorum Reprints, Collected Studies Series 648 (London: Variorum, 1999); Nina G. Garsoïan, Jean-Pierre Mahé and Robert W. Thomson, *From Byzantium to Iran: Essays in Honour of Nina G. Garsoïan.* Occasional Papers and Proceedings 8 (Atlanta: Scholars Press, 1997).

[3] Archbishop Maghak'ia Ōrmanian's three volume *Azgapatum,* still the most complete history of the Armenian Church, makes the union of church and state clear in its title, which can be translated roughly as *National History.* Published in Beirut in 1959–1961, it has since been reprinted and to it has been added a fourth volume which attempts to bring the history to the last quarter of the twentieth century. It has never been superceded, but it has also never been translated. There are, however, excellent studies of individual time periods, events, and personalities in the Church's development. See, for example, Nina G. Garsoïan, *Church and Culture in Early-Medieval Armenia.* Variorum Reprints, CSD 648 (London: Variorum, 1999). Ōrmanian's shorter work, *Hayastaneayts' Ekeghets'i (The Armenian Church)* appeared in French as *L'Église arménienne, son histoire, sa doctrine, son régime, sa discipline, sa liturgie, sa littérature, son present* (Paris, 1910) and has been translated into English (Brookline, Massachusetts, 1954). A series of essays covering a wide range of topics is in preparation by the Armenian Studies Program at the University of Michigan as the enhanced Proceedings of the conference *Where the Only-Begotten Descended: The Armenian Church through the Centuries,* Ann Arbor, MI April 1–4, 2004.

who have a longer, less interrupted, experience of patristic scholar-ship and related disciplines.[4] In its pages, and in those of Armenia's ancient sister churches' writings, we have a significant portion of the 'trunk', so to speak, which connects Christianity's Jewish roots with its modern branches. Without an examination of this 'trunk' the transition from root to branch cannot be adequately understood. As it grows and deepens, study of Armenian literature will inevitably make great contributions to an understanding of Christianity as a whole; all the more so as works of certain early Church Fathers which have otherwise been lost in their original languages have not infrequently survived in an Armenian version.

From the moment of the invention of the Armenian script in ca. 405, it was put to work in the service of the Armenian Church, whose interests at that time coincided largely with those of the Armenian State. The need to forge an independent Christian identity motivated the powers of both institutions. In the fifth century, Armenia's territory lay between the two great empires of Byzantium and Sasanian Persia. On the one hand relations between Armenia and Sasanian Persia were politically tense be-cause, as mentioned above, the Sasanians had been responsible for ending the Arsacid dynasty's rule in Persia, and a cadet branch of the Arsacids then ruled Armenia. Over and above the lingering political animosities of the dynasty, Christian sectors of Armenian society also resented the presence among them of adherents to the Persians' Zoroastrian faith.

Byzantium, on the other hand, was usually at enmity with the Persians, and too close an alliance with it would bring

---

[4] Events of the twentieth century damaged Armenian Christian studies to an extent that will take generations to repair. The century began with the genocide of Armenians living in the Ottoman Empire and went on to bring a portion of the Armenian homeland under Communist hegemony. Although many fine minds worked in Armenian scholarship at the cultural heart of Armenia, the study of theology and church-specific matters was not an avenue of research that could be pursued to any great degree until recently.

unfortunate repercussions from Persia. In addition, the exact color of Byzantium's Christianity was changeable; for example, as Arians and Orthodox succeeded one another on the Imperial throne, Armenian kings wishing to show loyalty to the Empire by maintaining the Emperor's Christianity found themselves at odds with hierarchs at home, for whom Arianism was not an option. Armenian hierarchs felt, too, that an overly close relationship with Byzantium's religious hierarchy would involve the Armenians in disagreements over doctrinal issues that were not necessarily germane to Armenia's own spiritual life. In short, Armenia needed to forge an identity which, ideally, would be neutral enough not to be unacceptable to either the Byzantines or the Sasanians, and which would give Armenians the opportunity to distinguish themselves from their neighbors without alienating them.

The alphabet, a tool in the forging of this identity, was invented by a civil servant turned scholar monk, Saint Mesrop Mashtots', who with the support of both the country's king and its catholicos enlisted a cadre of clerics like himself to research existing models, to refine the new set of symbols once it had been decided upon, and then to spread its use across the region.[5]

---

[5] The story of how Mesrop Mashtots' invented the alphabet is told by his disciple, Koriwn. A new English translation of Koriwn's *Life of Mashtots'* is in preparation by A. Terian. The story is also told, though in less detail, by Movsēs Khorenats'i in his *History of the Armenians*, translated by Robert W. Thomson. 3:52-54. See also P. Peeters, "Pour l'histoire des origines de l'alphabet arménien," *Revue des études arméniennes* 9 (1929) 203-237, and J. Marquart, *Über den Ursprung des armenischen Alphabets.* (Vienna, 1917); M. Mkryan, "Hay zhoghovrdi kazmavorman ev hay grakanut'ean skzbnavorman harts'ĕ" [The question of the Armenian people's formation and the beginning of Armenian literature], *Banber Erevani Hamalsarani* 1967/1, 29-56. A discussion of the alphabet's historical development, accompanied by rich illustrations, has recently appeared: Michael E. Stone, Dickran Kouymjian, and Henning Lehmann, *An Album of Armenian Paleography.* (Aarhus: University Press, 2002). Mesrop Mashtots' is also credited with the formation of an alphabet for Georgian, and another for Caucasian Albanian.

With the new alphabet spread a flood of Christian ideas, written and thereby to a large degree standardized, in Armenian. Translations of the Bible, liturgical writings, and patristic works were produced with impressive speed, giving Armenians access in their own language to the thinking of the universal Church.[6] Original works soon followed; histories, geographies, hymns, encomia, homilies, liturgies, canons, and letters.[7] Further waves of translation would follow periodically, as would great efflorescences of original writing and thought.

By the time its alphabet was created, Armenia had already been christianized officially for a century—since the days of Saint Gregory the Illuminator at the beginning of the fourth century. But it had in fact been christianized, at least in part and unofficially, much earlier. Thus Armenia already possessed a developed Christian tradition before it possessed the ability to express that tradition in writing in its native language. Relations between Armenia and Christian communities in Mesopotamia, Syria, and Jerusalem hark back to the second century if not earlier, and Armenian Christianity bore the

---

[6] Efflorescences of translation activity would occur again in the eighth and twelfth centuries, some of it undoubtedly related to increased ecumenical activity between the Armenian and Syrian Churches, as well as between the Armenian and Byzantine and, in the twelfth century, the Armenian and Roman Churches as well. For one recent study of the latter period, see Boghos Levon Zekiyan. "Un dialogue oecuménique au XIIe siècle: les pourparlers entre le Catholicos St. Nerses Snorhali et le légat impérial Théorianos en vue de l'union des églises arménienne et byzantine," *Actes du XVe Congrès International d'études byzantines. IV Histoire. Communications* (Athens, 1980) 420–441. An English translation by Y. Kutchukian of the ecumenical correspondence of Catholicos Nersès Shnorhali with annotation and introduction by R. Ervine is forthcoming as vol. 2 of his *Correspondence* (vol. 7 in the St. Nersess Armenian Seminary's AVANT series). For bibliography on the Unitor movement and its efforts to bring Armenians into communion with Rome, see R.W. Thomson, *A Bibliography of Classical Armenian Literature to 1500 AD*, 206–207.

[7] For a collection of excerpts of Armenian classical writing, see Agop J. Hacikyan *et al.* (eds.), *The Heritage of Armenian Literature*, vols. 1–2 (Detroit: Wayne State University Press, 2000, 2002). The editors have generally chosen works of historical rather than theological interest, but the collection is nonetheless impressive.

marks of its southern heritage for centuries,[8] even as it developed a new relationship with the Christian Empire of Byzantium.

In addition, Armenia was already involved in Christian ascetic lifestyles long before it had an alphabet. By the fifth century a number of monastic foundations laid claim to considerable antiquity; several traced their origin to the late apostolic age.[9]

---

[8] E. Ter Minassiantz, *Die armenische Kirche in ihren Beziehungen zu den syrischen Kirchen bis zum Ende des 13. Jahrhunderts.* Texte und Untersuchungen 11/4 (Leipzig, 1904).

[9] The history of monasticism in Armenia is only beginning to be studied. Eminent historian Nina G. Garsoïan prefers to distinguish between an earlier period of eremitic life in Armenia and a later development of coenobitic life; she reserves the term "monastic" for the latter. We await her study in the forthcoming number of *Revue des études arméniennes.* (In this present work, I use the term "monasticism" in a much broader sense, embracing all of single/singular religious life. Preliminary work on the Syriac connections of Armenian eremeticism has been done by Edward G. Mathews, Jr.; see his 'The Early Armenian Hermit: Further Reflections on the Syriac Sources', *St. Nersess Theological Review* 10 (2005) 141–167. See also the sources listed in n. 10, below.

According to tradition, Hogeats' Vankʻ was one the monastic institutions of Armenia to claim apostolic origins. The Apostle Bartholomew is credited with having founded the nunnery in Armenia in the late first century. Bartholomew is said to have brought to Armenia a portrait of the Virgin Mary. It had been given to him as a gift because, unlike the other disciples, he had been absent when she died. This portrait was brought to a spot south of Lake Van called Darbnakʻar, where a temple to the pagan goddess Anahita was located. Here a famous convent of women was built, called Hogeats' Vankʻ. The names of the first abbesses there are mentioned in a sermon on the Assumption: they were 'the sister of Yusik and the sister of Ormzdat and the sister of Maqowdowr'. According to the same sermon, one of Bartholomew's disciples was left with the congregation as its priest. The tradition is also mentioned in Movsēs of Khorenatsʻiʻs 'Patmutʻiwn Srbotsʻ Hṙipʻsimeantsʻ' (History of the Hṙipʻsimian Virgins) as well as in a pseudepigraphical letter attributed to him. Movsēs Khorenatsʻi, *Matenagrutʻiwnĕ* (Works) (Venice: 1865) 297–303. See also Melikʻ Pēylikʻjian, 'Sarkawaguhiner hayotsʻ Vankʻerēn nersʻ' [Deaconesses in Armenian Convents], *Hay Khosnak* (1933) 132–136. Even when the portrait of the Virgin was no longer to be seen there, pilgrimage to the shrine continued. A modern tradition, mentioned by Jerusalem's Patriarch Torgom Gushakian, said that the nuns sealed the portrait in a wall to prevent its theft. See J.-M. Thierry, 'Monastères arméniens de Vaspurakan', *Revue des études arméniennes* n.s. 4 (1967) 167–186.

The history of Saint Gregory the Illuminator's early ecclesiastical foundations included descriptions of the brotherhoods he established,[10] and the fifth-century historian Eghishē offers an exhortation to monks already seasoned in the life.[11] Armenian monasticism felt a conscious connection with Egyptian monasticism,[12] and Armenians participated in the early monastic movements of both Palestine and Egypt.[13]

[10] For the foundations of Saint Gregory the Illuminator, see Agathangelos, *History of the Armenians*, translated by Robert W. Thomson, §810–815, 831 [hereafter, Agathangelos]. See also Hagob Thopdschian, 'Die Anfänge des armenischen Mönchtums mit Quellenkritik', *Zeitschrift für Kirchengeschichte* 25 (1904) 1–32; and Erwand Ter-Minassiantz, 'Einige Bemerkungen zu Dr. H. Thopdschians Artikel "Die Anfänge des armenischen Mönchtums"', *Zeitschrift für Kirchengeschichte* 25 (1904) 626–630. See also G. Amaduni, *Monachismo. Studio storico-canonico e fonti canoniche.* CCOF Serie 2, fasc. 12, Disciplina armena II (Rome, 1940) and Dionysius the Areopagite, 'Mystery of the monastic consecration, that is of monks', in Robert W. Thomson, *The Armenian Version of the Works attributed to Dionysius the Areopagite.* CSCO 489/Scriptores Armeniaci 18 (Louvain: Peeters, 1987) 77–80.

[11] For a French translation see Bernard Outtier, 'Une exhortation aux moines d'Élisée l'arménien' in *Mélanges Antoine Guillaumont: Contributions à l'étude des christianismes orientaux*, Cahiers d'orientalisme 20 (Geneva: Patrick Cramer, 1988) 97–101. Simon Weber, *Ausgewählte Schriften der armenischen Kirchenväter* 2 (Munich 1927) 287–298 provides a German translation.

[12] In addition to Ter Minassiantz (above, n. 8) see R. Draguet, 'Une lettre de Sérapion de Thmuis aux disciples d'Antoine (AD 356) en version syriaque et arménienne', *Le Muséon* 64 (1951) 1–25; Louis Leloir, 'Solitude et sollicitude: Le moine loin et près du monde, d'après les Paterica arméniens', *Irénikon* 47 (1974); Louis Leloir, 'Les orientations essentielles de la spiritualité des pères du désert d'après les Paterica arméniens', *Revue de théologie et de philosophie* 24 (1975); Louis Leloir, *Désert et communion: témoignage des Pères du Désert, recueillis à partir des 'Paterica' arméniens* (Bégrolles-en-Mauges: Bellefontaine, 1978); J. Muyldermans, 'Fragment arménien du ad virgines d'Évagre', *Le Muséon* 53 (1940) 77–87; idem., 'Évagre le Pontique: Les *Capita Cognoscitiva* dans les versions syriaque et arménienne', *Le Muséon* 47 (1934) 73–106; Irénée Hausherr, 'Les versions syriaque et arménienne d'Évagre le Pontique', *Orientalia Christiana* 22/2 (1931) 69–118.

[13] John Moschos, *The Spiritual Meadow*, tr. John Wortley. Cistercian Studies Series 139 (Kalamazoo: Cistercian Publications, 1992) 113 mentions an Abba Sergios the Armenian, attendant to Abba Sergios the anchorite of Rouba from the days when

Monastic and eremetic lifestyles were to be an integral part of Armenian Christianity's self-expression across the centuries. A seventeenth-century map of Armenia shows the locations of several hundred monastic establishments and sanctuaries.[14] Even in the twentieth century, when first the Armenian genocide and then religious restrictions imposed by the Armenian Republic's communist regime all but obliterated Armenian monastic life, its few remaining bastions—primarily those outside the Armenian homeland in Jerusalem and Cilicia—continued to exert a profound influence on Armenian culture. And in the twenty-first century, a renewal of interest in monasticism has been one of the organic outgrowths of a renewed religious freedom.

Armenian monastic life does not seem to have constituted a withdrawal from the life of the world in the sense of creating a sharp division between the two. Monasteries were most often situated amidst a lay population; monks influenced kings, and kings retired to monasteries. Monks were consulted on the problems of the outside world, and monasteries were considered important sources of healing. In addition, monasteries were major landowning institutions and played a significant role in agriculture.

---

they were in the vicinity of the Dead Sea. According to Theodoret of Cyrrhus, *History of the Monks of Syria*, tr. R.M. Price. (Kalamazoo: Cistercian Publications, 1985) 61, the successor to Theoctetus at the cenobium of Publius of Zeugma was the Armenian Theodotus, 'Who was full of such spiritual grace that when he prayed all those present simply listened in silence to his sacred words, thinking the listening to be an earnest prayer'. Euthymius, the ruins of whose monastic foundation in the Judean wilderness still stand today, was an Armenian and entertained groups of Armenian pilgrims. R.M. Price (ed.), *Cyril of Scythopoplis: The Lives of the Monks of Palestine*. Cistercian Studies Series 114 (Kalamazoo: Cistercian Publications, 1991) 49. On Euthymius' monastery see Yiannis E. Meimaris, *The Monastery of Saint Euthymios the Great at Khan el-Ahmar, in the Wilderness of Judaea: Rescue Excavations and Basic Protection Measures, 1976-1979*. (Athens: 1989).

[14] Gabriella Uluhogian, *Un'Antica Mappa dell'Armenia: Monasteri e santuari dal I al XVII secolo*. (Ravenna: Longo editore, 2000). Narek is number 482 in the list of sites.

While it is sometimes mentioned in the Armenian sources that a particular medieval monastic community followed a particular rule—one that derived from Basil, for example[15]—the relative rarity of such comments testifies to a general lack of reliance on written codes for ordering Armenian monastic life. And although certain communities were formed by members of an older monastery who moved out specifically to form a new group, there were no monastic orders in the western sense.[16] Much more significant was the relationship between a revered monk or hermit and his disciples, a relationship which created genealogies of holiness, so to speak, which passed from one spiritual generation to the next a way of life inculcated by personal example.[17] Monastic life gave rise to a kind of literature within the literature, as bits of advice were passed down in more permanent form.[18]

---

[15] The congregation of Kamrjadzor, mentioned again below, followed the ascetic writings of Saint Basil, as did the monastery of Narek. J. Gribomont, *Histoire du texte des Ascétiques de saint Basile.* Bibliothèque du Muséon 32 (Louvain, 1953).

[16] Entrance into a monastic community was, however, marked as a formal occasion. For a liturgy on the reception of monks (men and women alike) see *Mayr Ts'uts'ak Dzeṙagrats'* [Grand Catalogue of Manuscripts] vol. 3. (Venice: 1966) cols. 26–27; for the ordination of a person 'worthy of religion, of mature age', see cols. 30–33.

[17] This was still the case in the twentieth century in Jerusalem's Armenian Monastery of the Saints James. There each aspiring young monastic was assigned to attend to the needs of an older, experienced member of the brotherhood, thereby both providing for the needs of elderly community members and permitting the young aspirant to learn by observing how his father mentor lived the life. See Louis Leloir, 'L'accompagnement spirituel selon la tradition monastique ancienne principalement arménienne' in *Mélanges Antoine Guillaumont, Contributions à l'étude des christianismes orientaux.* Cahiers d'orientalisme 20 (Geneva, 1988) 84–96.

[18] Yovhannēs Gaṙnets'i, *Xrat Krōnaworats'* (Advice to Religious) (1652) 291–316, in *Sion* (1953) 318–321. On the Armenian *Lives of the Fathers* see Nira Stone's study of J 285, *The Kaffa Lives of the Desert Fathers: a Study in Armenian Manuscript Illumination,* CSCO 566 Subsidia 94 (Louvain, 1997). The *Apophthegmata Patrum* also were translated into Armenian—in a rather idiosyncratic recension of the version arranged by subject matter.

The monastic life was informed by the notion of 'the angelic life'. This multi-faceted ideal included celibacy, of course, and it also influenced the regimen of monastic prayer, which sought to imitate the ceaseless prayer and praise of the angels and their alacrity in the divine service. Ultimately, it was felt, humankind was intended to take the place of the fallen angels: by its obedient devotion to God's praise, humanity would restore the nine ranks of the heavenly hosts to their original and proper number of ten. This restoration to glory would give humanity the added satisfaction of repaying Satan with poetic justice for his original jealousy of Adam's glory, a jealousy which had issued in mankind's expulsion from glory. It is not surprising that monastics, who were seen as having attained the quality of angels while still in the flesh, were frequently well-known as miracle workers.

As well as being centers of ascetic endeavor, angelic life, and social influence, monasteries were also the seats of Christian thought and learning. The *vardapets*, as Armenian calls the doctors of the Church, were most often monastics. These men were held in reverence as being the living repositories of the traditional teaching of the Church, both catholic and Armenian, on a wide range of topics from scriptural exegesis to world history and geography to canon law.[19] Throughout the middle ages, they issued compendia of knowledge, including history, mathe-

---

[19] The word *vardapet* means a doctor of the church, a person officially licensed to teach. In recognition of his high level of erudition, a *vardapet* received the preaching staff. This sign of authority was a staff somewhat shorter than a bishop's crozier and without a crook, on which the *vardapet* could lean while preaching. For the importance of the *vardapet* in the Armenian Church, see Robert W. Thomson, 'Vardapet in the early Armenian Church', *Le Muséon* 75 (1962) 367–384. Boghos Levon Zekiyan, 'Armenian Spirituality: An Attempt to Define Some of Its Main Features and Inner Dynamics', in R. Ervine, ed., *Worship Traditions in Armenia and the Neighboring Christian East* AVANT 3, (Crestwood, New York: St Vladimir's Seminary Press, 2006) 265–286, calls the uniquely Armenian institution of the *vardapet* the 'most fitting expression on the grounds of the institutional Church, of the privileged link between theology and spirituality'. (279)

matics, and geography as well as theology, law, and philosophy, and they educated the young. They were also the vanguard of contemporary thought in their day. Viewed as at least potentially inspired, they were entrusted with the application of tradition to non-traditional situations and issues, such as interfaith relations and ethical problems. Their influence extended far beyond the monastery walls; *vardapets* tutored royalty, offered predictions of the future to inquiring nobility, and had considerable value as hostages. It was they who built new structures of thought and spirituality on the foundations of the past.

It went without saying then that the *vardapets* were men of letters; transmitters of ideas across generations and across geographical distances. In fact, of the fifty–odd writers from the fifth to the tenth centuries whose work we have (together with at least some biographical data), a mere three were, so far as we can tell, laymen.[20]

THE LIFE AND TIMES OF SAINT GREGORY OF NAREK (*c.* 945–1003)

Gregory of Narek, to whose *Commentary on the Song of Songs* the present work is devoted, was a monastic and a priest. He also calls himself a teacher, albeit 'the least of teachers'; others did not hesitate to call him *vardapet*. The details of his biography are sketchy, and apparently have always been so. With a fitting monastic humility, he does not give particulars of his own life and accomplishments, though a certain amount can be gleaned from his writings and those of his contemporaries.

Gregory's birth is variously calculated to have taken place between 940 and 951.[21] Whatever his exact date of birth may have

---

[20] Even the one woman writer from this time period, the hymnographer and musician Sahakduxt Siwnets'i (675?–736?), was a hermit.

[21] In favor of the later date is a statement in the *Synaxarion* that Gregory died young, 'having not yet completed the usual course of life'. Some of those who

been, it is clear that from an early age Gregory lived and worked in the newly-founded monastery attached to the village of Narek, on the south shore of Lake Van (fig. 1 map; plate 1 photo of Narek). Gregory describes the monastery as 'many-mountained and hard-pedestalled'. Built of white stone, it stood on a hilltop with the village of Narek spread out down the slopes below. Later, Gregory's oratory, a cliff or rocky outcropping with nine stone rooms, would be shown a little to the north of the monastery, on the shores of Lake Van.[22]

The monastery of Narek was one of the new foundations which sprang up as part of a resurgence of monastic life in the tenth century. The historian Step'anos Asoghik includes Narek in a list of such institutions:

In this time the order of religious life flourished . . . and brotherhoods sprang up in many places, and members

---

prefer an earlier dating cite a colophon, penned by Gregory's older brother Sahak, to the *Commentary on the Liturgy* written by their father in 950. In that colophon, Sahak refers to their father Khosrov as 'Bishop of Andzewats'ik'', a rank which he attained as a widower. This assumes that the colophon and the *Commentary* were both produced at the same time, and that Gregory's birth must have preceded their father's elevation by at least several years. M. Mkryan, *Grigor Narekats'i* [Gregory of Narek] (Erevan 1955) 114.

[22] *Ibid.*, 117–118, probably based on a statement in the periodical *Azgagrakan Handēs* (1911) 41. Information on the founding of Narek's monastery, including readings of inscriptions there, was compiled by Fr. Hamazasp Oskian, *Vaspurakan-Vani Vank'erĕ* [Monasteries of Vaspurakan-Van] I (Vienna 1940) 189–200. He describes the monastery's twin churches of Saint Sanduxt and the Theotokos and the locations of the tombs of Gregory, John, and Anania. Oskian traces the history of the monastery into the modern period. Primarily using evidence from colophons, he points out periods of activity in the early fifteenth, late sixteenth, and eighteenth centuries, and describes nineteenth-century pilgrim quarters, an abbot's residence and a school. According to the *Geography* of the thirteenth-century writer Vardan the Great, the monastery contained relics of Saint Thomas and Saint James (of Nisibis?); French translation by J. Saint-Martin, 'Géographie du Vartabied Vartan', in his *Mémoires sur l'Arménie*, 2 (Paris 1819) 406–471.

came together for the love of Christ. First, the famous congregation of Kamrjadzor in the province of Arsharunikʻ. And in the province of Shirak, the monastery called Hoṛomos was built by John . . . Also at the same time Narek was constructed in the province of Ṛshtunikʻ, with the same rule,[23] with a large population of worship-enhancing singers and literary men.

He goes on to list monasteries in the provinces of Taron, Derchan, Karin, and Vayotsʻ Dzor.[24] Some are said to have been 'large'; the number of brothers at Kamrjadzor is specifically given as three hundred. Other monasteries founded at around the same time in Armenia's northern kingdom included Haghbat and Sanahin, both of which soon became famous centers of learning and guardians of tradition.

Narek was thus part of a larger monastic movement.[25] From Gregory's point of view, however, it was also a family monastery. Its founder was his maternal cousin, Anania, who became his teacher. Gregory's fellow monastics included his own eldest brother, John.[26] It has been held that, although John predeceased Gregory, he first succeeded Anania as abbot. The future historian and bishop Ukhtanēs, who may have been another relative, was also a member of the brotherhood.

---

[23] Presumably, the ascetic writings of Basil.

[24] Stepʻanos Asoghik, *Patmutʻiwn Tiezerakan* [Universal History] (Saint Petersburg, 1885) [hereafter, Asoghik] 3:7, 173–174.

[25] Its inception is also roughly contemporary with the first monastic foundations on Mount Athos.

[26] Their middle brother, Sahak (see n. 21 above), appears to have remained with their father, though in what capacity is unclear. In colophons Gregory refers several times to his elder brother, John, as more worthy and erudite than himself. At the end of his *Encomium on the Holy Theotokos*, for example, Gregory describes John as 'in the same order, more knowledgable and gifted philosopher than myself by far in all respects'. *Writings*, Venice: 1840, 422. (For full bibliographical reference, see n. 61, below.)

Gregory of Narek had the good fortune to live between interesting times. Narek was in the province of R̊shtunik', at the
southern end of the Armenian homeland and within what had
become the Artsrunid kingdom of Vaspurakan.[27] From the middle
of the seventh century, Armenia had been ruled by the Muslim
Caliphate. In 858, however, prince Ashot Bagratuni gained recognition as Armenia's prince of princes, and in 885 became the
country's king.

At the death—a mere generation later—of Ashot I's successor,
Smbat I, the southern region of Armenia around Lake Van broke
away and became an independent kingdom under its first king,
Khach'ik-Gagik Artsruni. Rivalry between the Artsrunids—who
traced their ancestry back to the regicide sons of Sennecherim of
Assyria—and the Bagratids—who traced theirs to King David of
Israel—was sometimes fierce, despite not infrequent intermarriage
between the two families. During the period of Gregory's life and
work, however, the political situation was relatively peaceful, both
in the narrow realm of Armenian internal relations, and in the
broader realm of relations with neighboring powers.

The tenth century was consequently marked by growing prosperity, flourishing trade, urban development and an efflorescence
of the arts.[28] The eleventh-century historian Aristakēs Lastiverts'i

---

[27] R̊shtunik' enjoyed a certain amount of notoriety among the Armenian provinces. According to the history of the fifth-century writer known as P'awstos, it had
been the scene of a stand-off between its cruel prince Manajihr and Saint Jacob
of Nisibis Although the prince won the battle, so to speak, he lost the war: Jacob
cursed him, his family and his province. R̊shtunik' rose to prominence in the early
seventh century when its prince T'ēodoros became for a time the overseer of the
country. *The Epic Histories Attributed to P'awstos Buzand (Biwzandaran Patmut'iwnk'),*
tr. Nina G. Garsoïan, Harvard Armenian Texts and Studies 8 (Cambridge: Harvard
University Press, 1989) [hereafter, P'awstos] 3:x.

[28] Gregory's lifetime also coincided with the conversion of Russia to Christianity,
with the Persian literary revival centered on the work of Ferdowsi (935–1020), and
with the life of Symeon the New Theologian (949–1032), also a noted poet. The
Armenian Bagratid kingdom had its capital at Ani, whose architectural remains

describes the city of Artsn, on Lake Van's north shore, as being 'like the city set on a hill . . . decked out like a bride', full of clement princes, just judges and church-building merchants.[29]

The period of peace and creativity was not to last. By the end of Gregory's life in 1003, pressure from the east was building as newly arriving groups of Turks strained the resources of the Armenian kingdoms to resist them. But Gregory did not live long enough to see the end: it would be 1025 before Vaspurakan's last Artsrunid king, Senek'ērim, exchanged his kingdom for the region around Sebastia, within the protection of the Byzantines.

The details of Gregory's physical biography seem not to have been important to the establishment of his reputation for sanctity or to the popularity of his writings. This is evident from the earliest biography of him which survives. It appeared in 1173, attached to the earliest extant manuscript of his *Book of Lamentations* (Matean Oghbergut'ean), the work for which he is best remembered.[30]

The biography occupies a single sheet in the manuscript. Its author was the spiritual and ecclesial prodigy Nersēs of Lambron (1153–1198), who would be ordained bishop of Tarsus, at the age of twenty-two, a mere two years after penning the biography. The miniatures adorning the manuscript make it clear that Nersēs was more interested in Gregory's spiritual development than in the actual details of his life. The manuscript contains four miniatures depicting Gregory. Three of these are captioned. The first shows Gregory as 'philosopher'; the second, as 'vigil keeper'; and the third as 'ascetic'. The fourth bears no title. It depicts Gregory

---

are impressive even today, and its population of some 100,000 made it the rival in size of the greatest Mediterranean metropolises of its time.

[29] Aristakēs Lastiverts'i, *Patmut'iwn* [History] (Tiflis, 1912) 78.

[30] The manuscript is number 1568 in the collection of the Matenadaran in Erevan.

in a garden, kneeling before Christ. The series, in the opinion of scholar James Russell, visually describes Gregory's development from scholar to mystic, wordless in the paradise of Christ's presence.[31]

The written content of Nersēs' brief biography of Gregory is spare. The most important of Gregory's biographical details are alluded to only very obliquely. The first paragraph of the written biography places Gregory's life in the chronology of the larger world: he was the contemporary of the Byzantine emperors Basil II (976–1025) and Constantine VIII (976–1028). There is nothing unusual about a biographer's conveying this information. Nersēs goes on to place Gregory within the reign of the Artsrunid king Senek'ērim (968–1026). Again, ignoring the fact that Gregory's life actually spanned the reign of four kings, one of whom commissioned one of Gregory's more important works, and focusing only on the king who was in power at the time of Gregory's death is not in and of itself illogical.

But in the same sentence Nersēs places Gregory in the reign of Catholicos Vahan I of Siwnik' (968–969). This is certainly unusual, and must have drawn the attention of Nersēs' contemporaries. Vahan reigned for only one year. Most of Gregory's younger years were lived under the reign of Vahan's predecessor, Catholicos Anania Mokats'i (941–965), and his mature years under the reigns of Vahan's three successors, Step'anos III of Sewan (969–972), Khach'ik Arsharuni (973–992) and Sargis I of Sewan (992–1019). It seems that Nersēs of Lambron, desiring to highlight the spiritual greatness of Gregory, quite pointedly chose to pass over several rather painful episodes of both a personal and a church political nature in the monk's relationship

---

[31] *Grigor Narekats'i, Matean Oghbergut'ean* [Book of Lamentations], introduction by James R. Russell (Delmar, New York: Caravan Books, 1981) [hereafter, *Matean*] xviii–xix.

with the hierarchy of the Church whose devoted son he was, and whose beloved saint he was to become.

While the secular political situation in Gregory's lifetime was stable and prosperous, there was considerable upheaval in religious life and church affairs. On the one hand, it was an era replete with figures of remarkable sanctity. Both the tenth-century historian Asoghik[32] and the thirteenth-century historian Matthew of Urfa give lists of notable holy men who lived in this period: Basilios the Elder and his disciple Step'anos the Spiritual; Grigor the married priest; David the Poor (also known as David Leatherfoot); Petros the Exegete—and Anania the Philosopher of Narek.[33] An emphasis on personal asceticism and holiness is clear: although all the men listed above were viewed as *vardapets*, only two are characterized as intellectuals. The rest were known for their ascetic feats. One Moses, in particular, was lauded for having imitated his Old Testament namesake's forty-day fasts. The pursuit of individual ascetic holiness extended to those in the secular realm as well. The Bagratid king Ashot III, the Merciful, was said to have dined daily with the poor and the sick, for whose needs he cared personally.[34] The presence of Gregory's great uncle and mentor among these holy individuals is significant, especially in light of his unfortunate involvement in the other face of Armenian religious life, the church political aspect.

In the broader ecclesiastical political sphere, there was conflict between the non-chalcedonian Armenians and their Chalcedonian Christian neighbors in Byzantium. Thanks to the Byzantine

---

[32] Asoghik 3:7.

[33] Matt'ēos Uṙhayets'i, *Zhamanakagrut'iwn* [Chronography] (Jerusalem: St. James Press, 1869) 215.

[34] The description of Ashot's pious sharing of his princely table with the poor echos the description of the charity of Catholicos St. Nersēs I, surnamed the Great (353–373) in P'awstos IV, iv. On the importance of a ruler's role in protecting the poor, see Nina G. Garsoïan, 'Sur le titre de *Protecteur des pauvres*', *Revue des études arméniennes* 15 (1981) 21–32.

Empire's political dominance, Armenians who persisted in their non-chalcedonian convictions were persecuted with considerable vigor in many parts of the Byzantine territories, though the emperors of the period were themselves Armenian by ethnic origin. Conversions of Armenians to Chalcedonian Christianity were numerous. As bishops were among the converts, painful rifts and ruptures were caused between sectors of the Armenian church hierarchy, between bishops and populations of the faithful who did not share their hierarchs' views, and between sectors of the lay population.[35]

Whether or not this broader conflict directly impacted Gregory's life is not clear. Perhaps as late as the year 1000,[36] he produced a work entitled *On the Cross of Abarank'* in which he lauds an invasion of northern Armenia by Emperor Basil II, and—unlike his great uncle Anania and his fellow monastic, Ukhtanēs—he never produced any writing of a specifically anti-chalcedonian nature.[37] The common pejorative term *duophysite* does not occur in his writings, nor is Chalcedon mentioned.

There was, however, another level of conflict which did touch Gregory intimately. A rather widespread grass-roots movement,

[35] For more on Chalcedonian and non-chalcedonian Armenians in this period see K. Maksoudian, 'The Chalcedonian Issue and the Early Bagratids: the Council of Shirakawan', *Revue des études arméniennes* 21 (1988–1989) 333–343; and V.A. Arutjunova-Fidanjan, 'The Ethno-Confessional Self-Awareness of Armenian Chalcedonians', *ibid.*, 345–363.

[36] According to his unofficial notes, the late curator of manuscripts for Jerusalem's Saints James Monastery, Archbishop Norayr Bogharian [=Pogharian], tentatively dated this work to 983.

[37] Anania's *Enddēm Erkabnakats'* [Against Duophysites] has never been published. The second volume of Ukhtanēs's *Patmut'iwn Hayots'* [History of Armenia] (Vagharshapat, 1871) deals with the seventh-century split between the Georgians and the Armenians, which occurred when the former accepted Chalcedon and joined the Byzantine fold. There is an English translation (to be used cautiously) by Fr Zaven Arzoumanian, *Bishop Ukhtanes of Sebastia, History of Armenia Part II* (Fort Lauderdale, 1985).

already active before his lifetime, questioned the authority of the clergy—from the catholicos on down—and the traditions of the Church. Tension between the church hierarchy and lay populations who expected them to maintain a high standard of spiritual example and leadership was certainly not unique to this era. But in Gregory's time, there was an especially broad spectrum of people calling for church reform with varying degrees of zeal.

At the extreme end of that spectrum were violent elements. The historian Step'anos Ōrbēlian recalls in graphic detail an armed rebellion which took place in 915 against the Bishop of Siwnik' and his monastery seat at Tat'ew.[38] Accompanying a monastic revival under its bishop Yovhannēs, the Tat'ew monastery received large gifts of land from the provincial nobility. Among those land gifts was the fortress of Ts'ur. We are told by Step'anos that the residents there were 'godless, brazen and thieving'. In a nighttime attack, they robbed the monastery church and workshops, as well as the cells of the monks, wounding some monks and putting others to flight. The attackers intended to capture and assassinate the bishop, who, fortunately for him, happened not to be in residence at the time. The historian goes on to say that the bishop cursed the fortress, producing an earthquake there, but ultimately had to resort to secular force to wipe out the fortress and remove its inhabitants. Though the violence might well have been prompted by discontent at having their land placed under monastic control, the inhabitants of the fortress also seem to have had a religious complaint. It is specifically said that they seized the silver vessel containing the holy chrism and 'poured it down the cliff'.

The province of Siwnik' continued to prove a thorn in the flesh of the church authorities. Catholicos Anania of Mokk' (941–965) encountered a rebellion there which threatened to remove from

---

[38] Step'anos Ōrbēlian, *Patmut'iwn Nahangin Sisakan* [History of the Province of Sisakan] (Paris, 1859) 1:48.

his jurisdiction the Church of the Caucasian Albanians, together with the province of Siwnik'. A certain Yakob, bishop of Siwnik' in those days, spearheaded this movement. Holy chrism began to be distributed among bishops in Armenia's northeast by the Albanian catholicos, whose seat was nearer to the region than that of the catholicos of Armenia, who at that time resided on the island of Aght'amar in Lake Van. Catholicos Anania, as he tells us in his own words, went with an entourage of bishops to Siwnik' and convened a synod there with the assistance of the local prince, who favored reunification with the Armenian Church. One of the issues before the synod was the 'reinstatement' of the repentant Albanian catholicos. This Catholicos Anania and the Armenian loyalist bishops rejected. As a result, the separatist hierarchy of Albania and Siwnik' continued in opposition to Anania, despite his vigorous anathema, until their deaths.[39]

Underlying the issue of Siwnik' and Albania's secession, and particularly that of the independent distribution of the essential holy chrism by the Albanian catholicos, was the question of the authority of the episcopate and the position of the catholicos as chief bishop among his episcopal brothers. The Armenian Church is not completely pyramidal in its authority structure, though it is hierarchical, and the degree of authority actually exercised by any given catholicos seems to have been determined by a variety of factors.

Questioning of authority and jurisdiction—to say nothing of open secessionist tendencies—is enough to make any hierarch uneasy. Catholicos Anania was no exception. And as this question directly affected Gregory of Narek's own family, we will return to it momentarily. But it is important first to add another complicating element to the conflict.

---

[39] Anania Mokats'i, 'Yaghags Apstambut'ean Tann Aghuanits" [Concerning the Rebellion of the Albanian House] *Ararat* (1897) 129–144.

Questions of religious life, Christian teaching, and the place of the Church in both were already to be found in abundance at the very time these questions of authority were being raised. Dissenters from mainstream Armenian Christianity appear to have been particularly abundant in the tenth century. Many were plain layfolk, albeit some were layfolk of exalted rank; but some were from among the church hierarchy itself.

A case in point was that of Bishop Yakob of Hark', a contemporary of Saint Gregory of Narek. His episcopal see lay slightly to the north and west of Lake Van. An ascetic of considerable reputation, he disagreed with his Church's teaching on several points. We are told by the historian Aristakēs that Yakob and his entourage were characteristically to be seen 'in rough garments, simple, severed from pleasant, rich foods, and they ever occupied themselves with singing the Psalms'. By reason of his piety, Yakob's influence was such that 'those who were haughty with pride because of their authority humbly gave themselves over to obedience to him; so much so that, had he ordered them to give up the ghost, there was not one who would have resisted, or even have presumed to open his mouth and let out a peep'.[40] Apparently, Yakob held his clergy to a high standard as well, defrocking those who were found unworthy. This, the historian says, proved pleasing to the people.

Yakob's teachings on two points were troubling. First, we are told, he ordered the Eucharist to be celebrated only three times in the year. Second, he taught that having confessed one's sins was not in and of itself sufficient grounds for admittance to communion. In addition, he set out to abolish the very popular custom of accompanying requiem masses with the ceremonial slaughter of animals (called *matagh*) which would be cooked and distributed to the community on the occasion. It seems evident

---

[40] Aristakēs, xxii.

that the ascetic bishop interpreted this custom as a sacrifice, a kind of posthumous expiation for the sins of the deceased, and considered it unchristian: 'His henchmen would ridicule this, and bring before him animals and say, "Oh, poor beast. If your master sinned in his day and died, what sin have you committed that you should die with him"'?[41]

The historian goes on to say that Bishop Yakob's teaching was divisive. He was protected by the nobility of his province, but Catholicos Sargis Sewants'i (992–1019) had him imprisoned sometime in the last decade of the tenth century. When Yakob succeeded in fleeing, he went first to Constantinople, but later returned to the area of T'ondrak.

His choice of refuge was telling. T'ondrak, which lay just north and east of Lake Van, gave its name to a large, dissenting group who rejected the ordained priesthood, and indeed all of the sacerdotal trappings of liturgy and sacrament, including the mainstream Church's monopoly on sanctioning marriage. Its adherents, moreover, opposed the acquisition of worldly goods and appear to have stressed ascetic principles and a high moral character. It was a rather fluid group, with a variety of ideas; some apparently preached what we might today call a return to Christian basics and a cleansing of the Church from the perceived greed of monks and clerics, while others washed their hands of the established Church altogether.[42] The dissenters were from all social classes. It was to their sphere of influence that Bishop Yakob gravitated, as did princes and women of im-

---

[41] *Ibid.*

[42] Gregory's *T'ught'* . . . *i Hoyakap* . . . *Uxtn Kjaway* [Letter . . . to the Wonderful . . . Congregation of Kjaw] mentions that the T'ondrakites considered themselves true to the primitive spirit of Christianity, calling themselves 'the people who have not swerved in faith'. For the full reference to this work see below n. 52.

portant families. In Gregory's days, the presence of this element in Armenia was a significant factor in the life of the Church.[43]

The social implications of the T'ondrakite movement worried secular and religious authorities alike. A catholicos like Anania Mokats'i may well have realized that there was a real need to reform certain practices and abuses of his clergy. But to the ears of a hierarch sensitized by the erosion of his and his Church's authority through secessions political and ideological, any criticism must have sounded threatening. After all, the lines between adherents to and dissenters from the established Church were not at all clearly drawn. To what point did a critic remain a loyal son of the Church, and when did his criticism put him beyond the pale? And if beyond the pale, what types of dissent constituted heresy?

It was in this rather tense and sensitive period that Gregory of Narek's father, Khosrov, was consecrated as bishop.[44] Having become a celibate clergyman following the death of Gregory's mother, he was promoted to the episcopate, probably by Catholicos Anania of Mokk', and became bishop of Andzewats'ik', while two of his sons entered Narek's monastery under the tutelage of

---

[43] On dissenting groups in Armenia, and on their connection with similar thinkers in Byzantine imperial territory, see Nina G. Garsoïan, *The Paulician Heresy: A Study of the Origin and Development of Paulicianism in Armenia and the Eastern Provinces of the Byzantine Empire.* (The Hague-Paris: Mouton, 1967); Vrej Nersessian, *The Tondrakian Movement* (Alison Park, Pennsylvania: Pickwick Publications, 1988); P. J. Alexander, 'An Ascetic Sect of Iconoclasts in Seventh Century Armenia' in *Late Classical and Medieval Studies in Honor of Albert Mathias Friend, Jr.* (Princeton: Princeton University Press, 1955) 151–160; K. Ter Mkrttschian, *Die Paulikianer im byzantinischen Kaiserreiche und verwandte ketzerische Erscheinungen in Armenien* (Leipzig, 1893).

[44] While there was an effort made by G. K'iparian, 'S. Grigor Narekats'i ew Erg Ergots'i Meknut'yunĕ' [Saint Gregory of Narek and the *Commentary on the Song of Songs*], *Bazmavēp* 109 (1961) 1–10 to dissociate Gregory of Narek from the son of Bishop Khosrov of Andzewats'ik', no substantial evidence was presented in support of that revisionist idea.

Anania, their mother's cousin. Bishop Khosrov authored both an
Explication of Church Orders and a *Commentary on the Eucharistic
Liturgy.*[45] These may originally have formed a single volume, produced around the year 950. He was clearly both an erudite and
a deeply spiritual man. It was perhaps his erudition that led him
to side with Bishop Yakob of Siwnik' in the latter's altercation
with Catholicos Anania. Although it is mostly Anania's viewpoint on the situation that we now have, it seems that Khosrov
agreed with Yakob's assessment that election to the catholicosate
conferred no rank higher than that of the episcopate.[46] Thus the
catholicos, especially as far as his bishops were concerned, was
first *among equals.*

For Anania, beleaguered as he was and in need of ways and
means by which to assert his authority over recalcitrant clergy,
such a declaration by a respected bishop whose see was among
those geographically nearest to the center of catholicosal authority on Aght'amar, was not welcome. Khosrov was invited to
review his opinion. He found it to be sound, if inconvenient,
and did not retract it. The Catholicos felt he had no alternative
but to remove Khosrov. He anathematized him as well, thereby
elevating disagreement over an ecclesial-political matter to the
rank of heresy.[47] There is no record of the anathema ever having

---

[45] This work appeared in English translation as *Commentary on the Divine Liturgy by Khosrov Anjewats'i,* tr. S. Peter Cowe. (New York: St. Vartan Press, 1991).

[46] There is confirmation of this to be found in the historian Kirakos of Gandzak's *Patmut'iwn Hayots'* [History of Armenia] (Erevan: 1961) 85. The historian,
representing the viewpoint of some three centuries after the events described,
supports Catholicos Anania's decisions in the matter, and also mentions other
lesser points in Bishop Khosrov's teachings that were open to criticism.

[47] Russell places this unfortunate event in 953. Anania's 'Patjaṙ yaghags zKhos-
rov nzoweloyn Andzewats'wots' Episkoposn' [Rationale for the Anathematizing of
Bishop Khosrov of Andzewats'ik'], *Ararat* (1897) 275–277, gives the date as 954.
In the 'Rationale', Catholicos Anania also cites other unusual teachings of Khosrov.
These included regulations for the cutting of younger children's hair and for the
growing and braiding of the hair of older youths: these regulations were based

been lifted; technically, at least, one of the Armenian Church's most celebrated commentators on her central liturgical sacrament was left beyond the pale until his death, somewhere around the year 963.

Catholicos Anania may have found Bishop Khosrov's refusal to compromise with the practical exigencies of the day all the more aggravating because, according to some, Khosrov's cousin by marriage, Anania of Narek, had been a classmate of the Catholicos in their youth. In fact, both men bore the same name. The suspicion of disloyalty—and possibly worse—certainly extended from Khosrov to Anania and Anania's monastic foundation—and, inevitably, to Khosrov's son Gregory, who was living his monastic life there.

Catholicos Anania heard rumors that Narek's Anania outstripped his episcopal cousin Khosrov in error and was in sympathy with the T'ondrakite movement.[48] The catholicos wrote the

---

on Khosrov's understanding of etymologies of Armenian words for 'child' and 'youth'. Khosrov was also said to have taught that a cross was worthy of reverence whether or not it had been blessed by a priest. Anania remarked, 'We forgave him these'. But the notion that the catholicosate held no higher rank than members of the episcopate, and the logical counterpart of that idea—that the episcopate was not inherently a higher office than the priesthood, but that all three designations reflected different functions of the sacerdotal office—was more than Anania could allow. He wrote a formal rebuttal of Khosrov's opinions, 'Yaghags or asen t'ē mi patiw ē hayrapetin ew Episkoposin' [Concerning Those Who Say that the Rank of Patriarch and of Bishop is One], *Ararat* (1897) 277–280. On the antiquity of such an egalitarian stance towards the clerical ranks see §219.8-9 of *Macarius of Jerusalem: Letter to the Armenians (A.D. 335)*, introduction, text, translation and commentary by Abraham Terian [AVANT 4]. (Crestwood, New York: St Vladimir's Seminary Press, 2008; in press).

[48] Khosrov's perceived errors did not include T'ondrakite sympathies. He is quoted as condemning either the T'ondrakites, or a group like them, because of the extreme reverence in which they held their leaders: 'They pray wherever they find it convenient, and what is worse, they worship not God but a man created in His image, since for prayer they gather in the houses of the elders of the village in order to pray not to God but to them, as though they were putting them above

monastic scholar what was, apparently, a blistering letter demanding that Anania recant—though Anania had not been examined
to determine whether or not he was, indeed, in error.

When he received the letter, Anania was, it seems, deathly ill.
But, stung to the quick, he wrote the reply himself, refuting the
Catholicos's accusations,[49] taking the Catholicos to task as one
who had known him intimately 'by parentage and province, race
and taste, training and shared life', yet had failed to know him
at all. Writing the response must have stirred up Anania's blood,
because he survived his illness and went on to outlive Anania the
Catholicos by at least fifteen years. Among Anania of Narek's
writings there was also a work *Against Smbat the T'ondrakite*,
mentioned in the twelfth century by the great Catholicos Nersēs
Shnorhali.[50] Although this work has not survived, and it is not

---

God' (quoted in Garsoïan, *The Paulician Heresy*, 162, with a reference to M 8075,
fol. 159). Gregory's letter to the congregation of Kjaw, cited in Garsoïan, *Pauli-
cians*, p. 500, also says that 'they dared to call the head of their abominable sect
a Christ', and relates that one of their leaders, Smbat by name, was challenged
by his assassin to rise from the dead as Christ had; the assassin was even willing
to give him a month—rather than a mere three days—during which to perform
the resurrection.

[49] *Gir Xostovanut'ean* [Writ of Confession], *Ararat* (1892) 1–18; also as a pam-
phlet: (Vagharshapat, 1892).

[50] In his *T'ught'k' Endhanrakank'* [General Epistles] (Jerusalem: St. James Press,
1871) 269. Such a work was also mentioned by Step'anos Asoghik in the eleventh
century: he described Anania as 'a great philosopher, who . . . wrote a book
against the sect of the T'ondrakites and other heretics', Asoghik 178. Prior to that,
Gregory of Narek's younger contemporary, Gregory Magistros, who was assigned
to remove the T'ondrakites from Armenia, noted the existence of Anania's work in
his 'T'ught' aṙ asorwots' episkoposn' [Letter to the Syrian Bishop] in K. Kostanianz
(ed.), *Grigor Magistrosi T'ght'erě* [Gregory Magistros' Letters] (Alexandropol, 1910)
153. In addition to writing against the T'ondrakites, Anania also wrote two works
against the Chalcedonian confession, one entitled simply 'Enddēm Erkabnakats''
[Against Duophysites], found in SJ 963, 429–456 and the other, *Hawatarmat* [The
Root of Faith]. The latter is no longer extant, but the historian Ukhtanēs in his
History, written for Anania, reminds Anania of the time when he presented the
work to the Catholicos Khach'ik (973–992). Ukhtanēs, 11–12.

clear whether it was written before or after his accusation by the Catholicos, it did make Anania's opposition to the sect clear.[51]

Since Gregory himself would later author a letter refuting any connection between his own views and those of the dissenters,[52] it seems clear that the accusation of T'ondrakite sympathies extended to him as well and was sufficiently serious to require a response.[53]

In spite of these unfortunate events, the orthodoxy and personal sanctity of Gregory's family were recognized by their contemporaries, and certainly by succeeding generations, as is obvious from the list of holy men, cited above, in which Anania of Narek's name appears. There is also an hagiographical story, with a number of variants, which shows the level of sanctity attributed to the Narekats'i's. The same story, in several versions, is recounted of both Anania and Gregory. According to one rendition of the story, Anania (or Gregory) was called to defend his faith before an unnamed Catholicos. Anania (or Gregory) mildly invited the two bearers of the message to stay for a meal; he offered them roast squab. Upon being reminded by them that it was a fasting day, he told them to bid the birds fly away. They could not. But when Anania (or Gregory) commanded them to do so, the birds immediately flew off. According to another variant, the protagonist of the story, incarcerated prior to his trial for heresy, asked for squab

---

[51] For more on Anania see H. H. T'amrazyan, *Anania Narekats'i. Kyank'ě ev Matenagrut'yuně* [Anania of Narek, Life and Literary Work] (Erevan, 1986).

[52] 'I hoyakap ew yakanawor Ukhtn Kjaway' [To the Wonderful and Notable Congregation of Kjaw], *Bazmavēp* (1893) 59 and 113. The letter also appeared in the first edition of the *Girk' T'ght'ots'* [Book of Correspondence] (Tiflis: 1901) 498–502. An English translation of the letter was published in Frederick C. Conybeare, *The Key of Truth: A Manual of the Paulician Church of Armenia* (Oxford: Clarendon Press, 1898; repr. Elibron Classics, 2004), App. I.

[53] Mkryan, 122 n. 15, confirms this.

for dinner. When he realized that it was a fast day, he bade the
birds fly away, which they did.[54]

In a more prosaic vein, the twelfth-century chronographer
Samuēl of Ani would say that 'the holy man of God Gregory of
Narek . . . shone like the sun in wisdom and virtue'. And around
the same time, his biographer Nersēs of Lambron called him 'an
angel in the flesh',[55] and incorporated the entirety of Gregory's
prayer 'All-powerful benefactor . . . ' into his own *Commentary
on the Divine Liturgy.*[56] The fourteenth-century *vardapet* Matt'ēos
Jughayets'i said that one stanza of Gregory's was 'better than all
the Psalms of David'.[57] In addition, Gregory's tomb was reputed
to have healing powers.[58]

At the time when Gregory began to write, however, the traditions and the stories of sanctity were yet to come. It was in
the shadow of the painful suspicions against his family, and his
father's death under anathema, that his spirituality and his literary gift developed. In almost all his writings, a gentle defense of
his family is clear. In his *Story of the Cross of Aparank'*, mentioned
above, he says, 'I Grigor, least of *vardapets* and most junior of

---

[54] Echoes of the incident in the Infancy Gospel, when Christ bids clay pigeons
fly away, are obvious. (See Abraham Terian's annotated translation, *The Armenian
Gospel of the Infancy*, forthcoming from Oxford University Press.) Russell, *Matean*
ix–xiii, gives more of the Gregory legends, and points out a Sufi parallel to the
story of the clay pigeons.

[55] 'Atenabanut'iwn' [Oration], printed as an addendum to his *T'ught'k'* [Letters],
published together with those of Catholicos Grigor IV 'The Youth' (*c.* 1133–1193).
Grigor Kat'oghikosi Tghay koch'ets'eloy Namakani [The Correspondence of Catholicos
Gregory Surnamed 'The Youth'] (Venice, 1838) 157.

[56] Nersēs Lambronats'i, *Meknut'iwn Pataragi* [Commentary on the Liturgy]
(Venice, 1847).

[57] Quoted in L. Khach'ikyan, 'Matt'ēos Jughayets'u Kyank'n u Matenagrut'yunĕ'
[Matthew of Julfa's Life and Writings], *Banber Matenadarani* 3 (1956) 57–84;
here, 82.

[58] Roupen Racoubian, *Grigor Naregats'i* [Gregory of Narek] (New York: Koch'nak,
1939) 24–26.

philologists, am son of the daughter of the brother of the father of Anania, spiritually adorned and intellectually astute philosopher, praised and renowned for the purity of his religious life'.[59] In his poetry, Gregory speaks of his father's faith. Indirectly, he defends the faith of his teacher Anania as well: in his *Book of Lamentations*— of which more will be said below—Prayers 33, 34, 75, 92, and 93 are notable statements of the family faith. Also, several of the *Bans*, or Prayers, in the *Book of Lamentations* are meditations specifically on the Church as the eternal expression of Christ's body, and the church as physical structure. These underline Gregory's devotion to the very institution which the T'ondrakites rejected, and are thus also implicitly in defense of his family's orthodoxy.

THE COMMENTARY ON THE SONG OF SONGS IN THE CONTEXT OF GREGORY'S OTHER WRITINGS

While a full study of Gregory's writings is outside the scope of this book, his other works should be mentioned briefly in order to put his *Commentary on the Song of Songs* in context.[60] All but three works are undated.[61]

---

[59] Gregory, *Writings* (Venice, 1840) 422. See n. 61, below.

[60] Scholarly literature on Gregory's writings is not particularly extensive. The following are recommended as a starting point for those able to read Armenian and wishing to read further: P. M. Khach'atryan and A. Ghazinyan, *Grigor Narekats'i Matean Oghbergut'yan* [Gregory of Narek, Book of Lamentations] (Erevan, 1985); Armine K'yoshkeryan, ed., *Grigor Narekats'i Tagher ev Gandzer* [Gregory of Narek, Taghs and Gandzes] (Erevan, 1981) [hereafter, *Tagher ev Gandzer*]; V. Aṙak'elyan, *Grigor Narekats'u Lezun ev ochĕ* [Gregory of Narek's Language and Style] (Erevan, 1975). For some works in western European languages, see the brief bibliography which follows the notes. The reader is referred to R.W. Thomson, *A Bibliography of Classical Armenian Literature to 1500 AD*, 228–133 for a more complete listing of works.

[61] Most of Gregory's works were collected in G. Awetik'ean, *Grigori Narekay vanic' vanakani Matenagrut'iwnk'* [Writings of Gregory, a Monk of Narek Monastery],

The Book of Lamentations[62]

The most famous of Gregory's writings is his *Book of Lamentations*, a book of ninety-five prayers in three hundred sixty-seven sections. It was his last work, written during the extended illness which preceded his death. Gregory relates that he destroyed it— and then was forced to rewrite it, just as Moses had been obliged to rewrite the tablets of the Law. Its completion date is given as 1002. The prayers vary in mood and imagery; they display a keen sensitivity to the human being's separation from God who is 'unapproachably distant; immediately near'. At the same time, they also display a joyful hope, an overwhelming realization of divine grace, much rumination on Gregory's own shortcomings and on the mystery of human nature and the human condition in general, meditations on divine light, expressions of the many ways in which the spirit may be wounded, exquisite descriptions of what it feels like to be consumed in the fire of God. Each prayer is called a *Ban*, that is, a unit of thought.[63] The faith with which they are suffused is far from calm; it is not steady, nor is it even consistently sure. It is, in the final analysis, honest.

The language of the Prayers is complex and studiedly abstruse.[64] It also evinces great creativity. Though not all the words

---

2 vols. (Venice, 1827); a more complete collection was published as *Srboy Hōrn meroy Grigori Narekay Vanits' Vanakani Matenagrut'iwnk'* [Writings of Our Holy Father Gregory, Monk of Narek Monastery] (Venice, 1840).

[62] There are some one hundred fifty manuscripts of the *Book of Lamentations*. Its most recent translation into English was produced by Thomas Samuelian, *St. Grigor Narekatsi: Speaking with God from the Depths of the Heart* (Yerevan: Vem Press, 2001), with a pocket edition appearing in 2002. The introduction, notes and general format are aimed at encouraging use of the book for private devotion.

[63] *Ban* is the Armenian equivalent of *logos*, and is also applied to Christ, the *Ban* of God.

[64] Interestingly, the same might be said of language favored by Gregory's younger contemporary, Gregory Magistros, whose letters and poetry are especially challenging reading.

Gregory coined therein have made their way into standard Armenian vocabulary, he unquestionably enriched the way Armenians thought about and used their language.[65] To express the inexpressible, to clothe the Word, he created a new world of words.

In his introduction to the *Book of Lamentations*, Gregory called its Prayers 'powerful medicaments for incurable wounds, effective drugs for invisible pains'. In addition, several of its *Bans* are specified as being intended 'for various types of healing' (28f, 35a, 42b, 43a,b) or 'for defense from a demon'. These statements, perhaps in combination with the arcane nature of his vocabulary and the depth of his mystical thought, opened the way for Gregory's poetry to be used quite literally for healing. The prayers are still today read by clergy over the sick; Russell mentions a copy of the *Book of Lamentations* which contained a handwritten list of specific *Bans* that served this purpose. The uses to which the *Book of Lamentations* has been put also included several which fall clearly into the realm of magic.[66]

The Story of the Holy Cross of Aparank'[67]

This piece, together with its accompanying *Encomium on the Holy Cross* and *Praise of the Theotokos*, is written in the same style as the *Book of Lamentations*, which it preceded by some twenty years. The receiver of the three part work, Bishop Step'anos of Mokk', and indeed the audience intended for the encomiastic retelling

---

[65] For a listing of some words belonging to each group, see Russell, *Matean* xiv–xv.

[66] *Ibid.*, xiii.

[67] Gregory, *Writings*, Venice: 1840, 371–390; the accompanying encomia *On the Cross* and *On the Theotokos* are found on 390–406 and 407–421, respectively, while the colophon is recorded on 422–423.

of the story, must have been of considerable erudition, with an appreciation for poetic style.[68]

The story commemorated is that of a military man from Mokk', of noble class, whose deceased uncle, one Bishop Dawit', enjoyed recognition as a holy man. The nephew took a bit of soil from his uncle's grave with him to Byzantium, where miraculous events occurred. The co-emperors Basil and Constantius honored the see of Mokk' and the grave of the saintly bishop by sending a relic of the Cross there, together with other relics. At the final deposition of the holy gifts in the Church of the Theotokos, the kingdom of Vaspurakan was represented by three royal princes, Ashot, Senek'ērim, and Gurgēn[69] Artsruni. The event took place in 983, which is likely also to have been the date of Gregory's composition.[70]

The *Praise of the Theotokos* which accompanies the *Story of the Cross* contains a notable litany of the Virgin's types, including many uncommon ones: she is the true Letter of the foreshadowing Law, the rooster crowing in night's darkness, gold of Ophir from earthly dust, the divine King's robe of light.

Encomium on the Patriarch Jacob of Nisibis[71]

Written in thirty sections, this extensive praise of one of Armenia's most revered saints[72] also displays the poetic qualities

---

[68] The Mekhitarist scholar Gh. Alishan, *Hayapatum* [Armenian History] (Venice: 1901) 88, lauds the literary quality of this work: 'It is a soaring history; it soars not only in its significance, but in its style; to translate this work with equivalent depth and elevation would be, it seems to me, impossible'.

[69] Gurgēn will be mentioned again below as the commissioner of the *Commentary on the Song of Songs*. He was also the founder of Holy Cross at Abarank'.

[70] Mkryan 133–134.

[71] Gregory, *Writings*, Venice: 1840, 424–438.

[72] The connection between Jacob and the Ark of Noah was especially important for Armenians, who considered the region of Naxijewan [First Descent] to have been where Noah and his family first descended from the Ark. *P'awstos*, III.x.

of Gregory's mature work, though there are no indications of its date. It is addressed to the Church as 'Holy Sion', and, in fact, the first four sections are devoted to an exaltation of the Church, setting the stage for Gregory's presentation of Jacob as the Church's most exalted saint. The audience, familiar with the hagiographical details of Jacob's life, would have been able to fill in the oblique references to his many miracles. It closes with a request for the saint's intercession. Although this encomium is more predictable in its treatment of the saint's virtues than was the *Praise of the Theotokos*, it still represents a stylistic *tour de force*.

Encomium on the Holy Apostles[73]

In its address to the apostles as 'flowers of the Cosmos and beloved trees of Paradise', this slightly shorter encomium calls upon phraseology from the *Frequently-related Discourses* of Saint Gregory the Illuminator, a source for which Gregory had a particular affinity.[74] The mystical value of the apostolic number twelve is considered from the point of view of its factors as 3 x 4 and as 5 + 5 + 2; the larger group of the 70 is also touched on. One is tempted to speculate that the drier, 'more academic' language of this work[75] marks it as earlier than the *Encomium on Jacob of Nisibis*, which it precedes in the Venice 1840 printed edition, but this is speculation.

---

[73] Gregory, *Writings*, Venice, 1840, 424–438.

[74] In discourses 7 and 10 Gregory the Illuminator refers to holy spirits as 'colorful Trees' and 'breathing Trees'. *Girk' or koch'i Yajakhapatum* [The Writings Referred to as 'Frequently Related'] (Istanbul, 1737) [hereafter, *Discourses*].

[75] Mkryan 138–139.

Writings in the Gandz, Tagh *and* Meghedi *genres*[76]

Gregory is credited with having invented the poetical form known
as the *gandz*. Whatever the actual derivation of the word in its poetic usage, in normal speech it carries the meaning of 'thesaurus'
or 'treasure'. Each *gandz* of Gregory's work begins with the word
Gandz, offers some type of play on the word, and is structured
around an acrostic spelling out the phrase, 'A Song of Gregory'.

There are three representatives of this genre which are universally acknowledged to be from Saint Gregory's pen: the *Gandz*
on the Coming of the Holy Spirit (which begins, 'Treasure of
light . . . '), the *Gandz* on the Church (which begins, 'Treasure
of good to be desired . . . '), and the *Gandz* on the Holy Cross
(which begins, 'Treasure ineffable, greatness concealed . . . ').[77]
More meditative than the encomia, these *gandzes*, like the shorter
poems written in the forms *meghedi* (melody) and *tagh* (hymn)
are among Gregory's finest writings.

The *tagh*, of which some two dozen examples have been collected, represents Gregory at his most succinct, and shows his sense
of imagery at its most dense and idiosyncratic. His *tagh* on the last
words from the Cross presents the dying Christ as an attacking lion
('I speak of the Lion's roar, crying from the four-winged cross . . . ')[78]
and is written from the point of view of a soul in hades; another on
the Crucifixion is a meditation addressed to a bird perched on the
arm of the cross.[79] Gregory's own visions seem to have provided the
material for a number of these most beloved songs.[80]

---

[76] In addition to *Tagher ev Gandzer*, which is devoted entirely to Gregory's
writings in these genres, a number of these works also appear in *Writings*, Venice:
1840, 455–482.

[77] *Tagher ev Gandzer* gathers together 11 *gandzes*, in addition to 27 hymns.

[78] I thank Abraham Terian for a typescript of this unpublished translation.

[79] *Tagher ev Gandzer* 237–238.

[80] For studies of individual *taghs*, see James R. Russell, 'The Song of Christ's
Ascension (Tagh Hambarjman) of St. Gregory of Narek', *St. Nersess Theological*

Letter to the Congregation of Kjaw[81]

In addition to his poetical and encomiastic works, two pieces of hortatory writing are attributed to Gregory. At an unknown point in his life, Gregory authored a letter to the abbot of the congregation of Kjaw. Apparently, the abbot suspected Gregory of T'ondrakite sympathies. In response, Gregory points out to the abbot that, while Gregory himself is innocent of any such sympathy, there are suspect elements among the abbot's own monks. In the very politest and most careful of terms, Gregory shows how unclear the line between orthodoxy and sectarian thinking can be.[82]

A Brief Word of Advice on Orthodox Faith and the Pure and Virtuous Life.[83]

This quite lengthy work in seventy-five sections is found at the end of the Venice 1840 edition of Gregory's collected works. Its heading says that it was requested by an individual named Vardan. Following a standard introduction in which the author explains

---

Review 2:2 (1997) 114–131; and T. van Lint, 'Grigor Narekats'i's *Tagh Yarut'ean*. The Throne Vision of Ezekiel in Armenian Art and Literature I', in V. Calzolari Bouvier, J-D. Kaestli and B. Outtier, edd., *Apocryphes arméniens: transmission — traduction — création — iconographie. Actes du colloque international sur la littérature apocryphe en langue arménienne* (Genève, 18–20 septembre 1997) (Lausanne, 1999) 105–127.

[81] *Bazmavēp* (1893) 59 and 113. Also *Girk' T'ght'ots'* (Book of Correspondence). (Tiflis, 1901) 498–502.

[82] Included in the Venice 1926 edition of the *Book of Lamentations* 477–492 is a writing entitled 'Discourse Concerning the Church, against the Manichaeans Who Are Policians [sic]'. This work is not included by N. Bogharian in his listing of Gregory's works. *Hay Groghner* [Armenian Writers] (Jerusalem: St. James Press, 1971) 157–159.

[83] *Writings*, Venice: 1840, 483–533. Again, Bogharian does not include this work in his list of Gregory's writings.

why one must respond to those who request information, there is a detailed exposition of the faith: first, of those articles that are essential to Christian confession, including belief in the Trinity and the mysterious sufferings of the Son ('Being uncontained and boundless in Nature, he was on the cross *and* at the Father's right; in the grave *and* upon the cherub throne'). Then, the articles of faith on whose exact details Christians can and do differ, while remaining, nonetheless, Christian. The major part of the work, however, is devoted to a discussion of right living, and is based on an understanding of the spiritual and the physical senses and their proper functions, a theme which derives from Gregory the Illuminator's *Frequently-related Discourses* and which will recur in Gregory's *Commentary on the Song of Songs*, as will be pointed out below.

SOME ASPECTS OF SAINT GREGORY'S COMMENTARY ON THE SONG OF SONGS

The *Commentary on the Song of Songs* was the earliest of Gregory's works.[84] It dates to 977. Gregory's biographer Nersēs characterizes the work only as 'brief'. This is true—at least in comparison with two of the other Armenian commentaries on the book, of which more will be said below. Despite the fact that it was written in Gregory's youth and composed for a layman, however, it is not a simple document. And Gregory was to ruminate on the themes introduced in it for the rest of his life. They surfaced from time to time in his other writings, reaching a mystical maturity in his final work, the *Book of Lamentations*.

---

[84] Gregory's authorship has been disputed. K. K'iparian (see n. 44 above) prefers to attribute it to a married priest from Narek, also named Gregory. The basis for this seems to be the difference between the straightforward language of the *Commentary* and the artistic vocabulary of the *Lamentations*.

Allusions to the Song of Songs in Gregory's Other Works

References to the Song of Songs are scattered throughout Gregory's writings.[85] In his *Encomium on the Holy Cross* he uses Song 1:7 in a list of prophecies concerning Christ as the Shepherd. His description of the Virgin Mary in the accompanying *Encomium on the Theotokos* uses Song 4:14 with its list of fragrant spices in a depiction of the Virgin as a divine censer. Song 1:13 is also used in the same *Encomium*.

Jacob of Nisibis, in the *Encomium* dedicated to him, is described in terms of Song 4:2/6:8; he is 'like the sheep of the

---

[85] There has been no study as yet of the Song of Songs' role in Armenian patristic literature. However, it does appear that references to the Song of Songs are comparatively rare in Armenian writing. The references that do occur are found in a wide variety of contexts. Vardan Aygekts'i (1170?–1235), in his *Aghot'agirk' Surb Tegheats'* [Holy Places Prayerbook] (Istanbul, 1737; 1841) uses Song of Songs 5:6 as a refrain, a metaphor for the pilgrim soul's seeking of Christ as the pilgrim travels from shrine to shrine.

In the early seventh century, John of Mayrivank' (575?–640?) referred to the Song of Songs as the Blessing of blessings, and noted that myrrh in the Song of Songs symbolizes the death of Christ. He saw Song 5:1 as an expression of the intentionality of Christ's descent into the tomb. 'Yovhan Mayrivanets'i, "Verlutsut'iwn Kat'oghikē Ekeghets'woy ew or i nma yawrineal kargats'" [John of Mayrivank, Analysis of the Catholic Church and the Orders Created Therein], *Sion* (1967) 70–75.

Sahak Vardapet Mṙut (820?–890?) in his *Exposition* written in refutation of the 'Nestorian duophysites', focused on Song 2:3. Interpreting the apple as Christ, Sahak said: one can no more separate the elements of Christ's nature than one can separate the four elements which make up an apple. *Bats'ayaytut'iwn . . . jshmarit ughghap'aṙ dawanut'yan Hayastaneayts'* [Exposition . . . of the Armenian Church's True, Orthodox Confession] in *Girk' T'gh't'ots'* [Book of Correspondence] (Tiflis, 1901) 413–482; also published separately, ed. N. Bogharian. (Jerusalem: St James Press, 1994). For the full quotation, see n. 126, below. A body of Armenian prayers attributed to Ephrem the Syrian cites Song 5:1 (Prayer 1), and refers to the south wind as the Holy Spirit, just as Gregory does in his commentary to 4:16. (I thank Edward G. Mathews, Jr. for an advance reading of his forthcoming publication of the prayers.)

In a macabre fashion, Song 2:13 served as the rationale for branding heretics on the face with the image of a fox.

Proverb writer, bearing twins, none barren'. The apostles, too, in their *Encomium*, are called 'offspring of the hart', referring to the hart's propensity for treading on serpents, an element in Gregory's exegesis of Song 2:17 and 7:1.

The *Gandz on the Holy Church* speaks of the faithful as a 'sealed door of cedar', combining Song 8:9 and 4:12. Gregory's *Tagh* with the opening line *Hawun, hawun . . .* , combines Song 2:14, 4:8 and 6:13 in the space of four lines. In addition to these lesser citations from the Song, there is a *tagh* for Christmas which, in an extended passage, speaks of the newly born Christ child in the words of the Song. It concludes in the words of Song 2:1 and 4:4 :

> How beautiful, how praiseworthy,
> the Child unattainable, timeless.
> He is the mountain tower,
> lily of the valleys,
> flower of the fields.

The Song of Songs also appears twice in Gregory's *Brief Word of Advice on Orthodox Faith*. Early in the exhortation he quotes Song 1:3-4, applying it to those who have 'drawn Life to themselves'. Towards the end of the work, he brings together multiple allusions to Christ as the Groom and the Church as the Bride. Following a quotation from the Gospel of John he goes on, 'not to mention the Song of Songs, which from start to finish rings changes on this same idea; through corporeal things it impresses upon us the spiritual'. The love of groom and bride, as the greatest example of earthly love, was the only thing that could viscerally express the love of Christ for the Church.

Interestingly, in his final work, the *Book of Lamentations*, Gregory makes use of the Song no less than seven times.[86] Prayer/

---

[86] All English translations of selections from the *Book of Lamentations* are taken from Samuelian, *St. Grigor Narekatsi: Speaking with God from the Depths of the Heart*, 2001.

Ban 46A uses Song 1:7—'The image of the shepherd's tent in the Song of Songs aptly applies to me, for I do not know or understand by whom, in whose image, or why I was created'. In section D of the same *Ban*, Gregory asks himself, in the words of Song 5:3, 'Why did you put off the clothes given you and put on the cloak of sin? Why did you infect the purity of your feet by taking the path of the fallen?' Rather than being simple quotations, the references to the Song include echoes of his own exegesis on the verses alluded to. Prayer/*Ban* 75, one of several meditations on the nature of the Church, refers to the Bride's maidens as the assembly of the patriarchs (§J), an exegetical theme featured in the *Commentary*.

Prayer/*Ban* 52A uses Song 2:9, but focuses on the explanation that the metaphor of the Nephew's peering 'through the window' depicts our partial knowledge:

> Lord, with a new showering of grace and streams
>   of mercy from on high,
> who delights in pouring forth enlightenment
>   miraculously without end,
> more abundantly than upon the nations of old
> and opened and broadened those narrow windows
> through which knowledge glimmers as Solomon said,
> for him and with him for me a wretched sinner.

In words reminiscent of his *Brief Word of Advice on Orthodox Faith*, Gregory's *Ban* 93 H ('A Prayer of Instruction on Holy Chrism, the Light-giving Oil of Consecration') combines Song 8:2; 1:2; 4:4,10; 5:1; 3:6; 4:14 and says,

> In praise of Christ's bride, the holy Church,
> the Song of Songs, from beginning to end,
>   explains the divine mystery,
> comparing incarnation to spiced wine,

and virtue to myrrh mixed with choice oil
and perfect morals to a sweet perfume of myrrh
      and incense
mixed with delicious powders.

Section I of the same *Ban* refers to Song 2:5 and 6:2, concerning the oil or balsam, 'that fine substance, filled with your Spirit, whose light enables us to see your finer, higher, ungraspable element, praised Lord'. Section K, carrying on with the metaphor of oil as applied to Christ's nature, takes in Song 2:1; 1:3,4.

Instead, turning your name [anointed one] into reality,
You mixed yourself into this pure oil,
    making it radiant with heavenly light.
And although the savors of your sweetness are beyond
expression and cannot be compared to anything,
although you have variously been referred to
as the flowers of the field or the lilies of the valley,
exquisite nard or sandalwood mixed with aloe,
the scent of saffron, the blossoms of the vine or a
      fine wine,
you, Lord beyond understanding, deemed it fitting
that your name be glorified simply as 'oil poured out',
for you are the consummation of all things
and lacking in nothing. . . .
With Solomon the anointed and adopted of God,
I sing with the mouth of a bride to you,
    you heavenly bridegroom,
a song of praise and thanksgiving,
yearning with the fervent desire of my heart
for your sweet scent more than for any incense.
In the inspired words of the wise man
    and the theological evangelist,

let us hasten in your footsteps and the trace of
    your scent,
like one who has the words of eternal life. . . .

The overarching theme of Gregory's *Commentary on the Song
of Songs* is this understanding of the Incarnation; it is as if in
his last work he returns to his beginnings, giving deeper, poetic
expression to what he had first said in simple prose.

GREGORY'S COMMENTARY IN THE CONTEXT OF OTHER COMMENTARIES ON
THE SONG OF SONGS

When Gregory wrote his *Commentary on the Song of Songs* he was
stepping into a tradition of exegesis that stretched back to Hippolytus and Origen, and had an entire companion literature,
so to speak, in Jewish tradition.[87] As investigation of Armenian
biblical exegesis is in its infancy,[88] it may be possible to tell in

---

[87] Both Origen and Hippolytus on the Song of Songs were translated into
Armenian. M4066, dated 1283, contains them both together. See the recent com-
pilation of information on Armenian biblical commentaries, Eznik Petrosyan and
Armen Ter-Step'anyan, edd., *Surb Grk'i Hayeren Meknut'yunneri Matenagitut'yun*
[Bibliology of Armenian Commentaries on the Holy Scriptures] (Erevan, 2002).
On Hippolytus, see G. N. Bonwetsch, *Hippolytus Kommentar zum Hohelied*. Texte
und Untersuchungen 23, no. 2 (Leipzig, 1902). Fragments of Hippolytus' *Com-
mentary* are to be found in two later Armenian commentaries, those of Vardan the
Great Arewelts'i (1200?–1271) and Gregory of Tat'ew (1344?–1409), of whom
more will be said below. Robert W. Thomson says that the Origen commentary
on Song of Songs referred to by Gregory is not genuine (Hamam, *Commentary on
Proverbs*, Armenian text, English translation, introduction and notes by Robert W.
Thomson [Hebrew University Armenian Texts and Studies 5], Louvain: Peeters,
2005, 9, n. 51). He refers the reader to J.-P. Mahé, 'Origène et la baleine; un fragment pseudo-origénien *Sur Job et le Dragon* en traduction arménienne', *Revue des
études arméniennes* 14 (1980) 345–365.

[88] Three important studies on Armenian exegesis are M. Ē. Shirinyan, 'Me-
knoghakan zhanri kazmavorumĕ ev zargats'umĕ Hayastanum', [Formation and

future what literature Gregory had to draw on when composing his *Commentary*; for the moment, we must rely simply on what he himself tells us.

At the outset of his prologue, Gregory contrasts his own capacities with those of his fellow Gregory, bishop of Nyssa, and implies that he is following Nyssa's work. In fact he will mention Nyssa by name six more times throughout the *Commentary*. And as the annotations to Gregory's text will show, he does make frequent use of the Cappadocian in his exegesis, though he is not slavish about it. That Gregory should choose Nyssa as his main source is not surprising. Nyssa, like the other Cappadocians, enjoyed great status in Armenia, and his work on the Song of Songs had been extant in Armenian for a considerable time. A manuscript copy of his *Letters on the Song of Songs*, copied in Taron in 951, was the only manuscript to be found whole in the cave-repository opposite the great monastic school of Haghbat when it was investigated in the eighteenth century.[89] And the eighth-century translator, commentator, and bishop Step'anos of Siwnik' used it in his work, *On the Incorruptibility of Christ's Flesh*.[90]

Development of the Commentary Genre in Armenia], *Ashtanak* 3 (2000) 36–64, and Robert W. Thomson, 'Homilies and Biblical Commentary in Classical Armenian Writers', in R. Ervine, ed., *Worship Traditions in Armenia and the Neighboring Christian East* (Papers of the St. Nersess Armenian Theological Seminary, 40th anniversary symposium) (Crestwood: St Vladimir's Seminary Press, 2006) 175–186; *idem.*, 'Is There an Armenian Tradition of Exegesis?', *Studia Patristica*, 41: *Papers presented at the 14th International Conference on Patristic Studies held in Oxford 2003. Orientalia*, F. Young, M. Edwards and P. Parvis, edd., Louvain: Peeters, 2006, 97–113.

[89] Fr Tachat Eartĕmian, 'Hayastani vank'erun iravichakĕ Hayr Ghukas Inchichiani *Hayastan* ashxatut'yan mēj 1600–1800 tarinerun' [The Actual State of Armenia's Monasteries in Fr Lukas Injijian's work *Armenia 1600-1800*], *Bazmavēp* (1999) 13–62; here, 54–55. Another tenth century MS is M 2684, dated 973.

[90] Galust Ter-Mkrtchian, *Step'anos Imastaser* [Step'anos the Philosopher] (Vagharshapat, 1902) 25. Step'anos was the translator of Nyssa's *On the Nature of Man*; it is not clear, then, whether he used Nyssa's *Letters on the Song of Songs* in Greek or Armenian, or whether he was perhaps himself responsible for their translation.

Gregory of Narek did not choose to enrich his *Commentary* with references to other commentators on the Song.[91] Instead, he chose to refer to the orations of Gregory Nazianzen (whom he mentions thirteen times by name), to 'the universal teacher' John Chrysostom (seven times), to an unidentified 'Basil' (three times) and to Gregory the Illuminator (fourteen times).[92] One is tempted to speculate that, rather than rely on works which would have been read only in the course of higher biblical studies, Gregory deliberately chose texts which would have been familiar to persons at a rather lower level of religious education.

Unlike Gregory of Nyssa, whose *Letters on the Song of Songs* represent the final distillation of a long career, Gregory of Narek's *Commentary on the Song of Songs* is the first fruit of a youthful thinker. He must have been between twenty-five and thirty years of age when he wrote it. Both men wrote at the request of an interlocuter. Unlike Gregory of Nyssa, whose work is addressed to the learned deaconess Olympia, however, Gregory of Narek produced his commentary for a youthful man of the world and future king.

As we mentioned above, the study of Armenian exegetical works is in its infancy, and such points may be clarified in the future.

[91] It should be said here that Robert W. Thomson, the person who has done the most to advance Armenian exegetical studies in the West, has compared the content of Narek's *Commentary* with those of Hippolytus, Origen, Philo of Carpasia, Theodoret of Cyrrus, Eusebius of Caesarea, and Procopius of Gaza, in his invaluable article, 'Grigor of Narek's Commentary on the Song of Songs', *Journal of Theological Studies* 34 (1983) 453–496; rpt. in Robert W. Thomson, *Studies in Armenian Literature and Christianity* (London: Variorum, 1994) as article 18 (hereafter, Thomson, 'Song').

[92] It is interesting to note that *The Teaching of St. Gregory* includes one clear reference to the Song of Songs. This is a paraphrase of 1:1-3, found in §440, where the Church is described as the Bride. Robert W. Thomson, ed., *The Teaching of Saint Gregory*. AVANT: Treasures of the Armenian Christian Tradition 1 (New Rochelle, New York: St Nersess Armenian Seminary, 2001) [hereafter, *Teaching of Saint Gregory*].

The circumstances in which Prince Gurgēn Artsruni made his request that Gregory enlighten him on the meaning of the Song of Songs are not known to us. In fact, little is known about Gurgēn[93] apart from his regnal dates (999–1003), the names of his brothers, Shahnshah and Senek'ērim, and the fact that he was son of Abusahl, a king who had been active in church politics. We do know that the paths of the prince and the monk crossed again in 983, when the Holy Cross of Abarank' (to which Gregory dedicated the work of the same name referred to above) was dedicated.

The nature of Gurgēn's query concerning the meaning of the Song appears to have been simple enough: what place does an overtly erotic writing have in the canon of Scripture—a question that also troubled many before and after him, Christians and Jews alike. But it seems that the question was not asked lightly, and that the prince was reasonably learned. In the course of the *Commentary*, Gregory several times refers him to the text of Gregory of Nyssa for further details. Hence, one would expect that the prince had access to it. Gregory's allusions to the Theologian, Chrysostom, Basil and Gregory the Illuminator also imply that the prince had enough familiarity with the writings in question to be able to follow Gregory's train of thought.[94] In addition, Gregory makes

---

[93] What little is known of Gurgēn (or Gurgēn-Khach'ik) we owe to Asoghik 3:xliii, xlvi and to Vardan Arewelts'i, *Hawak'umn Patmut'ean* [Collected History] (Venice, 1862) li. Gregory's *The Story of the Holy Cross of Abarank'* mentions Gurgēn (as Gorgēn) on p. 387, and says that his baptismal name was Khach'ik. Gregory goes on to describe Gurgēn and his brother as 'good men and pious, exceedingly wise and gifted, and as it happened, most desirable of face and stature. And in love of the saints, honor of the chosen, respect for the meek, receptivity to the orthodox, in adornment of churches and giving luster to the holy places and Christ's crosses, and in reverence to the martyrs, . . . unequalled and without parallel'. Gurgēn may not have been the only intended recipient of the *Commentary*, as Gregory several times refers to his 'hearers' in the plural.

[94] For general information on Armenian familiarity with the fathers of the universal church see J.-P. Mahé, 'L'Arménie et les Pères de l'Eglise: Histoire et

more than two hundred fifty direct citations of Scripture, as well as a number of oblique allusions to it, so, presumably, Gurgēn was scripturally literate.

Gregory suited his exegesis to the special situation of a man in authority, such as Gurgēn was. From the outset, the piety of the Old Testament kings David and Solomon is stressed. Speaking of Song 5:5, 'I rose to open for my nephew', Gregory reminds the prince that while there have been royal persons who have lived to repent in their last hour, there are others who have greeted their last hour with the confidence that comes from having lived an upright life. The prince can choose to which of those two groups he will belong. And in Chapter 8, commenting upon the verse 'He gave his vineyard to husbandmen', Gregory develops a beautiful explanation of the 'spiritual husbandry' which a person in authority should exercise over his family and other subject persons who, after all, constitute Christ's *vineyard*, in which a king is merely a functionary from whom an account of harvestable fruit will be required.

The royal reader is also exhorted to love the Church in terms which are a virtual apology for the orthodoxy of Gregory's own

---

mode d'emploi (Ve-XIIe siècle)' in J.-C. Fredouille and R.-M. Roberge, edd., *Le documentation patristique. Bilan et prospective* (Laval/Paris: 1995) 157–179; J. Muyldermans, 'Repertoire de pièces patristiques d'après le catalogue arménien de Venise', *Le Muséon* 47 (1934) 265–296; and Robert W. Thomson, 'The Fathers in Early Armenian Literature'. *Studia Patristica* 115 (1975) 457–470. On the Armenians and Gregory the Theologian in particular, see G. Lafontaine and B. Coulie, *La version arménienne des discours de Grégoire de Nazianze.* CSCO 446, Subsidia 67 (Louvain, 1983) 103. The Center for the Study of Gregory of Nazianzus at the Catholic University of Louvain has several volumes on the Armenian corpus of the Theologian forthcoming; for recent updates visit http://nazianzos.fltr.ucl.ac.be. See also Kim Muradyan, *Grigor Nazianzats'in Hay Matenagrut'yan mēj* [Gregory of Nazianzus in Armenian Literature] (Erevan, 1983). A more complete listing of studies relative to Nazianzus in Armenian may be found in Nishan Baljian, 'An Armenian *Encomium on the Theoleptic Holy Cross* attributed to Gregory the Theologian', *St Nersess Theological Review* 11 (2006) 160–183, n. 1.

attitude towards the Church as a divine institution. In his commentary on 6.8 he specifically says that prayers should be performed in church, not in 'unsanctified places' or given over to 'the vulgar people'. The seriousness of removing oneself from the arms of the Church is spelled out: 'Those whom Satan has found outside their Mother, who is the Church, he takes captive, like a slave trader who steals children whom he finds far from their parents'. Moreover, in the context of 7.1 he warns against those who, 'now, too, . . . impart erroneous teaching' concerning behavior, food, creation, and the last Judgment.

Gregory's youthful age at the time of the *Commentary*'s composition, and the status of its commissioner, both set it apart from the two other full Armenian commentaries on the Song of Songs written in the middle ages.[95] Neither of these has as yet been published, so what is said here concerning them is tentative, but they are clearly quite different in nature from Gregory's work.[96]

The commentary by Vardan Arewelts'i (1200?–1271) was written towards the end of his life (1265) for a fellow *vardapet*, Kirakos of Gandzak (1203–1272). It is replete with references to Origen, Hippolytus, Nyssa and Gregory of Narek, and is twice the length of Gregory's opus. Written for an erudite colleague, it appears to

---

[95] More modern commentaries were written in the seventeenth-nineteenth centuries by Khach'atur Ērzrumts'i (1666–1740), Yovhannēs Vardapet (perhaps Mrk'uz, 1642–1716), Yakob Kaḷnets'i Simonian (18th c.), Archbishop Petros Berdumian (1720?–1787) and Abraham Kostandnupōlsets'i (19th c.). Those by Ērzrumts'i and Simonian were published in the 18th century, while that of Berdumian appeared in *Gandzasar* 2 (1992) 220–252, edited by Mik'ayēl Ajapahian.

[96] Gregory's biographer, Nersēs of Lambron, appears to have written a continuation of Hippolytus' commentary (he also wrote a commentary on Proverbs, Ecclesiastes and Wisdom), which appears in M4066, dated 1283. Fr N. Akinian, 'Nersēs Lambronats'i: Keank'n ew Grakan Vastaknerě' [Nersēs of Lambron: Life and Literary Works], *Handēs Amsōreay* 68 (1954) 85–251, mentions manuscripts in Vienna and Berlin, but without much detail. The exact nature of this work remains to be investigated.

contain none of the moral discourse that marks Gregory's work so clearly.

Gregory of Tat'ew (1344?–1409), a prolific exegete and educator, wrote his *Commentary on the Song of Songs* in 1405. Like Vardan before him, Tat'ewats'i produced the work towards the end of a long career. It accompanied his *Commentary on Proverbs, Ecclesiastes and Wisdom,* dated to the same year. The content of his *Commentary on the Song of Songs* is carefully laid out in points and headings. This would seem to hint at its having been designed as a textbook, and a long section on the nature and importance of *vardapets,* which falls near the beginning of the work, points to an intended audience of aspiring church doctors.

THE TEXT OF THE SONG OF SONGS EMPLOYED BY GREGORY

While a detailed examination of the Armenian texts of the Song of Songs is better left to biblical scholars, some comments must be made concerning the biblical text which Gregory uses as the basis for his commentary.[97]

First of all, it is a longer version of the Song of Songs than the one contained in either the Hebrew or the Septuagint text. Six additional verses appear at the conclusion of the Song in the Zohrab edition of the Armenian Bible,[98] with the heading, 'Found elsewhere in this same book'. These six verses are commented upon by Gregory in the prologue to his commentary, where he treats them as a kind of christological preface to the text proper. A fourteenth-century manuscript of Vardan's commentary (M1121) includes a quite lengthy exegesis of these verses, but places it at

[97] See Sebastian Euringer, 'Ein unkanonischer Text des Hohenliedes (Cnt 8 15–20) in der armenischen Bibel', *Zeitschrift für die alttestamentliche Wissenschaft* 33 (1913) 272–294 [Hereafter, Euringer].

[98] Ed. Hovhannēs Zohrabian (Delmar, New York: Caravan Books, 1984).

the end of the work, after the colophons, making it appear as a separate item. There, the heading speaks of 'fathers of the Church' as the commentators on the verses, rather than of Vardan in particular, so it may have been appended to Vardan's actual work by a later copyist. In the commentary of Gregory of Tat'ew the extra verses also appear at the end of the commentary, but in that case they are clearly included as part of the main work.

Gregory's Song of Songs also includes the rubrics identifying the *dramatis personae*, and describing the action. These are commented upon as part of the text.[99] While the style of commentary used to explain the rubrics, as well as the rest of the text, might be termed 'allegorical', there is no simple, one-to-one correspondence between the elements of the text and what they signify, apart from the consistent interpretation of the *Groom* as Christ. Yes, the *Bride* is the Church, particularly gentile believers, but the Bride is also the individual faithful person. And the faithful, corporately or individually, are also represented by the *garden*, the *vineyard* and the *meadow*. The *maidens* who are mentioned from time to time are the angels, but they are also representative of several other classes of persons: 'those who have become like children in regard to sin', the ancient saints (patriarchs, prophets, apostles, fathers), and the contemporary ones as well; the *friends of the Groom* have the same symbolism. The angels are also intended under the guise of *the watchmen* or *the guards*; and the *daughters of Jerusalem* can be either the angels or the class of righteous human beings. The *mother* can be either the Church or God (who is also symbolized by *the powers of the field*) or Sion, and the *queens, concubines and princesses* are all the 'mother's children'—that is, they are both the children of the Church and the

---

[99] Euringer compares the rubrics of the Armenian with those of the Codex Sinaiticus 272 (fourth century). On the rubrics, see Jay Treat, "Lost Keys. Text and Interpretation in Old Greek Song of Songs and its Earliest Manuscript Witnesses," Ph.D. dissertation (University of Pennsylvania, 1996), especially ch. 3–4.

children of the Holy Spirit. The *mother's son,* however, is Satan, who is also symbolized by *the north* and *the terrors of the night.* The *mother's chamber,* as well as the *city street* and the *square,* all symbolize heaven.

There are a dozen or so verses in which Gregory's text deviates noticeably from that of the Septuagint. In one instance (7:4a) a phrase is omitted. In a second instance (4:4) the interpretation is not affected—the substitution of *in Talpiot* for the words *for an armory* does not seem exegetically significant. However, the remaining discrepancies cause an obvious difference in the understanding of the text:

2:7/3:5	*do not rouse or wake my love, until he please* Arm: arise, *arouse love while he wishes*
3:10	*a pavement of love, for* the daughters of Jerusalem Arm: *he spread out bejeweled love from*
4:1	thine eyes are doves, *beside thy veil* Arm: *from your silence*
4:3	like the rind of a pomegranate is thy cheek *without thy veil* Arm: *except for/apart from your silence*
6:3,9	beautiful as Jerusalem, *terrible as armies set in array* Arm: *recounted as a wonder*
7:5	Thy head upon thee is as Carmel, and *the curls of thy hair like scarlet; the king is bound in the galleries.* Arm: *the tresses of your head like purple, like a king with his crown on his head, at the race course*
7:9	and thy throat as good wine, *going well with my kinsman, suiting* my lips and teeth Arm: *going with my Nephew in uprightness, sufficed with*

7:13	O my kinsman, I have kept them for thee
	Arm: what my mother gave me will be laid
	up for you, my Nephew
8:1	I would that thou, O my kinsman, wert he
	that sucked the breasts of my mother
	Arm: Who will cause you, my Nephew, to
	suckle at my breasts?
8:8	what shall we do for our sister, in the day
	wherein she shall be spoken for?
	Arm: *when it shall be manifest to her?*

In two places, the Armenian text uses a word which can have two meanings, and Gregory chooses to interpret the meaning which does not match with the Septuagint's commonly understood meaning. One of these occurs in 7:1— 'The joints of thy thighs are like chains'. The word for *thigh* in Armenian (*bardz*) can also mean *pillow*, and it is on the latter meaning that Gregory chooses to base his interpretation.

The other occurs in 5:14—'his hands are as turned gold set with gems of Tarsus'. The word for *gem* in Armenian (*akn*) can also mean *eye*, and that is the meaning which Gregory's chooses as the key to his interpretation of the verse. In making this choice, Gregory may have been influenced by Gregory of Nyssa's interpretation which, drawing on 1 Cor 12:21, briefly describes the relationship between the *hands* and the *eyes* in the Body of Christ.

The Role of Scripture in Gregory's Exegesis

Armenian exegetes took for granted the existence of different, equally valid versions of Scripture.[100] Gregory says in several places

---

[100] They also sometimes made up their own, rewording a text to bring out the meaning on which they were working at the time, making a specific exegetical or

that translation from Hebrew to Greek and from Greek to Armenian has significantly changed the language of Scripture as an Armenian would read it. This was not necessarily a drawback; the realization that there are several valid translations prevents one from attaching too much importance to a literal reading of one's own version, which can lead to a too narrow and restrictive understanding. Multiple versions, on the other hand, could bring out otherwise obscure facets of the rich meaning of Holy Writ. Even when people are using versions of Scripture which tally in every respect, one ought to realize that 'Scripture can be interpreted in many ways'.

Armenian exegetes had absorbed the totality of Scripture to an extent that is hard to imagine today. The Bible (independent of any issues over what might constitute its canon) was conceived of as a panoramic whole; thus, a reading of any one portion of it had necessarily to be produced against the backdrop of the entirety of Holy Writ. The Song of Songs, while it might be remarked upon briefly as a singular literary piece, was also an integral part of what was generally considered to be the Solomonic *corpus*, and that set of writings was itself only one segment of the Old Testament. The function of the Old Testament was both historical and prophetic: it looked back over God's involvement with humanity in general and the Chosen People in particular; and it looked forward (albeit in a veiled way) towards the fulfillment of that involvement, in the Incarnation, the history of the Church, and the ushering in of the eternal Kingdom at the eschaton. Hence any plausible reading of the Song of Songs would naturally reach back to Adam and forward to the next world. The notion that the history of

---

homiletical point. Vardan the Great rewrote the Psalms extensively in his commentary on them, using his own version as one among several whose lexical depths he mined for sparkling gems of divine wisdom. Resemblances between this type of exegetical reworking and targum have been noted, but a comparison of the two awaits further study.

Israel prefigured the history of the Church, which prefigured the ultimate reality of the eternal Kingdom, was one that filled the medieval mind with joyful awe at that unfolding, and inspired Christians to search the Scriptures for as much information as possible on the perfection still to come.

One of the things that held the panoramic vista of Scripture together in the mind of exegetes was the repetition of motifs; not simply of major types—like the sacrifice of Isaac and its New Testament fulfillment in the crucifixion of Christ—but repetition of names, numbers, and individual words or phrases. Exegesis was associative. Accordingly the title *Song of Songs* would be illuminated by a consideration of its relationship to similar phrases, such as *Holy of holies* or *Blessing of blessings*. The fact that *breasts* come in pairs automatically led to the connection of that image with other paired things: the testaments, for example, or the two tablets of the Law. The odd juxtaposition of *breasts* with *wine* caused the exegete to ponder the relationship between *wine* and *milk* in terms of other scriptural allusions to those drinks. The simple mention of *flocks* associated with the Groom led to commentary on Christ as the Shepherd and to musings on the fate of sheep and goats in parables of the Last Judgment. These connections may seem artificial at times. For example, the comment on Song 1:9, comparing the Bride to a *horse of Pharoah*, led both to commentary on Moses' rod and Pharaoh as counterparts of the cross of Christ and Satan respectively, and to a comparison with other 'resting places' of God.

A single word could be as evocative as an entire image: the single word *desirable* in 5:16 calls forth references to the *desire* of Herod and of Zaccheus to see Jesus, and to the *desire* of the disciples, in the future, to see 'one of the days of the Son of Man'.

Such an associative approach to the exegetical process led inevitably to the weaving together of a large number of biblical quotations or allusions in close proximity to one another, creating a kind of brocaded fabric, every fold of which reflected some element of the others. Gregory's scriptural citations number more than two hundred fifty, more or less evenly divided between the Old Testament, the Gospels, and the Epistles. This distribution is what one would expect in a discipline that seeks parallels between the former times of salvation history, the incarnation of Christ, and the history of the Church.

THEMES IN GREGORY'S COMMENTARY

While the *Commentary* speaks for itself, and while a good number of its interesting features will be pointed out in the notes to the text, it may be well to highlight here a few of the major themes in Gregory's thinking as exemplified in the *Commentary*'s pages.

On the broad canvas, Gregory writes, the Song of Songs

> shows us the brilliant adornment of the Church through the cross and the altar, the body and blood of the Lord, the holy font, and the sacred chrism, the Old and New Testaments, apostles and prophets and *vardapet*s, priests and hermits, virgins and martyrs, Christian kings and all pure peoples who were to be planted in the Church, together with other ineffable and unspeakable gifts. (Prologue)

But punctuating that grand panorama are certain motifs whose recurrence creates specific patterns or sub-themes within the larger picture.

The Incarnation

The whole of the Song of Songs revolves around the Incarnation. In his commentary to the additional verses of the Song, Gregory specifically says that the birth of the incorruptible, living and eternal Word of God re-establishes the body 'without blemish, spotless, luminous' that humanity possessed before eating of the forbidden fruit: this restoration of flesh's original glory through the incarnate flesh of the Word is the 'Blessing of blessings'.

Because of the Incarnation, we have seen the invisible *ointment poured forth*—the name of God—insofar as it is possible to see it (*Commentary* 1.3). Gregory's interpretation of the continuous, spiralling ascent in both the Bride's understanding of the Groom and her transformation into his beauty, depends on the descent of the Groom into flesh. But that is only the beginning: the Incarnation propels those who begin with even the most rudimentary recognition of Him into a spiralling ascent in understanding and love for the Incarnate Word. That ascent was the pursuit of Gregory's own life; he felt, too, that it was the pursuit of Christians throughout the Church's entire history. The growth into one's own true beauty—and, above and beyond that, into an awareness of one's own true beauty, especially as it appears in the eyes of God—was made possible by the Incarnation and by our awareness of its significance. The Incarnation makes possible a reciprocal love between God and humankind, makes it possible for humanity to 'feed' God with love, and to enjoy God's joy in that love.

The first turning in the upward spiral of love, beauty, and awareness begins in Chapter One of the Song, as Gregory describes it in his *Commentary*. There the Bride realizes that a change has taken place in her: her blackness has been transformed. She begins her pursuit of the Groom by asking where he shepherds his flocks in the shadowless light. He responds by telling her to 'know herself' and describes her as a horse and a dove; she is the vehicle of the divine, like a horse; and she should emulate the dove's purity and faithfulness. In the light of this realization, the Bride is able to regard her Nephew in a new way (*Commentary* 1.16-17).

The second turning of the spiral occupies Chapter Two. Here, the Groom reveals himself as the lily, and says that the Bride, too, is a lily (Song 2:1-2) She responds with a recognition that He is also like the apple tree. This new recognition overwhelms her; she is established in it with apples and wine (2:4-5). Then in a second moment of insight, she recognizes that she has heard His voice in many places already (2.8-9); as a result of this, he can now speak more fully and directly to her, inviting her into the springtime vineyard (2:10-13).

Chapter Three initiates yet another new upward movement in understanding and love. In verse 1, the Bride is shown as having mastered the metaphors—the lily and the hart, for example—with which the Groom has described himself. She begins to realize, however, that, wonderful and meaningful though these images are, they are no more than metaphors; there are unspeakable things yet to be communicated to her by him. She sets out on her quest through the city (3:2-3) until she is able directly to *seize* him (3:4-5). The Groom praises the new beauties which she attains through this new, more direct approach to himself (3:6), and the angels begin to describe to her new mysteries (3:7-11).

Chapter Four is devoted to the Groom's revealing to the Bride her new beauty in more detail, as her new level of awareness of the Groom also entails a new level of self-awareness. Gregory reads the chapter as a paean of praise sung by God to humanity, by Christ to the Church.

In accepting the praise offered her by the Groom, the Bride in Chapter Five has a new revelation: it is possible for her to offer him joy. Whereas in Chapter Two he invited her into the garden, the roles are now reversed, as she begs him to *come down and eat*, and he does so with delight (5:1). He offers her a new intimacy, *knocking at* her *door* (5.2), and she realizes that everything she has seen or understood to that point is still only the merest hint of his true beauty (5.4-8). The rest of the chapter is given over to her description of him as *altogether desirable* (5:16-17).

Chapter Six and the first part of Chapter Seven are again devoted to the Groom's praise of the Bride's new level of awareness

and love. Her response begins in 7:9, where a new kind of togeth-
erness is apparent. Rather than one inviting the other into the
garden, she now says, 'Let *us* go to the vineyard' (7.11-12).

After an opening dialogue in which the Bride takes the initia-
tive (8:1-2), the strength of their mutual love is described in Chapter Eight as *strong as death* and unquenchable. The conclusion
deals with the passing on of that love to others, and describes the
means by which she can help them, in their turn, to understand it.
There is an open invitation to enter into that highest mystery, an
invitation to participate in that eternal growth in understanding
of self and God, compared to which 'the things which have been
said by Solomon pale' as does everything else.

The Qualities of Christ as Groom

The upward spiral of new revelation is powered by the fact that
for Gregory, although the knowledge of Christ is unattainable, it
is also intimate: he cannot be understood except through one's
own love. The *watchmen* to whom the Bride appeals in 3:3 have
nothing to tell her about the Groom: He is instead seized directly,
by faith (3.4).

Christ is eager to acquaint those who love him with themselves, and to make their beauty obvious to others as well (3.6).
He not only loves them, but indwells them (3.7) and seeks them
out to the extent of becoming like them and sharing their existence, which entails a suffering not native to his divine nature
(3.11; 5.2). He is not only not removed from them, but he finds
nourishment and satisfaction in their love (4.11; 5.1; 8.1) and
openly delights in them (7.2-12). His love is ever wakeful towards
them, and 'to benefit from it requires only willingness on our part'
(8.5). Swift and observant as the hart (8.14), innocent (5.13),
sweet in gentleness (5.16), Christ rescues even lowly sheep from
avaricious shepherds (6.1-2). And most importantly, his love
inspires, elicits and rewards reciprocation.

The Qualities of Human Spiritual Beauty

If deep learning is not a necessary ingredient in the transformed beauty of the Bride / Church / believer, then what are that beauty's salient characteristics? Beauty begins with the recognition of the Groom's love (1.7), which produces the humility of self-knowledge (1.8). A dove-like love of purity (1.10) and an acceptance of relationship with the Groom make the believer fragrant to others, with the fragrance of virtue (1.14; 4.10).[101]

The beauty of virtue consists in pure-eyed vision (1.17; 4.1), being beyond all passion (4.2), having a homely and unsophisticated manner like a pomegranate's skin (4.3) concealing luscious nourishment that is, nonetheless, visible on the face (6.6). It is adorned with the shield of perfect faith (4.4), washed spotless through Christ's blood (4.8; 6.5; 8.1). Spiritual beauty irrigates the virtuous fruits of others' gardens (4.15). It makes one into Jerusalem, the abode of Christ (6.4). It is a beauty that grows tall like the cypress and makes the flesh as incorruptible as the spirit (6.10). It is, in short, the beauty of Christ himself (6.5).

The Elusive Vision of God

The Incarnation opened the road of ascent to the divine and made it possible for humanity to be transformed into the beauty of Christ and restored to the original glory of the first creation. But there is a tension inherent in the Incarnation: in Christ, the

---

[101] In a similar vein, John Chrysostom, in his *Homily* 5 on Genesis, says that 'merely by your comportment you will benefit those with whom you associate: by sharing in converse with you they will partake also of the spiritual fragrance that accompanies you, and of your excellent way of life'. St John Chrysostom, *Homilies on Genesis 1-17*, translated by Robert C. Hill, The Fathers of the Church 74 (Washington, DC: The Catholic University of America Press, 1999) 69.

Christian experiences God both as proximate and, at the same time, as completely Other. He is intimately near and infinitely unattainable. Gregory of Narek's whole life was to be an experience of the never-ending road that led deeper and deeper into the understanding of and love for God—a road which, in fact, has no ending, inasmuch as its destination is the Infinite himself.

What Gregory would express in poetry at the end of his life, he said at the very outset of his career here in his exegesis of Song 5:4. Seeing not the Groom himself but merely his *hand through the hole* of the door, the Bride confesses that her *belly is moved*. While Gregory has, in discussing the previous verse, made reference to the Incarnation as just such a *glimpse* of the divine, here his commentary consists of a wonderful affirmation that no matter how ineffable one's experience of the divine may be as one progresses through life, 'compared to what he will show us and give us knowledge of in the life to come, these are like a person seeing only the *hand through a hole*, or like a drop of water compared to the water of the sea, or like a lamp compared to the sun, or like a babe in its mother's womb compared to an old man'.

Indeed, while the whole *Commentary* pivots on the Incarnation, its various strands are woven into a picture of the stages in the Bride's increasing awareness—her discovery, at every turning, that however overwhelming her love and her realization of love may become, it is still nothing. In the words of one of the desert fathers at the end of his life, she comes to the end only to find that she has made no more than a beginning: 'I recognized him, and I was united to his love, and I was ebullient with his commandments. And thinking that I had attained something, I recognized myself to be all the more distant from attainment' (5.6).

Gregory's desire to draw Gurgēn along the infinite road of God's love for us and ours for God, is both positive and joyful in its longing. The road to death is the road to an opening of eternity in the inner person, constrained though that may be by time: 'Now it is clear that first it is needful to die, and to "put to death the members of the flesh" (Col 3:5), as the same Apostle affirms, and then there will be an entering of God and the divine mysteries into man' (5.5).

Whether Gurgēn was drawn into that eternal cycle of death and new birth, discovery of abundance and realization of nothingness, we do not know. But that cycle—embodied in and made possible by the descent of the Incarnation and the human ascent whose path it opened—and the tensions which drive it, are the fundamental concern of the *Commentary*.

Humanity and the Angels

Speculation on the exact nature of the relationship between the angels and human beings, who were made 'only a little lower than the angels', was a frequent occupation of medieval Christian thinkers. Once a connection had been established between the *maidens* in the Song of Songs and the angels, a commentary on the work became a good vehicle by which Gregory could expound his understanding of the angelic nature, with its limitations, and the exaltation of humanity to a rank that would no longer be even 'a little lower' than theirs.

The first human beings lost their original, created glory through the jealousy of a fallen angel, Satan, whose very desire to see man evicted from that created glory caused his own fall from glory, and that of his cohorts. To be forced to witness a return of humankind to its original state would have been in and of itself sufficient punishment for Satan. But God went farther. Because one entire class of angels had been lost by the plunge into the abyss of the satanic legions, man would be reinstated in their place, making once again complete the nine ranks of angels alluded to by Paul, and bringing their number back to ten, the number of perfection. In the commentary on 5:3 the Bride is depicted as saying, 'I . . . have been dressed in light and been given the authority to direct myself toward heaven and to join the ranks of the angels'. And in the commentary on 8:5 Gregory says that Christ, 'Taking us by the hand, has led us into the place of the fallen angels, with the result that the ones whom Satan could not bear to see in Paradise, he should see occupying his own place in glory'.

But that was not all. The angelic nature is not perfect. It is modest, as are all females (1.6), but its knowledge is limited. The nature of God, which is concealed from our imperfect sight, is also concealed from theirs, although not to the same degree. The Bride is unable to learn of the Groom from them (3.3). On the contrary, the angels learn of the Incarnation of Christ from us humans; 'You have given us soul and heart to see what we had not known; that is, the provident love which He has displayed towards humanity—birth through the font, adoption, and the kingdom as well—which He accomplished through the death on the Cross', the angels / friends of the Groom say to the Bride in the commentary on 4:9. And on 5.17, Gregory says, 'The One who is invisible to them they desire to see in the flesh, who was seen by us in the flesh, having been among us. Through us they came to learn of His descent from heaven and His incarnation, and they still continue to learn'.

Clearly, God loved human beings more than the angels, for he took our nature, not theirs, despite the fact that they, too, had fallen. Their function is to minister to us, whether as nations, provinces, cities, or individuals (5.7). Humanity's destiny is not only to fill up the ranks of the fallen angels, but to become like God himself, a destiny beyond the angelic, leading to a remarkable intimacy with God. Speaking of the Bride's beauty and of how the Groom desires it, Gregory says that this is 'exactly as the Theologian said—"Gazing upon God, to become God". This shows that those who look to God and draw near to him, acquire God's beauty, just as a wick, by approaching the lamp, is transformed into its same light' (6.4).

God as Mother

Over and above the predictable identification of the Church as Mother Sion, and her font as the womb from which all Christians are born, there is from the outset of the *Commentary* a recurrent image of God as Mother. This does not diminish God's fatherly role, but rather adds another dimension to it. In speaking of the sub-title to the Song of Songs, Gregory says that 'we beseech our Parent to kiss us with maternal love'; this is immediately followed by a reference to the father's kiss of the returning prodigal son. Satan, who was created by God, as was humanity, is spoken of as our 'mother's son' (1.6), and in the commentary on 3:4 heaven is our 'mother's house'.

These two images—of God as Mother and Church as Mother—do indeed overlap. In 7.13, 'the mother is the holy Catholic Church and the Holy Spirit, . . . and Christ'. But the image of God as Mother is very clearly spelled out. Commenting on 8:5, Gregory speaks of Christ as having come from 'the Mother of All, who is his begetter by nature and ours through grace'. He goes on to say of Solomon that

> He uses the word *travail*; *travail* is indicative of a *mother*; therefore it is Christ's Father and ours that he referred to as *mother*. The Father, however, was *in travail* through His messages in the Law and the Prophets, and *gave birth to* His children through water and the spirit (Jn 3:5), as brothers of Christ. So our Mother is One—the Father Begetter, the omnipotent God.[102]

---

[102] The image of God as Mother would later be taken for granted by Vanakan Vardapet (1181–1251) who, in his unpublished *Harts'munk' ew Pataskhanik'* [Questions and Answers], in preparation by the present writer, takes students to task for finding the application of feminine imagery to God strange or offensive.

The Significance of Numbers

One of the adornments of medieval biblical interpretation was its resonance with the numerical truths revealed in the structure of the universe. Although Christianity applied the ideas of Pythagoras in ways that the ancient pagan sage would not have recognized, the belief that the microcosm and the macrocosm were reflected in one another by means of the numbers which governed them both was something the two intellectual traditions shared.

In the tenth century the basics of biblical arithmology already had a long exegetical history and were taken for granted.[103] While Gregory does not indulge in arithmological explanations to the extent that others do, they are still among the elements of his interpretation. In the introduction to his *Commentary* Gregory says that the phrase 'our eyes by fifties', found in the additional verses to the Armenian Song of Songs text, implies the imperfection of human vision, whereas 100, as the square of 10, would imply perfection. In this he is drawing quite specifically on the ancient idea that 10 is perfect because it is the sum of the first four integers (just as 3 and 6 are also perfect, being the sum of the first two and the first three integers respectively)—perfect because four is the least number of points needed to create a three dimensional figure in geometry. The same reasoning is used again in 8.12, where Gregory expounds on the 'thousands for Solomon' to be rendered to him by the keepers of his vineyard.

The fact that there are *sixty queens* mentioned in 6:7 can be interpreted in two ways, Gregory tells us: if we look at sixty as 12 x 5, it denotes the persons who, by the right use of their *five* senses, were chosen by God from among the *twelve* tribes of Israel. If we

---

[103] On the use of numbers in Armenian patristic writing see Robert W. Thomson, 'Number Symbolism and Patristic Exegesis in Some Early Armenian Writers', *Handēs Amsōreay* 90 (1976) [hereafter, Thomson, 'Number Symbolism'] 117–138.

regard it as 6 x 10, it can be extrapolated to 6,000, the number of years in the history of the Old Dispensation, with which the *queens* are identified. Likewise, the number 80, assigned to the *concubines* who represent the more numerous gentile believers, can be extrapolated to 8,000, and the *concubines* are to be crowned in the eighth millennium.

By virtue of their occurrence in Scripture or theology, certain of the ancient significant numbers took on new weights of meaning in a Christian context. In 8.12, the vineyard keepers themselves receive 'two hundred', signifying the *two* natures which they possess.

The Importance of the Church and Her Doctors, the Vardapets

According to the prologue, *vardapets*, doctors of the Church, are one of God's ineffable gifts to the faithful. They are part of the *palanquin* of Solomon; that is, they are the 'resting place' of God. And what is more, they constitute one of the three essential parts of that palanquin, identified by Paul in 1 Cor 12:28 as 'apostles, prophets and teachers (*vardapets*)' (3.10).

The role played by the *vardapets* was one of great importance. In Gregory's imagery they are not, as one might assume, the *mind* of the Church. Instead, Gregory identifies them as Christ's *jaws*, whose function it is to take in the Word, ruminate on it, and produce it in digestible form for the rest of the Body. But they are not to do the Body's digesting for it:

> Instead, they dispense the knowledge of Scripture at an intermediate level of instruction, so that it may neither be despised as something negligible, by being too easily acquired, nor cause despair among those who desire to learn, by its unintelligibility (5.13).

Their function is to induce the other members of the Body to put forth the effort required to digest the Word for themselves and make it their own. This image goes a long way towards explaining why there are very few simple, straightforward works produced by Armenian *vardapets*; their role was not so much to make plain as it was to allure through explanation.

Gregory goes on to say that the *vardapets* are also Christ's *lips*, 'pouring forth myrrh in abundance'. That is, they are not dispensing information to the faithful, *per se*; they are attracting the faithful to the beneficial death (symbolized by the myrrh) necessary to growth in grace:

> a complete death—mortifying the thoughts of the mind, so as not to think on things earthly but on things heavenly; mortifying the belly by restricting its intake of foods; mortifying the eyes by gazing not with lascivious appetite, but on legitimate beauty and on the face of the longed-for Groom, Christ (5.17).

People who have been attracted to greater love for Christ by the *vardapets*, then go on to lead the angels into more perfect praise.

In the end, however, everything the *vardapets* say is incomplete and indirect compared with Real Knowledge. *Vardapets* should never lose sight of the fact that Christ is the True *Vardapet*, whose instruction is a process that will go on throughout eternity (8.14). The earthly *vardapets* are on an equal footing with everyone else where the love of God is concerned. God finds the *vardapets* beautiful, not because of their teaching or the depth of their understanding, but because they have desired him (7.6-7), and He 'goes about' with them as they cultivate compassion for all humanity and bear the fruit of virtue (7.12-13). In other words, God's relationship with them is neither more nor less special than the relationship He has with any other willing believer. They simply fulfill a unique function in the Church body.

The *vardapets* are able to serve the Church because she alone bears in her *breasts* the essential nourishment of Christian life:

> Now, as those who are estranged from their mother's milk and from her nourishment die, so also those who are estranged from the Church and Her breasts—that nourishment by means of Scripture which is the Church's *breasts*—and do not enter into Her with desire and longing and are not in Her fed with Scripture, cannot live, but die an eternal death (6.8).

The Church is Mother in the same way that God is Mother: without God we have no existence; without the Church, we are no Christians; we cannot be born as children of God in any other way than through her font. She is the corporate Bride of Christ; the individual believer cannot be wedded to Christ except as part of her. We have noted above that Gregory was careful to assign a clearly unsurpassable status to the Church partly because of the church political situation in which his family found itself. But there is no question that, quite independently of his encounters with the Church Temporal, his mystical reverence for the Church Ideal was genuine and lifelong, and that as a *vardapet* he felt his connection to Her nourishment most strongly.

The Example of Saint Gregory the Illuminator

While there have been many saints who exemplified the spiritual beauty which is Christ's own, Armenians resonated in a special way with the spiritual qualities of Gregory the Illuminator, who had brought about the official, state christianization of Armenia at great personal cost. Son of the regicide who had done away with Armenia's king Khosrov Arshakuni, Gregory had indeed undergone transformation from a political to a spiritual life. In addition, he had endured more than a decade of imprisonment following a remarkable number of inventive tortures devised for him by Khosrov's son, Trdat. Gregory of Narek was aware that he shared the Illuminator's name, and found it significant that the name means 'wakeful'; plays on the word occur from time to time in his writing.

Gregory the Illuminator is listed just after the Theotokos and the Protomartyr in the commentary on 6:1, putting him in the company of the apostles, among the *sixty queens*. The Illuminator is not only quoted more often in the *Commentary* than any other Church Father, but he also serves as an example of special devotion to Christ. In Gregory's commentary on 2:5, it is Gregory the Illuminator who exemplifies the extent to which a person may be ravished by the love of Christ—to the point that suffering of no matter what intensity appears to be bliss if it is endured for the sake of Christ. In 5.8, as well, it is Gregory the Illuminator who is given as the first example of a saint who was overwhelmed by the love of Christ and who, as a result, received from Christ the power to endure. The possibility of dying to suffering while remaining alert to the divine is also illustrated by the Illuminator; as Gregory comments on 5:2, 'By putting to sleep the natural passions, he was a partaker in Christ's death with wakeful mind'.

The Possibility of Losing What One Has Gained

Gregory of Narek was keenly aware that one must not rest on the grace of God *as if on a bed* (3.1). There is, in fact, 'no rest' for those who set foot on the path of eternal growth in grace: quoting the Theologian, he avers that 'one must be ever moving towards virtue, and agile' (4.9).

Indeed, those who have once scented that fragrance of divine virtue never desist from the pursuit of it (1.4). There is, however, always the possibility that one may lose by lack of vigilance what one has gained through the combination of divine grace and one's own efforts. Lack of vigilance results in dire consequences. As Gregory says in his commentary at 5.2, 'Now, preserve that which you have received; that is, the innocence of a dove and that perfection, and do not lose it again, for there will be no second Cross, and no second death for your sake'. Even bishops and *vardapet*s, to say nothing of royal figures like Gurgēn and simple believers who have been joined to Christ through baptism and have set out on the road of Bridehood, can fail to attain their lofty destiny. And if it should happen that they 'thereafter separate themselves from Him', they will find that they have 'dissolved the love of Christ their Groom and the vow which they made to one another', and have instead been 'wedded to Satan, the teacher of evil'. Gregory felt that those who turn their back on the divine love lavished on them—as depicted in the Song of Songs—'will rightfully receive unfailing torment'. The Upright One has loved us. He requires the same love from us, his beloved (1.4). To spurn divine love, ineffable beauty, and the prospect of ever increasing proximity to the Divine is, in the end, to reduce oneself to a sub-human level.

The Beauty of Human Love

This love is possible because the beauty of divine love has been made clearly manifest—even to the eyes of a fallen humanity—in the beauty of married love. Yes, there is a certain sense in which 'we ought first to bewail our licentious ways', which have 'constrained the Holy Spirit to relay these ineffable things' to us so indirectly as to portray them in the guise of human affections. Yet this marital love, which is 'second-best' insofar as it is a metaphor, is a wonderful and perfect mystery in its own right.

One can negate the beauty of married love by approaching the married state unworthily. But Gregory's paean to the love of husband and wife, given in the Prologue, makes clear that the love ordained by God from the very outset of human existence was intended as a motivation to devotion and sanctity second to none. Married love is a gift of the Holy Spirit; it leads to the heights of self-sacrifice—as indeed it did in the case of Adam and Eve, when Adam chose to sacrifice his own life in Paradise rather than be separated from Eve. And Adam realized prophetically that human salvation was to come through the vehicle of a woman's love, a recognition reflected in his choice of a name for his wife: 'Life'.

The love of parents for their children, too, is a divine force within human life: 'Wherever holy love resides, be it parental or marital, or the like, *rivers* cannot *deter it,* neither can sword nor fire nor death' (8.7).

In addition to these human to human loves, every human being is endowed with an innate love for God. This love, Gregory asserted, 'cannot be sapped'. The human impulse to that divine love 'overcomes fire and water and bonds and flayings and imprisonment and wife and children'.

Glorious in and of itself, then, all human love of this kind leads naturally to the divine.

A Note on the Translation

This translation is based on the text of the 1789 Venice edition. The Venice 1840 edition has also been consulted, but the translation into modern Armenian (Beirut 1963) was not used.

Because the reader of this volume will not have the Armenian text available for examination and comparison, every effort has been made to insure that the English translation is understandable in and of itself and that its literary tone is equivalent to that of the Armenian. (Citations of works available only in Armenian have also been avoided in the footnotes.) Armenisms have been kept to a minimum; the lengthy, clause-laden sentences of proper Armenian classical style have been broken up to make the meaning more accessible in English. However, certain vocabulary essential to the commentator's thinking has been retained: the Armenian term *Nephew* has been kept in rendering the common English term *Beloved,* and the text of the Song has not been altered in any way that would bring it in line with standard English versions based on the Hebrew, or indeed with the Septuagint. In biblical citations, numbering of the psalms follows that of the Septuagint.

Words taken directly from a verse of the Song which is being commented upon, are italicized wherever they occur in the interpretation.

Transliterations have been made following the system established by the Library of Congress.

Since Robert W. Thomson has already produced a listing of parallels between Gregory of Narek's commentary and that of Gregory of Nyssa, the numbering used by Thomson has been included in the square brackets in the text.[104]

---

[104] The numbering is explained in Thomson, Song.

Commentary on Solomon's
Song of Songs

elucidated by the inspired
Lord Gregory, spiritual teacher,
son of Bishop Khosrov

Prologue

Your pious majesty's command, O royal lord, was more forceful and higher than our capacity, for such a request—to comment upon the Song of Songs—is a matter for those who are Solomon-like in spirit. If Gregory of Nyssa, who was a perfect doctor of the church and indwelt by the Spirit, was deterred from completing a commentary on this book, how much much more shall I, who am ignorant in every way and devoid of the grace of the Spirit, be incapable of following the thoughts uttered by the solomonic spirit! Particularly since there is no little condemnation and punishment for those who, in order not to appear ignorant, distort the words of Holy Writ through alien interpretation and with vainglorious pride display as true things which are nothing of the kind. Nonetheless, since we are commanded to be obedient to the orders of kings, I make so bold as to say what my weak mind is capable of attaining to, hoping in the Holy Spirit, and carrying out the command of him who said, 'Remain subject to kings'.[105]

Now, first and foremost I rejoiced that you have evinced such an intention to examine Scripture, and to attend to learning; this betokens a fear of the Lord and an alienation from vile concerns,

---

[105] The phrase is an echo of the following, though it is not an exact quotation of any of them: Titus 3:1; Col 3:22; Eph 6:5; Heb 13:11. It is especially true to the spirit of Rom 13:1-8. The same quotation is repeated in the Colophon.

idle speculations and sin-loving ways, and an approach to that
bliss of which the Prophet says, 'Blessed is the man who has not
walked in the way of the wicked', and so on.

A little farther on he remarks, 'But he meditates on the law of
the Lord day and night'. And then, adding the reward of meditat-
ing on the law of the Lord, he says 'He shall be like a tree which
is planted by the rivers of water' (Ps 1:1-3). For as a tree which is
planted by the rivers of water is never withered, so also is the one
who examines the injunctions of God and is attentive to them
day and night. He likewise will remain ever green in this life, and
whatever he does God will prosper, as he prospered David himself, who was a king. Great king that he was, he spurned the cares
of war and all bodily necessities, and thought only on the things
of God. Because of this, he remained invincible to his enemies.

See the same in Solomon; how universal a king he was! And
yet his continual concern was for that which you are reading,
along with so many other writings that the world would not have
sufficed to bear them all, had all his writings survived. But since
the world was not worthy, and since it was not good for people
to acquire such boundless knowledge, God removed Solomon's
writings from the earth, because he had brought to light everything which God had done upon the earth. And had he not fallen,
he would have attained yet greater grace. Thus, it is right to emulate such kings, and insatiably to study the law of the Lord.

But for now, let that be, that we may involve ourselves in the
beginning of our commentary.

First, it is proper to say how the title *Song of Songs* is interpreted,
and thereby to learn about the limitless dignity of it. The *Song of
Songs* is the Blessing of blessings. In the same way we are used to
call the holy apse where the holy altar stands the *Holy of holies*, as
the Apostle himself says.[106] That is, if the church is holy the altar

---

[106] Perhaps a reference to Heb. 9:3 or 9:25.

is doubly holy and more so. This Song of songs, in a similar way, is above and beyond all songs and blessings; just as the Gospel is called holy and honorable above all writings in the New Testament, so this is above all writings in the Old. Concerning it, one must know that it was sung aloud in the temple, with greater suitability and prophetic inspiration than the Psalms of David, because the mystery concealed in its awesome words is ineffable.

And no corporeal being can comprehend it, except those who are in spirit like Paul, who was caught up into the third heaven and heard unutterable words which it is beyond the power of a human being to utter (2 Cor 12:2-4). For our ears cannot bear to hear the mysteries of God, just as our eyes cannot bear the sight of God.

Thus Solomon, desiring to relate the ineffable, did so by means of a corporeal parable: by means of groom and bride, nephew and princess, daughter and dove, breasts and incense, and oil poured out, apples, mountain goats, Solomon, king, the city of Jerusalem, a garden and such like things which the eye aspires to see and the ear enjoys and the mind desires. In just such a way do the parents of children conceal special things in a good-looking package so that [the children], seeing the exterior to be desirable, will consider what is inside to be the greater treasure, and will thereby be encouraged to preserve carefully what is within. Likewise a sweet and expensive unguent like nard, which Solomon specifically mentions, is contained in a vessel; moreover, its fragrance cannot last apart from that.

As the Lord Himself says in the Holy Gospel, 'Do not cast your pearls before swine' (Mt 7:6); that is, do not present ineffable things to weak ears. The same Spirit instructed Solomon neither to disseminate openly the things which he had seen by the Spirit's light, nor to conceal completely the mysteries of the Church and salvation and the incarnation of Christ and all that he suffered for love of humankind, and his death and resurrection, and his second coming, and the unimaginable rewards which are stored up for the saints, and the intensity of the saints' love for Christ, which they bore within themselves to the extent of suffering and death, loving Christ as He loved us (1 Jn 4:19); who in order to express His boundless love towards us was obliged to put on flesh, and even to spill his holy blood for us. He who as God would have been able by *fiat* to save us from Satan's clutches, did it through righteousness, and restrained him by force. He accomplished this quietly, and not through domination. Thus our servitude was to be redeemed both legally and mercifully; the death, that is, by which it was lawfully decreed for us to return to dust because of our disregard for the commandment not to eat of the fruit [of the tree of the knowledge of good and evil]. That just judgment he did not remove without the Law, although he had the authority to do so. Rather, he put on the flesh of Adam, and took upon himself his death, and redeemed us through righteousness. Moreover, he mingled mercy with righteousness and righteousness with mercy, and it was through all this that he displayed his love towards us, which is beyond telling.

All of this the Song of Songs relates; by parables, it shows us the brilliant adornment of the Church through the cross and the altar, the body and blood of the Lord, the holy font and the sacred chrism, the Old and New Testaments, apostles and prophets and *vardapets*,[107] priests and hermits, virgins and martyrs, Christian kings and all pure peoples who were to be planted in the Church, together with other ineffable and so inexpressible gifts. Yet, even he did not recognize the whole of it, nor was he able to acquaint us with it all; he could not even clearly express what he himself knew, but rather did so by analogy.

Should one then ask, 'How could he allegorize this using a bride and groom? How is it possible to signify the mystery of God by means of physical desire, and to illustrate the limitless love

---

[107] On the significance of the *vardapet* in the Armenian church, see above, n. 19.

of God by analogy with passionate love?' We ought first to bewail our licentious ways, we who are so far estranged from God's mysteries that the Holy Spirit, through Solomon, was constrained to relay these insupportable things to us by means of an animal desire. It is because of such realities that the blessed universal teacher John asserts that we ought to adopt such a saintly way of life that Scripture would become unnecessary[108]—as was the case for Noah and Abraham and his sons and grandsons, and as it was for Job and Moses and the apostles, who instead of Scripture had Him dwelling in their hearts, and He taught them and wrote on the tables of their hearts rather than in books (2 Cor 3:3).

We would thus have obtained a heart so illumined and angelic that we would have had no need of such parables of bride and groom to formulate the mysteries of Christ and the Church and whatever intelligible good things are in heaven. However, since we have lost that kind of dignity and have blinded those eyes, let us turn, sighing, to the second-best, and view the spiritual things through the physical, as Solomon, having received the grace of the Holy Spirit, relates them.

In addition, holy matrimony, and the love of a groom for his bride and of a bride for her groom, as it is free from defilement, is not foreign to the grace of the Spirit through whom its mystery is consummated in that of Christ and the Church. The Apostle, confirming the words of Solomon, says, 'This mystery is great. But I speak of Christ and the Church' (Eph 5:32). Thus, whoever defiles holy matrimony by defiled relations and evil acts, defiles the mystery of the Church and dishonors Christ, for [Christ and the Church] are the archetype of [marriage].

Let us expound yet more on the mystery set before us and show that God has love towards humanity as great as a groom's

---

[108] The source of this reference is unknown to me. It is my hope that readers more deeply versed in patristic literature than I will be able to identify some of the quotations which have eluded me.

for his bride. Isaiah says, 'As the bridegroom rejoices in the bride, so does the Lord rejoice in you' (Is 62:5). David himself also says this in his lament over Jonathan, 'Love of you pains me more than the love of women' (2 Sam 1:26).

Now, there is nothing more honorable or greater on earth than the love of a man and a woman. If to some individual it seems not to be especially great or important, it seems so because he has either not come to marriage in a sacred way or has not maintained his virginity in a holy manner, but by his prodigal defilements he has thrust away from himself the grace of the Spirit. Whereas all who approach marriage in a pure and spotless manner, and by the Holy Spirit's ineffable love are united to one another, are blessed with the blessing whereby Adam and Eve were blessedly united. Those who are united with this kind of love and blessing die for one another, literally to the degree that they will spill their blood for one another.

It is the case that for love of family many have fallen away from Christ and apostacized because of the persecutions of our time. But even Adam gave up Paradise and the light of glory for love of his wife and fell outside, not because he wanted to become God, but because it seemed to him too onerous to be separated from her love. He well knew that he would be punished by God—because he was not an ignorant person but rather was filled with the prophetic spirit—and he had not yet fallen from the grace of the Spirit, because he had not yet transgressed the commandment.

Even after eating the fruit, he did not completely lose the Spirit, but while he was in Paradise he understood through the Holy Spirit the ways of all living creatures; and when God brought them to Adam, he gave them names one by one according to their individual habits. While he slept, Eve was created and when He brought her to him, he prophetically declared, 'This now is bone of my bone' (Gn 2:23), and he foretold as well the procreative increase which would derive from woman, and the leaving of father and mother to go after one's wife, and their becoming one flesh (Gn 2:24).

Moreover, after eating the fruit, he prophetically recognized our salvation, which was to come through woman, that is, through the Holy Mother of God; for which reason he named his wife 'Life' (Gn 3:20). If this had not been so, how could he have called 'Life' her, who became the cause of death to all Adam's generations? The Holy Illuminator, too, says, 'Saying this, he understood all the deeds which were to be on earth until the accomplishment, even salvation through Christ'.[109]

Now if, when he had fallen from glory, he retained the spirit of prophecy, how much more must he have had it while he was yet in glory! Thus it is obvious that, as the Apostle says, 'Adam was not deceived' by the snake's lying promise through Satan, 'but the woman was deceived and transgressed' (1 Tim 2:14); Adam ate of the fruit in order not to be separated from his wife, and for love of her, not in order to become god—as the woman had eaten.

It is the same even now; for love of their wives men honor their wives' injunctions, knowing perfectly well that what they will is wrong and not appropriate, yet for love of them they are constrained to do it. Hence Solomon, being aware that in humans this love is greater than any other love, used it as a parable of the love of Christ and the Church for one another. Not that the love of God is simply equivalent to this one; God's love is greater than

---

[109] In *Teaching of St. Gregory* §264 and §276 there are statements similar to this. The idea that Adam was a prophet can be found in numerous sources and across many centuries. The thirteenth-century teacher Vanakan Vardapet, for example, in his *Questions and Answers* notes that Adam's identification of Eve was evidence that God had given him prophetic powers; the same idea is to be found in the *Cave of Treasures*, tr. E. A. Wallis Budge (London: The Religious Tract Society, 1927) 53, and in Saint Ephrem the Syrian's *Commentary on Genesis*, Syriac version (the Armenian version does not include it); K. McVey, ed., *St. Ephrem the Syrian: Selected Prose Works*, tr. Edward G. Mathews, Jr. and Joseph P. Amar. The Fathers of the Church, 91 (Washington, DC: The Catholic University of America, 1995) 150.

that of marriage, to the same extent that the inequality between God and humanity is great.

Nonetheless, anyone who reads this book needs to purify his mind and understanding of all thoughts of bodily marriage, and then to devote himself to the hearing of it. For this is Mount Horeb, where God dwelt, and just as when any beast approached that mountain it was stoned,[110] the same fate will befall anyone who approaches the revealed words of this book in an animal manner. For which reason we ought to place ourselves beyond all fleshly thoughts, closing the eyes of the body and opening those of the spirit, so that we may be able like Moses to ascend this conceptual mount where God lives, and to express, according to our ability, the secret, deep things of God which are in it. May the Holy Spirit lead us, giving to us a tongue to speak, and to you who listen, a mind to hear.

[110] An allusion to Ex 19:10-15.

Ecclesiastes

T hat is, the ingathering of the *Ecclesia*, which was divided into futile cults; it is the people that is called the *Ecclesia*, the Church.

[111]*I understood that the flesh strengthens youth.*

That is, the *youth* of Adam, aged by sin, attained to Solomon's knowledge through the Holy Spirit; the *flesh* is our own, which Christ was to put on. By means of that flesh was our decrepit nature strengthened to return to youth, putting on the glorious light of which it had been stripped.

He shall elevate it into our barns,

Whether you understand this as Paradise or heaven—both are possible interpretations—into it the Lord shall *elevate* us who

---

[111] Here the rubric *The maidens and the queens say* is omitted. (On the rubrics, see n. 99, above.) Vardan the Great authored a sermon on 'the Word of Solomon, "I knew that flesh [strengthens] youth"'; P'.P' Ant'apyan, *Vardan Arewelts'i, Kyank'n u Gorjunĕut'yunĕ* [Vardan Arewelts'i, Life and Work] (Erevan, 1989), vol. 2:324. The piece occurs in only one ms (M 5862) and comprises a mere three pages; nonetheless, its existence attests to the acceptance of the additional verses to the Song of Songs.

have been brought low through sin. And if anyone should ask who accomplished this salvation, he will hear—

> *our king,* Christ, *who sits on the throne like a date palm,*
> *golden and full of myrrh.*

The flesh reigning united with the Word of God *on the throne* of God, like *a golden date palm* pure of sin as gold is pure, foretells the divine united with the flesh, that is with the *date palm*. How is it that our flesh was called a *date palm*? It is because His flesh was unspotted by sin. For if David says 'The righteous flourish like a date palm' (Ps 92:12) because of their propriety, how much more would this metaphor apply to the divinized flesh! Because He suffered mortality, He is also *full of myrrh,* which was brought to Him by the very magi themselves as a gift, with the two other gifts, to foretell this; I need not remind you that He was wrapped in *myrrh* at His burial.

> *The king shall return thence to his youth,*

This utterance repeats the previous ones, which said that *the flesh strengthens youth.* Man is here referred to as *king,* because he was made in the image of God. *The king shall return thence to his youth;* that is, to the original glory which he possessed in Paradise.

> *my beloved to his chamber.*

Whereas in the preamble he called the Kingdom a *barn,* where the just are to be 'stored up', here he refers to it as a *chamber.* He is the *beloved* because He loved man more than the angels, by virtue of which love He put on our nature.

Sing his love.

That is, bless the love of Him who loved so much, who granted such gifts to us again by means of His death.

Even I am in the Psalter.

This sentence has two interpretations: one, that 'I am the One described in the Psalms. What I achieved in the direction of salvation, and what I suffered, is written in the Psalms'. I do not want to adduce witnesses in support of this interpretation one by one, since I am trying to be concise.

The second interpretation is that, 'If someone desires to sing and bless my love by means of the Psalms, it is I who instruct him, how he should bless Me'. The Apostle attests to this, saying, 'When one stands in prayer, we do not know how it ought to be, but the Spirit himself intercedes for us with soundless groaning' (Rom 8:26). In other words, when you groan in prayer the Holy Spirit wordlessly and soundlessly teaches you the words of blessing.

I shall sing with my companions;

That is, with the angels. How can the angels be called our *companions*? For one thing, we came into existence through the Creator, as did they; and for a second, we were not far from angelic glory, but 'only a little lower than the angels', as David says (Ps 8:6).

we shall sing and rejoice in the beloved King,

That is, when we receive again our lost glory we shall rejoice in our King, Christ, who loved us, and we shall sing to Him with blessing.

although we may be hidden from sight,

Hereby he expresses that although God is invisible to us because we have physical eyes, we shall bless Him unseeingly.

our eyes by fifties.

Among the numbers, ten is perfect. And if one counts higher, he returns to one, saying 'ten-plus-one' and so on. The Theologian affirms this too.[112] Now, what applies to the units, also applies to the tens—ten tens are a hundred, and five tens are fifty. One hundred is a perfect number, like ten; while fifty is half that number, like five is half of ten. Thus, humans have half eyes—that is, *by fifties*—not perfect ones. So how could one see what is concealed *from* our *sight*; that is, from our *fifties*? It is invisible even to the hundreds!—that is, it is also invisible to the angels. Albeit not to the same degree as it is for us, yet their vision also is imperfect.

The Lord created you and established you.

He made the first man, and He also re-established in that same glory the one who had fallen.

He prepared you from the womb;
your mother was the most beautiful among women.

---

[112] Gregory Nazianzen, *Oration* 45.xiv mentions the perfection of the number ten; its perfection was a standard topos of Christian arithmology, having been sanctioned by Philo, the foundation of so much exegetical thinking. See also R. Ervine, 'Vardan Vardapet's Sermon on the Ten Commandments'. *St. Nersess Theological Review* 8 (2003) 12–83, esp. 64–66.

The womb is the font, and it is the Church which is called *Mother* Sion, for 'Sion is called mother, and a man was born in her' (Ps 86:5).

> *A body shall be born for him without fault and without blemish,*
> *by another Providence.*

That is, by the Holy Spirit. The Apostle, too, says, 'Born again, not of corruptible seed, but of the incorruptible, living and eternal Word of God' (1 Pt 1:23).

> *For he had possessed such,*

That is, previously they had had a body without blemish, spotless, luminous, before he ate of the fruit.

> *and it was the blessings of blessings*

By saying *blessing of blessings*, he herewith adduces as evidence the words of his father David, 'The Lord said to me, thou art my son, and this day have I begotten thee' (Ps 2:7).

1.1 *The Song of Songs, which is Solomon's*

Solomon means *peace*. Thus, he symbolizes Christ, for 'He is our peace', as the Apostle says (Eph 2:14).

Now since we have been born a new generation, we beseech our parent to kiss us with maternal love, to bring us near to the divine mouth, so that when She kisses us, we may drink from Her mouth that which Her all-holy mouth said: 'If anyone thirst, let him come to me and drink' (Jn 7:37) [Nyssa 779a].

Because of that, it says:

— CHAPTER ONE —

1.2 Let him kiss me with the kisses of his mouth,[113]

Moreover, being the prodigal son, we are kissed by our heavenly Father, as the Gospel parable relates. So under the guise of the kiss, we beseech Him to increase 'the love wherewith He loved us' (Eph 2:4).

for your breasts are better than wine,

The commandments which are 'sucked' by the spirit from the *breasts* of Scripture, *are better than wine*; as the Prophet says, 'The words of your mouth are better to me than thousands of gold and silver' (Ps118:72). For the milk which flows from the breast is the cause of life, whereas wine merely gives strength.[114]

1.3 and the odor of your unguents is better than all fragrant incense.

Thus are the virtue and good works which emanate from the divine *unguent* [Nyssa 781B-C]; in other words, that which the Holy Spirit teaches to those who draw near and savor it.

Your name is like ointment poured forth;

---

[113] The awkwardness of the shift in English between Her/Him is less noticeable in Armenian, in which third person singular pronouns are not gender specific.

[114] In the poetical setting of his *Ban* 75.14 Narek states that the milk of Mother Church's breasts is Christ's blood. *Odes of Solomon* 8:14; 14:2; 19:1-4, uses the imagery of the breasts: 19:4 says 'The Holy Spirit opened Her bosom and mixed the milk of the two breasts of the Father.' James H. Charlesworth, ed., *The Old Testament Pseudepigrapha* (New York/London/Toronto/Sydney/Auckland: Doubleday, 1985) 2:752.

And as what is poured out of the vessel is unexaminable, and only by means of the vessel is the ointment in it recognized, by the same token the nature of the godhead is unfathomable and inconceivable and invisible, *like ointment poured forth.* Yet it perfumes the souls of the righteous [Nyssa 784A] and those who, in terms of sin, are like little children (1 Cor 14:20); the ointment, like its vessel, is precious.

Now, since the godhead's name is *like ointment poured forth,* and is unattainable by human knowledge, even by the perfect saints—and not only the saints, but also the entire panoply of the heavenly beings—nonetheless, by means of His union with our nature through the holy Virgin, we have seen the *ointment* insofar as it is possible to see it. This the Lord himself said to the blind man: when He asked, 'Do you believe in the Son of God?' and he responded, 'Who is he, Lord?' the Lord added, 'You have both seen Him, and the one who speaks with you is He' (Jn 9:35-37). He meant that, having seen the divinized flesh, he had seen the invisible *ointment* Himself.

therefore do the maidens love thee.

He identifies as *maidens* those who in terms of sin have become like children (1 Cor 14:20), and the angels as well.

> 1.4 *We shall run after you because of the fragrance of your ointments.*

Those who become worthy to sample the flavor of the Word of God, and to take in His fragrance, *run* insatiably *after the fragrance* of His *ointments,* and never desist from the pursuit [Nyssa 785A]. Even though it might happen that they suffer prison and bonds or be obliged to forsake their children, as the first saints who detected this *fragrance* took it upon themselves to do, they do not swerve.[115]

The bride tells the maidens concerning what the groom has granted her.

The Church and the people are called *the Bride*. And the *maidens* are the angels and saints; those who, as has been mentioned, have become as little children with regard to sin. So the Bride is addressing the *maidens*, that is, the first Fathers and the prophets and the righteous, and the angels as well.

The king led me into his chamber.[116]

In other words, 'He translated me into the Kingdom, to His abode;[117] thus, in the stead of Paradise, our natural abode from which I was expelled, He has given me that which is even better'.

The bride addresses the maidens, and they say:
We shall rejoice and be glad in you,
and we shall love thy breasts more than wine.

---

[115] *Teaching of St. Gregory* §440–441 are devoted to the image of the Bride as the Church of the gentiles. There Song 1:1-3 is quoted; in that context, the *breasts* are the testaments, 'which give drink to all the ignorant with the spiritual milk of knowledge'. The *ointment* reveals 'the anointing of Christ and his name', and the kiss is the sign of their mutual love.

[116] Verses 1-4 of this chapter appear in *Teaching of St. Gregory* §440, where they are addressed by Christ to the faithful.

[117] At this point Thomson, 'Song', references Procopius of Gaza, *Epitome in Canticorum* (PG 87:1552C), in which Procopius in turn quotes from Cyril of Alexandria. The ultimate basis for the identification of the chamber with the Kingdom lies in the eschatological exegesis of the parable of the wise and foolish virgins in Mt 25.

That is, the righteous join in the joy of the gentiles' salvation, and they *rejoice* mutually in the Saviour Jesus, and together they love the *breasts* of love, which are the commandments of God.

> *The maidens speak the name of the bride to the groom.*

The *maidens* mean the friends of Christ the Groom. Quite often, any commentary is superfluous!

> *Uprightness loved thee.*

David also says this: 'The Lord our God is upright' (Ps 24:8; 91:16). Now, if He who is upright has loved us, He requires the same love from you, His beloved.

> *The bride says,*
> 1.5-6 *I am black and beautiful, daughters of Jerusalem, like the tent of Kedar, and like the tabernacle of Solomon. Do not look at me because I am black, because the sun has looked upon me fiercely. The sons of my mother fought with me, and they set me as the keeper of the vineyard, so my own vineyard have I not kept.*

Now, if the words of the prophetic books do not coincide with one another, do not expect absolute precision. For the blessed universal teacher John says 'Translating from the Hebrew language into Greek, one cannot convey the meaning completely'.[118] Even more so in our circumstances; when translated

---

[118] The editor of the Armenian text (Venice 1840) cites John Chrysostom's *Commentary on Genesis* as the source of this quotation. In *Homily* 4 on Genesis, §9, Chrysostom makes a statement on the translation of the Septuagint and the effects of the translation on certain phrases; however, a much closer parallel is found in

from the Greek or the Syriac, the meaning is obscured in Armenian. Gregory of Nyssa says the same in this very commentary [Nyssa 796 A-B].

That notwithstanding, the gist of the utterance is this; when the maidens have said to the Bride—that is, to the gentile believers—'With what great love has the Upright One loved you! Therefore do not stray any more and move away from Uprightness', the Bride responds by praising Christ the Groom; she relates her earlier transgressions and the chastisements which she suffered. *I am black, and* am become *beautiful* now through His mercy, O *Daughters of Jerusalem*. It calls the righteous *daughters of Jerusalem*, and, as often occurs in the books of the prophets, it is usual to call the angels *daughters* as well, because they possess a modesty like that of women, inasmuch as the female sex is more modest than the male.

It says *like the tent of Kedar*. Kedar means 'dark'; that is to say, 'I was *the tent* of Satan, and through the mercy of God I am now fit to be *the tabernacle of Solomon*'. It says *the tabernacle of Solomon*, referring to the Temple; in other words, 'Now, like *the tabernacle of Solomon*, I have become God's house'. Hereby, it anticipates the Church of the gentiles [Nyssa 792 A].

Then again recalling her earlier ugliness, she adds, '*Do not look at me because I am black*', meaning the blackness of sin, '*because* having caught me in transgression, God *the Sun looked on me fiercely*'. By this she indicates the bitterness of the punishments which He inflicted upon her, and her expulsion both from God's presence and from Paradise. Because of whose transgression did

---

the *Second Homily On the Obscurity of the Old Testament*, where it is expounded upon at length. For a recent translation of the above, see St John Chrysostom, *Homilies on Genesis 1-17; Homily 4* is found on pp. 51–65; *idem., Old Testament Homilies*, translated by Robert Charles Hill, 3 volumes (Brookline: Holy Cross Orthodox Press, 2003): The *Second Homily on the Obscurity of the Old Testament* is found in vol. 3:25-51.

this come about? The Bride says, '*The sons of my mother fought with me*'. She calls Satan '*my mother's son*', for they were both made by one Creator.

And they set me as keeper of the vineyard, so my own vineyard have I not kept. This is what 'God set him in the paradise of delight, to dress it and keep it' (Gn 2:15) means. It is not as if Paradise, where all was enjoyment and divine protection, needed any dressing or keeping, other than his doing right, and keeping the commandment which He had previously taught him [Nyssa 797D].

> *The bride says to the groom,*
> 1.7 *Tell me, whom my soul loves, where do you shepherd, where do you rest your flock at midday, lest I become like one who goes after the flocks of your companions.*

Now, the Bride having recounted from what ugliness and blackness to what beauty she was transformed, the Groom being willing to forget the Bride's wickedness because of His love for her, she is likewise inflamed with love for Him. She beseeches the Groom to tell her what the path is along which she may be shepherded under the hand of her Shepherd, so that, going towards the shadowless Light she may remain invulnerable to the predatory Enemy.

At midday the sun's light is without shadow; for that reason she mentions noonday: 'Let me not be blackened by demonic ways of life with my previous companions in sin and stray from the place of good pasture'.

As the Lord Himself says in the holy Gospel, 'I am the good Shepherd' (Jn 10:14); 'Whoever enters in by me will be saved' (Jn 10:7-9), and so on [Nyssa 801A].

> *The groom says to the bride,*
> 1.8 *If you do not know yourself, O most beautiful among women, follow the footprints of the flock, and pasture your goats by the tents of the shepherds.*

The Groom answers according to the Bride's question, reminding her of the beauty which He has given her, and cautioning her to know herself; as the Prophet said, 'Look to yourself' (Dt 4:9). Now, he is saying 'Remember the previous gifts—that is, Paradise and glory—having received which you contaminated them through sin; you again found mercy, not by virtue of good works which you performed, but through me who, in your place, made recompense for your sins'. As the Prophet says, 'In my stead, the Lord recompenses' (Ps 137:8).

'But if you do not remember all this, and you do not look to yourself, and you do not humble yourself from your arrogance, and if like your forefather you are proud of your upright ways or your good works which you have done in your repentance from evil, and if you do not hereafter walk aright, you will leave my flock, who are fruitful in wool and milk. Instead of my flock you will join the herd of goats, who are unproductive, for they have neither wool nor milk; who have strayed from the good Shepherd's tent, following the tracks of strange flocks which think themselves to be the flock and which are not the flock. Thereafter you will not find the Good Shepherd again [Nyssa 804 C].

So be careful for the salvation which I have accomplished for you, fighting with the chariots and horses of the invisible pharaoh by my formidable power'. This is what it means when he says,

1.9 *I shall compare you, my Near One,*[119] *to my horse among the chariots of Pharaoh.*

'Overwhelming his chariots, I made you my Near One, carrying you through the sea of sin'.

Now, I am trying to be brief; if you desire to hear more extended statements, you should go to Gregory of Nyssa.[120]

The maidens say to the bride

These are the friends of the Groom, the apostles and prophets, and *vardapets*, who continually advise us to regard how much our re-creation excels the original creation by comparing it to a dove, a necklace, gold, silver and horses.

1.10 *For your cheeks are beautiful like a dove's,*

That bird loves purity. If its mate should happen to die, it never, until its death, unites with any other of its kind. So, by praising her *cheeks* as being *like a dove's*, he conveys that, 'You are the countenance and likeness of God, adorned with purity like a dove. The awe of His commandments adorns you like a circlet around your neck (Prv 1:9), pure and cleansed from sin, like gold and silver'. Metaphorically, that is; not actual silver and gold. For that spiritual beauty with which humanity is adorned, is beyond human thought.

He who has heard unutterable words (2 Cor 12:4), like Paul and his spiritual ilk, is also God's resting place, like a *horse*. Now, the maidens said this in support of the Groom's words comparing his *horse*, which fought with *Pharaoh*, to the Bride in virtue.

Those who are adorned with good works are shown to have attained to yet greater gifts; not only does He rest upon you like a *horse*, but He receives you into His bosom. As it continues:

---

[119] The Armenian *merjawor im*, here translated as 'My Near One', has meanings ranging from 'intimate' to 'closely related' (by blood or otherwise), to 'similar'.

[120] It should be noted that in Nyssa the point is quite different; he stresses the overcoming of subjection to evil by means of mystical wonder.

until the king shall receive you into his bosom.

It occurs to me, however, that you have not fully comprehended the commentary on these words. So let me perforce recapitulate:

I shall compare you to my horse among the chariots of Pharaoh,
O my Near One

Now, one must ask him about the *horse*, 'If it be yours, why is it *among the chariots of Pharaoh*? And who may *Pharaoh* be?' Listen, and I will explain it. God's *horse* is our human nature, because it was the resting place and abode of the godhead.[121] Like an obdurate *horse* it became arrogant in conceit, and through sin it turned into a steed of Satan, who is described as *Pharaoh*. With him Christ the Saviour fought by means of the cross. The prototype of that cross was the rod of Moses, which parted the sea and drowned *Pharaoh*, that is, Satan. [God's] image, which like a *horse* had been harnessed to [Satan's] *chariot*, He again gathered to Himself. This is that it means when it says, *to my horse among the chariots of Pharaoh*: the efficacious power of the godhead destroyed the chariots of *Pharaoh*.

Or again, 'That metaphorical *horse*, royally adorned and harnessed to *the chariot of Pharaoh*, was also Mine, for all creation is Mine. Now, I shall compare you to that adorned *horse* of Mine, which I rode so forcefully that they said, "Let us flee from the face of Israel"' (Ex 14:25).

Likewise, He made you His steed, adorned with a circlet, and the other things he listed in order, drowning the invisible *Pharaoh* in the fiery sea. Having decked you out in so much virtue, He took you, who had been His *horse*, to Himself; instead of riding you, He took you into His bosom, and even more, carried you on His shoulder, as the Lord says in the Gospel (Lk 15:5).

---

[121] In his *Encomium on the Apostles*, Gregory refers to them as 'steeds of the Word' (*Writings*, 435).

The bride says to herself and to the groom,
1.12-14 *My spikenard has sent forth its fragrance. My Nephew is a bundle of myrrh; he shall rest between my breasts. My Nephew is to me like a blooming cluster in the vineyards of Engedi;*

That is, among the luxuriant fruits of the vineyards.

First of all, know that the one called the Groom is also called her *Nephew*, for the Word of God became incarnate of the Jews, and the Jews and the gentiles are also brothers because they are both from Adam.

My Nephew is a bundle of myrrh; he shall rest between my breasts. This is what the word means in the Gospel: 'Whoever believes in me, has affirmed that God is true' (Jn 3:33) [Nyssa 824 C]. Now whoever believes in Him and gathers His commandment and the fear of Him into his heart is like precious ointment and fragrant incense, especially because he spreads that fragrance to others. As the Apostle says, 'We are a sweet savor of Christ to God among the saved, and among the lost' (2 Cor 2:15) [Nyssa 825 B].

There is, however, an animal which dies from sweet fragrance, like the sinners who do not accept the instruction of the fragrant Scriptures which *rest between the breasts;* that is, in the hearts of the saints [Nyssa 825 B]. Those who receive [that fragrance] will be translated from life to life, and those who do not receive it, from death to death (2 Cor 2:16). As Christ's great martyr Ignatius said, 'I bear in myself Christ'. Hearing this Trajan said, 'I give order to burn that Ignatius who bears the Crucified One in himself, so that the Crucified One will be burned together with him'.[122]

---

[122] The story is from the *Martyrdom of Ignatius*, the Armenian version of which is to be found in the series *Sop'erk'* 22 (Venice, 1861) 141–185, but there is no exact verbal parallel there.

The groom says to the bride
15.15 *Behold, my Near One, behold, my beautiful one, your eyes are doves.*

'Because you have come *near* to Me, and have become estranged from sin, you have received the previous beauty which you possessed in Paradise, and you have attained not to this gift alone, but by regarding Me you have received the *eyes* of a *dove*; that is, of the Holy Spirit'[123] [Nyssa 836 B]. For whatever a person looks at, he becomes in thought.

Now, if I do not prolong the words of my commentary, know that it is because I prefer brevity.

The bride says to the groom
1.16-17 *Behold my Nephew, and beautiful as well; there are canopies to our seat. The beams of our house are cedar; our rafters are fir.*

Once the Groom has shown her the eyes of the Spirit, pure as those of a dove, the Bride testifies, 'What I could not see then, when I had not been transformed into the nature of a *dove*, I can now see, having become a *dove*—my *Nephew*. For although you became *my Nephew*, taking on the flesh of my ugliness, yet you are *beautiful* to me because you mingled your divinity with my nature'. As the Prophet says, 'Fairer in appearance than all the children of men' (Ps 44:3).

There are canopies to our seat; that is, she calls Christ in His incarnation our *canopy* and *house* [Nyssa 836 B]. *The beams of our*

---

[123] Connecting the dove with the Holy Spirit is a commonplace. *Teaching of St. Gregory* §418 and 420 make this connection, while §603 deals with the dove's faithfulness to its nest and §605 ties the two concepts together. §606 uses Is 60:8 to apply the dove's qualities to the saints at the Second Coming, rising to meet the Lord.

house are cedar: that wood is sweet smelling and incorruptible, and good for building. Likewise the body of our Lord, 'Whose house we ourselves are' (Heb 3:6) [Nyssa 840 A], according to Paul, is good for building this *house*, or for purifying us to dwell there.

— CHAPTER TWO —

The groom says to himself and to the bride

The Groom more clearly reveals His beauty, invisible and inexpressible. What the Bride perceives dimly with the eyes of the Spirit, He relates:

2.1 *I am a flower of the fields, a lily of the valleys.*[124]

What an amazing thing! Like the bodily incarnation of the Lord, by which He brought the invisible into visibility for us, He tries by a similar metaphor to display the lovely adornment which the earth put on at receiving Christ. How the earth's appearance, crowned with flowers, delights the eye of the beholders, and the *lily* which is in *the valleys*! Just so are those who spread out their souls, like *fields*, for my habitation, and they burgeon because of Me, like *the valleys*. They flower around Me to the inutterable joy of the beholders'. And this is not all, but,

---

[124] Cyril of Alexandria, *Scholia on the Incarnation of the Only-Begotten* (Oxford, 1881), §10, also adduces this verse to describe Christ: 'In the Song of Songs our Lord Jesus Christ Himself has been introduced to us saying, "I am the flower of the plain, the lily of the valleys". As then the smell is something unembodied, for it uses as its own body that wherein it is, . . . so shall we conceive of the Nature of the Godhead in Christ too, that it sheds forth on the world the savour of His own more than earthly Excellence, as in the object of human nature. . . .'

2.2 Like a lily among the thorns, so is my Near One among the daughters.

'Not only am I the Groom beautiful after the manner of these flowers, but the Bride, who is near to me, becomes as beautiful *among the daughters* as *a lily among thorns*'.

He calls *daughters* those wedded to Satan; that is, the sinful. There is no need to explain *thorns*, remembering the parable in the Gospel of the thorns and the tares (Mt 13), which the Lord did not allow to be plucked up from among the wheat until the time of harvest, which is the end of this world. The Song of Songs, as well, considered it appropriate for the righteous to be among the sinners. First, because the way of life of the righteous would appear all the brighter, as the precious stands out amidst the cheap. And secondly, because the *thorns* may perhaps turn into *lilies*, seeing the worth of the latter.

The bride says to the groom
2.3a Like an apple amid the forest,
so is my Nephew among the sons.[125]

See how step by step she augments her praise of the Groom. He who was at first called *a lily* and *a flower*, now is *an apple*. A flower delights only the eye, whereas the apple delights the eye with its appearance, the palate with its scent, and then comes into its own as a food [Nyssa 844 B].[126]

---

[125] Because of a typographical (or perhaps scribal) error in the text, *usterats'* [sons] appears in the printed editions as *dsterats'* [daughters]. The word is correctly rendered at the end of the same section.

[126] The ninth-century writer Bishop Sahak Mṙut (*c.* 820–*c.* 890) in his long *Exposition of the Faith*, p. 89 (for full reference, see n. 85, above) makes the following comment on this verse:

Now, an *apple*, made of the four elements in combination as one, is a type of Christ. If you are able, separate the four contrary elements which have

What she spoke of there as *thorns* is here a *forest*—that is, people who are 'afforested', so to speak, with sin; as it says 'The wild boar of the forest laid it waste' (Ps 79:14).

He also calls the children of wicked fathers *the sons*.

> 2.3b *Under his shadow did I desire to sit down, and I*
> *sat, and his fruit was sweet in my throat.*

This does not need much interpretation. We who had made offerings to forests and leafy trees, having now made the acquaintance of the *apple* which was given to us from the Tree of Life, have taken refuge in *his shadow* with eagerness. We sit around Him with immovable faith: to *sit*, means not to 'stand up' for false doctrine.

And His fruit was sweet in my throat. Hereby you should understand the life-giving sacrament and the fruit from the Tree of Life, and also the words which were given to us by His divine mouth. Both interpretations are possible. As the Prophet says, 'Your words are sweet to the palate, sweeter than honey to my mouth' (Ps 118:103) [Nyssa 844 C].

> *The bride says to the maidens*
> 2.4 *Take me to the house of wine.*

She says openly, 'I am not satisfied by the bringing of the cup, or by the divine words. For I have an insatiable desire, and indolent ways. So *take me to the house of* these very good things,

---

been commingled and have become a single apple: isolate the wet and the dry, the cold and the hot. If you lack the ability to do even this, how much more impossible is it to separate Christ's combination of godhead and humanity commingled and become one Nature and one Christ, into two separate parts! Thus, if four physical elements united make one apple with one nature, how much more must the commingled union of incorporeal with corporeal, firmly conjoined, make a single Person and a single Nature, inseparable in its union.

for I have no great desire towards the Groom, and towards His commandments; if I see Him and hear them through you, I shall be satisfied'.

Wine is an occasion for gladness. In this life people like to cause forgetfulness of sorrow; for that reason she calls the giving of God's gifts *wine*.

Set love upon me,

Do not demand too much consistency between expressions, as I have previously stated; just grasp the explanation of them. Here, it says *set love*, just as it says in another place, *arouse love*. [Nyssa 845 B]

God is Love. Love is recognized as God's name; the Apostle says, 'God is love, and whoever remains in love dwells in God, and God in him' (1 Jn 4:12). So the Bride, warmed with love of the Groom, beseeches the friends of the Groom not to speak for Him distantly, as did the prophets, but in an apostolic manner to introduce her into the *house* of Christ, whom she described as *wine*. For by the sight of one another's faces is love of the beloved inflamed in both. This is what *set love upon me* means.

2.5 and establish me with ointments.

Mercy is called *ointment*. So this means, 'When I see the Groom, by the opening of my spiritual eye I shall recognize yet more the boundless mercy which He has worked for us, and I shall be the more *established*', and I shall discover it through mercy, as the Theologian says.[127]

---

[127] The source of this quotation is not known to me.

Pile up for me apples,

The beauty of good works is called *apples* [Nyssa 849 C-D]. For as by its appearance and scent an *apple* is appetizing even before one tastes it, likewise the sight of various virtues exhilarates those who see it.

for I am overcome by love.

Love dwelt among the saints with immeasurable celebration, through the coming of Christ. They who tasted the savor of that Love became insatiable; they were not satisfied with the various trials which they suffered, whether from Satan or from human beings, but they voluntarily added innumerable tribulations for themselves. They resembled the Prophet David, who, concerning the tribulations which come from others, said, 'The pangs of death surrounded me, and the sorrows of hell found me'. He increased his soul's tribulation yet more: as he adds, 'I discovered tribulation and difficulty' (Ps 114:3). Similarly, the Holy Illuminator and the great Paul and other saints like them considered the tribulations which came for Christ's sake[128] to be gifts, like *apples*; thus, Trdat said to Saint Gregory, 'Is that happiness?' and he responded, 'Yea, this is happiness'![129]

---

[128] An allusion to Mt 5:11.

[129] Agathangelos § 105. Saint Gregory the Illuminator there avows that the torture of being beaten over the head for Christ's sake is happiness. Armenians were in awe of the number and variety of tortures endured by the Illuminator. See A. Terian, *Patriotism and Piety: Medieval Panegyrics on St. Gregory the Illuminator* (Crestwood: St. Vladimir's Seminary Press, 2005). By the fourteenth century, commentary on the symbolism of Gregory's various tortures was being produced. For example, according to an unpublished sermon of Yovhannēs Kolotik (1370?–1443) found in J1327, 213, Gregory's having been suspended upside down symbolizes nine things, among them: the fact that human feet were originally intended to walk the upward path; the descent of Christ into the world; and the planting of the human 'root' [i.e., the head] in the ground of grace.

2.6 His left hand is upon my head and his right hand embraces me.

He repeats this in another place: 'Length of life is at *her right hand*, and on *her left hand* are glory and wealth' (Prv 3:16) [Nyssa 856 A]. Now this means that there is no other fulfillment for my love or expression of my heart but to cling to Him, and to see Him: though various trials and tribulations come upon me, he will hold *his right hand* and *his left hand* as my only shade and protection.[130]

The bride says to the maidens

The angels, and humans who have become angelic,[131] are called *maidens*.

---

[130] Perhaps an allusion to Ws 5:17.

[131] In Armenian, as in other traditions, there are many references to living 'the angelic life', in particular as a goal for monastics. Its desirable qualities included celibacy and continual worship of God. Ideas on the relationship between human and angelic life were connected to ideas on the parallels between the ranks of clergy and the ranks of angels, and, in broader terms, on the replacement of the class of fallen, faithless angels by the class of saved, faithful human beings. John of Mayrivank' (*c.* 575–*c.* 640) is one of the earliest Armenian writers on the latter topics ('Analysis of the Catholic Church', 70–75). He cites as authorities both Ps-Dionysus the Areopagite, and Saint Gregory the Illuminator. For the teaching of Gregory on the taking of human beings into the ranks of the angels see *Teaching of St. Gregory* § 364, 596 and 674. *Homily* 16 in Saint Gregory the Illuminator's *Discourses* also mentions the replacement of the fallen angels with 'the meek and humble' (p. 187b). See also *Teaching of St. Gregory* §640. Some centuries after Gregory of Narek, Vardan the Great Arewelts'i (1200?–1271) in his *Commentary on the Pentateuch* (M1267, 5r) wrote that 'man was accounted among the nine ranks of angels, as the tenth'. The Catholicos Nersēs Shnorhali (1166–1173), in the part of his pastoral encyclical addressed to priests, bases his explanation of the Armenian word for the season of Pentecost (*yinunk'*) on the nine (*inunk'*) ranks of angels, among whose ranks humans celebrate the wedding of Christ and the Church. *Ēndhanrakan T'ught'k'* [General Epistles] 64.

> 2.7 *I adjure you, daughters of Jerusalem, by the powers*
> *and the forces of the field, that you raise up and wake*
> *love, while he wishes.*

This world is referred to as a *field* [Nyssa 856 A]. Heaven is as
well.[132] And the *power and force of the field* is God, through whom
the world was established—and the heavens, too—and remains
bound together and locked[133] by the immovable *power and force*
of the field; that is, God.

It is the angels and humanity, who dwell in the *fields*, who are
mentioned as being *adjured*. Thus, 'by that *force* do I adjure you
to rise and pray, and to *arouse* that selfsame *love*, Christ, entirely'!
This is what the Lord Himself commanded us to pray: 'Thy will
be done', He said, 'on earth as it is in heaven' (Mt 6:10).

Thus, those who were *adjured* are the *daughters of* the heavenly
Jerusalem, the angels, and the saints who are from this earth.

> *Hearing the voice of the groom, the bride says*
> 2.8 *The voice of my Nephew!*

See how, though she recognizes the hidden things before confess-
ing them with her mouth, she pauses in announcing them, so
that others too may recognize His justice. For if He is merciful,
He is also just in judgment. Her calling out to Him, and her eager
pleading, are for the payment of our debts' account.

When the Bride, that is, the Church which is from the gentiles, cried out to the maidens to *take* her *to the house of wine*
and not away from the Groom's presence, as was appointed for

---

[132] This is apparently an allusion to the parable of the wheat and the tares (Mt
13:24-30, 36-43), and the parable of the treasure hidden in a field (Mt 13:44).

[133] References to the locks of the earth, heaven and hell are to be found in Jb
26:13; 38:6, and in Jonah 2:6.

transgressors,[134] and when she *adjured the daughters of Jerusalem to arouse love,* until His good will towards humanity might be accomplished, the Groom did not wait for the pleading of intercessors, but having heard the supplication of her who besought Him, He announced a reconciliation, and ran to meet her, as it says in the Gospel in the parable of the prodigal son (Lk 15). For He goes about seeking the ones who are worthy, and those who love Him and seek His will, having recognized it by foresight.

The bride says
The voice of my Nephew; behold he comes running
upon the mountains, skipping upon the hills.

She calls *voice* that which we heard from the prophets: 'As we have heard, so have we also seen' (Ps 47:8) [Nyssa 861 A]; that is, the Word of God 'Who in many partial ways and with many archetypes spoke to our fathers through the prophets, at the end of these days He spoke to us through His son' (Heb 1:1-2). This is what it means, *Behold he comes running upon the mountains, leaping upon the hills.* The tyranny of Satan he calls *mountains and hills,* which He trod down by His coming. As the Prophet said, 'The mountains and hills were moved, they shook, and trembling seized them' (Na 1:5).[135] The Lord gave to the apostles the same authority over mountains; not only to *skip upon* the *mountains* of sin, but even to send them into the sea (Mt 21:21) [Nyssa 861 D-864 A].

---

[134] References to banishment from the divine presence are many. Ps 50:13 comes to mind at once, as do the parables of the wedding guest without a wedding garment (Mt 22) and of the unprofitable servant (Mt 25). Jesus' description of the Judgment in Mt 25 includes the command to the goats on the left hand to depart from the Judge's presence.

[135] This may be a conflation of Na 1:5 and Ps 47:6, where the same vocabulary is applied to the kingdoms of the earth.

2.9 My Nephew is like a roe or a young hart upon the mountains of Bethel.

Though this is not particularly appropriate, she compares her Nephew to a *roe* because of its eyesight. Even before the creation He saw what pertained to humanity; as it says, 'Before He created you from the womb, I knew you' (Jer 1:5). Since there is no better sight among the beasts than the *roe's*, for that reason she makes it the metaphor for Christ's vision.

The *hart*, too, kills snakes, as the Lord did the invisible Serpent.

Upon the mountains of Bethel; in Hebrew *Bethel* means heaven, where He brings those who have been saved from the Serpent [Nyssa 864 B].

The bride gives a sign of the groom to the maidens
Behold, he stood behind our wall,

He calls the body which was from the Virgin, *wall.*

rising to the window,

He calls the prophets *the window.*

looking through the lattice.

That is, *through* the Law. In other words, in former times the light of the godhead shone upon us *through* these things; then, later, it did so through His coming in the flesh from the Virgin [Nyssa 864 C].

2.10 My Nephew answered me and said, Arise and come, my Near One, my beauty, my dove,

This is the call that came through Christ, who said, 'Come to me all you who labor' (Mt 11:28), and so on. He says *my beauty,* because of the washing of the *dove; my dove,* because of her having put on the Spirit; *my Near One* because we have become sharers in Christ's body (Eph 3:6).

> *for, behold, the winter has passed,*

He calls the idol worship which had spread worldwide, *winter.* It *has passed,* moreover, by the self same coming of the *Nephew,* who is Christ [Nyssa 865 C]. Likewise,

> 2.11 *the rains have passed; leaving, they have gone away.*

This stands for the deceit of Satan, who takes on the shape of a good thing (2 Cor 11:14). The *rain* is one of destruction, like that in the days of the Flood, by which the demons were expelled; that is, *leaving they have gone away.*

> 2.12 *Flowers have appeared in our land, the time for pruning has come.*

By this he indicates the beauty of the spring which came through Christ in the winter of persecution. He calls the crowd of the Just, flourishing in virtue and piety, *flowers. The time has come for pruning;* for cutting off and removing the polluted from among the saints.[136]

> *The voice of the turtledove was heard in our land.*

As birds in springtime twitter and are spread out across the land, so also at the coming of this spiritual springtime do the saints rejoice, especially the apostles and prophets, and *vardapets,* and those who through their preaching bless God night and day with

---

[136] This is perhaps an allusion to Jn 15:2,6.

angelic and spiritual songs. This is what *The voice of the turtledove was heard in our land* means.[137]

> 2.13 *The vineyards blossomed, and gave forth their fragrance.*

He refers to as a *vineyard* those faithful people who *blossomed* into a variety of diverse colors and fruits and *fragrances*; one person through martyrdom, another through various virtues, and yet another through good works.

> *Rise and come, my Near One, my beautiful one, my dove, my perfect one,*

He repeated the same original, previous words, affirming his call, '*Arise and come*, not through *the window* and *the lattice*—that is, through the prophets or the Law—but at this, My own call!' By repeating the words, he indicated that one does not come to a halt on the way to the Kingdom, so long as one is in the flesh. As the Lord says, 'Oh, rise, let us go hence' (Mt 26:46). This is also consonant with the Theologian's interpretation.[138]

> 2.14 *And come, my dove, under the shelter of that rock, near the retaining wall.*

See, although she has become a *dove*, yet he demands that she continually increase in purity, and not consider herself to be

---

[137] In his comments on this verse, Thomson points out a parallel with *Teaching of Gregory* §655–658 and the description of birds—not only turtledoves, but cranes and swallows—as images of the resurrection. Indeed, §641–658 are all descriptive of the resurrection as the Great Springtime. In his *Exhortation to a Virtuous Life*, Gregory of Narek calls the 'general resurrection' a 'spiritual springtime', when all those who have partaken in Christ's body and blood will 'bud, renewed truly and with immortal life' (*Writings*, Venice 1840, p. 490).

[138] The interpretation to which Gregory refers is not known to me.

perfect in purity; 'And let him who thinks that he stands take heed, lest he fall' (1 Cor 10:12).

Under the shelter of that rock. He calls Christ a *rock*, for the Apostle says, 'The rock was Christ himself' (1 Cor 10:4).

And he calls the commandments a *wall*, as it is in Scripture. Now, he orders her hereafter to conform with the Gospel and its preaching, and not with the Law [Nyssa 877 B-D]. To this the Apostle testifies: 'Christ is of no effect for you, if you are justified by the Law' (Gal 5:4).

And near the retaining wall. It is as if he says that by keeping the Gospel commandments you are not far from the Law: as the Apostle says, 'The fulfillment of the Law is Christ' (Rom 10:4). And the Lord Himself says, 'I came to fulfill the Law' (Mt 5:17). So by carrying out what has been fulfilled, you draw *near* to *the wall*, that is, to the Law.[139]

> *Show me your face, and let me hear your voice,*
> *for your voice is sweet, and your face is beautiful.*

These the Song of Songs says are the words of the Groom. Gregory of Nyssa divides it, and says it is the words of the Bride. [Nyssa 880 A-B] We agree with this.

Now, having become a *dove*, the Bride beseeches the *rock*, understood to be Christ, '*Show me your face*, and do not speak to me any longer through the prophets and the Law! Instead, insofar as you are visible to corporeal creatures, show me your face visibly, so that I may see it and be sated with your glory's appearing. Insofar as human hearing can bear it, let me hear your *voice* so that, grazing in the shade of your gospel preaching, I shall not go after a foreign shepherd. For if your *voice* was so enticing to me through the *window*—that is through the multitude of the proph-

---

[139] The identification of the Law with a wall is also found in Gregory Nazianzen *Oration* 45.xii.

ets—how much more shall it be so if I am made worthy of seeing your *face*, of hearing the good news of my own salvation?'

> *The groom says to the maidens*
> 2.15 *Let us catch us the little foxes that spoil the vines,*
> *so that our vines may flourish.*[140]

This He says to the angels, which are ministering spirits, sent for the service of humanity. On the other hand, He says it even more to the apostles, who became 'hunters' of the entire universe [Nyssa 881 A-B]. First they hunted the *fox* to destruction, expelling him from the vineyard. It is Satan that he calls a *fox*. A *vineyard* is what he calls the Church, which is the souls of the faithful—whom the apostles snatched from the claws of the *fox*, who was the opponent of the truth—so that they were transferred from death to life (Jn 5:24).

The Lord Himself too, when the apostles returned rejoicing and said, 'Lord, even devils obey us in your name', told them, 'Lo, I have given you authority to tread on snakes and scorpions, and on all the power of the enemy as well' (Lk 10:19). He who at another time called Satan a 'mountain' and a 'dragon' and a 'prince', here by contrast calls him a *fox*, and a small one at that, because of the awesome power which the apostles received over him.

> *The bride says this*
> 2.16 *My Nephew is mine and I am his, who shepherds*
> *among the lilies, until the day dawns, and the shadows*
> *disperse.*

The Bride, seeing herself liberated from the predations of the *fox*, joyfully gives herself to the One made earthly, who took down the

---

[140] The identification of the fox with Satan is also made in *Physiologus*: 'The scribe heard from the Lifegiver, "Foxes have dens"; and in the Song of Songs, "let us catch the little foxes that spoil the vineyards".' (Muradyan, *Physiologus*, 117. For full reference, see n. 142, below.)

wall of separation (Eph 2:14). And because the wall of the Law no longer divides her from the One she desires, then she says, 'I am my Nephew's, and my Nephew is mine' [Nyssa 882 D]. And again, 'Because I have tasted of His love and seen His alluring *face*, and heard His enticing *voice*, I am in Him and He in me.[141] So hereafter neither earthly desire nor need can separate me from Him'. This indeed came to pass, and we saw this demonstrated in the martyrs and the ascetics. As the Apostle says, 'Who shall separate us from the love of Christ? shall tribulation or difficulty, or persecution'? and so on (Rom 8:35).

> *Who shepherds among the lilies,*
> *until the day dawns and the shadows disperse.*

That is, no longer does He feed them with grass, which is the food of bestial men. It is the pleasures of the flesh which one refers to as 'grass'; however it is not with that, but rather with spiritual food, that He feeds them. Indeed all the saints ate and marveled at it, and spurned vain desires. They wait in the hope of the *dawning* of that *day* which is the final day, when they shall not be moved—in other words, they shall not pass away—forever. Then it is that the saints will slake the boundless thirst they have for Christ the Groom.

> 2.17 *Again, my Nephew is like a roe or a young hart*
> *upon the incense bearing mountains.*

This means, 'See the works of the wicked with your sharp eyes, you who sit in the heights, and trample the serpent and the dragon'. It is indeed the nature of *harts*, to tread on snakes and kill them[142] [Nyssa 884 C].

---

[141] An allusion to Jn 17:23.

[142] The enmity of the hart towards serpents /dragons is described in the *Physiologus*, which tells us that the hart blows water down the hole in which a serpent is

— CHAPTER THREE —

3.1 *On my bed at night I sought him whom my soul loves. I sought him and did not find him, I called him, and he did not answer me.*

These phrases require many words of explanation, and it is not to be concluded in a few. Nonetheless, I will relate a few; I refer those who desire more expansive statements to Gregory of Nyssa [Nyssa 892–893 C].

When the Bride's knowledge had progressed through the many metaphors that He listed, and she attained to the pinnacle of this knowledge of Christ at which we find ourselves, she thought that her knowledge had come to a resting point; as it were, 'Now I have arrived!' She became careless. Like a person tired and resting in *bed*, likewise she rested, as if *on her bed*, from having sought out great treasure—that is, the great, enlightened, true knowledge to which she had attained through her desire.

She rested, as if *on a bed*, and she did not recall Paul's saying, 'We know more or less, and we prophesy more or less' (1 Cor 13:9), and 'Now I understand more or less' (1 Cor 13:12). In comparison with the life to come, he calls this life 'night' (Rom 13:12), dark and tenebrous. The spirit is concealed by the body as if in a house, or even in a prison, invisible to those standing outside. The Prophet speaks of it as prison and bonds, saying 'You have broken my bonds' (Ps 115:16), and 'Lord, take my soul from prison, that I may praise your name' (Ps 141:8).

---

hiding, and then kills the emerging reptile with its hoofs. For a new edition and translation of the Armenian version see Gohar Muradyan *Physiologus. The Greek and Armenian Versions with a Study of Translation Techniques*. Hebrew University Armenian Studies 6 (Louvain: Peeters, 2005). For general notes on the work, see Ferdinand Holthausen, 'Zum Physiologus', *Anglia Beiblatt* 33 (April 1992) 102–103. For some patristic applications, see Ursula Treu, 'The *Physiologus* and the Early Fathers', *Studia Patristica* 24 (1993) 197–200.

Thus, *on my bed at night I sought him whom my soul loves, I sought him and I found him not, I called him, and he did not answer me* means that however much I seek God's power or the vision of His glory, or the greatness of His name, or the gifts which are prepared for the righteous, and the like, I find myself distanced therefrom. Having attained to the knowledge which is told us by the prophets and apostles and *vardapet*s through the Holy Spirit, and by the Lord Himself in the Gospel, all of this was accounted by perfect understanding as being no discovery at all.[143] Those who are knowledgeable of the world to come, those who are worthy of it, consider that it has not communicated, or even spoken, through these. For the corporeal tongue cannot utter the things of that life, as the Apostle Paul himself says: 'I heard unutterable words, which it is not right for man to utter' (2 Cor 12:4). (Here, *not right* is used with the meaning of *impossible*.)

> 3.2 *I rose and went about the city, in the squares and*
> *in the streets, and I sought him and did not find him.*
> *I called him, and he did not answer me.*

He calls the heavens *city and street and square,* and those in them are the angels, from whom she could obtain no knowledge of the supernal mysteries.

> 3.3 *The guards who were going about the city found*
> *me. I asked, Have you seen him whom my soul loves?*

They too, by not answering, made her understand that even they have not attained to this knowledge. For to whatever measure of knowledge a person attains, it is but the foundation of yet higher knowledge.

---

[143] Perhaps an echo of Phil 3:12.

3.4 When I passed a little beyond them, I found him
whom my soul loves.

There is a knowledge the attainment to an acquaintance with which blocks the seekers' discovery. It says, *'When I passed a little beyond them, I found* because at that point, I relied on faith and the Holy Spirit'. The words of Paul, too, are similar: 'When the world by wisdom knew not God, God was pleased by the foolishness of preaching to save those who believe' (1 Cor 1:21).

Having found the groom she says
I seized him,
and I did not let him go until I brought him into my mother's house
and into the room of her who conceived me.

He alludes to the *seizing* of faith, by which we bring Him in to our *Mother*, into the *house* and *the room of Her who conceived* us; that is, Paradise and Heaven.

The bride again adjures the maidens for a second time
3.5 I adjure you daughters of Jerusalem by the powers
and the forces of the field, that you arise, arouse love
while he wishes.

This I have once explained.[144] But see the augmentation of Christ's love in those whom He indwells: how insatiable it makes people! It is as though she had not attained to so much grace and knowledge: she repeats the adjuration which she had made in unattainment and ignorance; she *arouses love* as if she had not perfectly received it.

---

[144] See comments on 2.9, above.

> *The groom says concerning the bride*
> 3.6 *Who is this who comes up from the desert like*
> *pillars of smoke, scented with myrrh and frankincense*
> *and with all powders of sweet ointments?*

The Groom wishes to show off the beauty of the Bride—that is, of the faithful—by asking the angels, who are described as *maidens*, 'I know that she is black, having lost her form in Paradise; now, whence has she received this form and fragrance, having taken which *from the desert*, she *comes* to the heights of heaven?' He calls those who have deserted evil works *desert* [Nyssa 897 B]; there David also desired to fly with the wings of the Spirit. He describes her as surrounding herself with virtue and good works *like a pillar of* scented *smoke*, like *incense, and myrrh, and frankincense, with all the powders of sweet ointments*. *Myrrh* is the symbol of death; *frankincense*, of a fragrant way of life. Observe that the body of sin (Rom 6:6) must first be put to death and made a partaker in Christ's death, and by a fragrant way of life become the equal of Christ's purity [Nyssa 897 C-D], and then become a Bride and ascend to Christ the Groom.

> *The maidens say something like this*

Desiring to acquaint the Bride yet more fully with the Groom's beauty and propriety, they call the Groom *Solomon*, because Solomon means 'Peace'; that is, Christ, who became our peace, and broke down the dividing wall, and reconciled God to humanity (Eph 2:14-16) [Nyssa 897 D].

*3.7 Behold Solomon's couch, sixty soldiers round about
it of the valiant of Israel,*

Israel was divided into twelve tribes, and twelve fives is *sixty;*[145]
also, the senses in a person are five. Now, he wants to say that as
the twelve tribes became Israel through the Law, they each became
pleasing to God by being purified through the five senses.

In the literal realm, Israel were doers of the will of Solomon's
kingdom, and were his *couch;* likewise, here and now, the *couch*
of this *Solomon* is the entire universe, where the will of God rests
[Nyssa 901B-905A].

Soldiers round about it from among the valiant of Israel. In this
new *Israel, the valiant* are all the believing saints.

3.8 they all have swords and are studied in war.

This *sword* is 'the blade of the Spirit, which is the word of God'
(Eph 6:17), wherewith they were instructed to war against the
invisible Enemy.

Each man's[146] *sword was at his thigh,*

For 'it is not a battle against flesh and with blood', where it would
not be essential to have [the sword] with one at all times; rather, it
is inseparably fixed *at the thigh,* ready to fight 'against principalities and powers' (Eph 6:12).

because of the terrors of the night.

It is obvious that the one who fell from heaven is referred to as
terrors of the night.

---

[145] Arithmological interpretation was a standard of medieval exegesis, but
many variants were possible. Thus, in Hippolytus (358–359) this sixty refers to
the sixty fathers from Adam to Christ, but a little later (368) the same number
he interprets as being 10 x the 6 senses, i.e., ears, eyes, and nostrils. Cited in
Thomson, 'Song', 466–467.

[146] The translation assumes *ard* (now) to be a typographical error for *ayr* (man).

> 3.9-10 *King Solomon made himself a palanquin of the trees of Lebanon. Its pillars he made of silver, and its bottom of gold, and its covering of purple, and in the middle of it he spread out bejeweled love from the daughters of Jerusalem.*

I have often said that *Solomon* signifies Christ, for he was from the offspring of David, and a king who judged justly and made peace and built a temple [Nyssa 908A]. Nonetheless the words which concern him are few, while those concerning Christ are many, for He is the root of David, and King of heaven and earth, and more just in judgment, and merciful, and the occasion of peace for the whole earth, removing from the world idolatry and the discord between heavenly things and earthly. Thereby all the earth was made into the temple of God, through Christ, transforming the type, with its king and temples, into the Truth, which is the Church.

King Solomon made himself a palanquin of incorruptible wood: the *wood of Lebanon* is the gentiles. David too affirms it for you: 'He shall break the cedars of Lebanon' (Ps 28:5). And again, He will break them like the calf which Moses shattered (Ex 32:15-20)—Satan, that is, and those who work his will [Nyssa 912D]. Taking us out of idolatry, he made us his *palanquin*, for 'the Lord is holy, and he rests upon the holy' (Is 57:15); through Isaiah he says, 'Where shall I rest, and pause, if not in the meek and in the humble and those who tremble at my words' (Is 66:2). The Apostle also says, 'In the house of a rich man are vessels not only of gold and silver, but also of clay and wood', adding, 'If anyone cleanses himself from such things, he will be a vessel of honor' (2 Tm 2:20-21), and so on.

He showed that man is not like other plants and shoots which are for nourishment, but by his own will he may become gold, or silver, or an apple; he may produce bitterness, or sweetness, or thorns, as our Apostle and Illuminator says in his *Frequently Related*

Discourses.[147] Now, some of the *trees of Lebanon* become *silver* and some *purple,* transforming evil into good. It is appropriate for the *palanquin* to be understood as the Church, as well as the apostles and prophets and *vardapets* and virgins and saints adorned with various virtues who are within it. The Apostle expresses this by saying, 'These are whom God has set in the Church: first, apostles; second, prophets; third, teachers (*vardapets*)' (1 Cor 12:28) [Nyssa 913B-C]. Afterwards he lists more with them, but he does not count them individually, for the really honorable parts of the *palanquin,* that is, the building of the Church, are these three ranks.

> *Love from the daughters of Jerusalem.*
> 3.11 *Arise, and let us look, daughters of Jerusalem, at King Solomon with the crown wherewith his mother crowned him on the day of his wedding, and on the day of his happiness.*

Love from the daughters of Jerusalem: He calls the angels—fellow rejoicers, and fellow lovers, and fellow praisers with him—*the daughters of Jerusalem.* For His sake was Lebanon, "enforested" with sin, transformed into the *palanquin* of Christ, adorned with various virtues: with the *crown* of thorns, which *King Solomon,* that is, Christ, put on his head and blessed the earth, taking on his own head the curse which He had spoken, 'Thorns and thistles shall it bring forth for you' (Gn 3:18). The Holy Illuminator also interprets it thus.[148] Gregory of Nyssa says otherwise,[149] but we cite the latter more frequently than the former.

---

[147] Though the *Discourses* are cited here, the reference appears to be to *Teaching of St. Gregory* §650.

[148] The source of this reference is not clear. Thomson, "Song" refers the reader to *Teaching of St. Gregory* §348, but the discussion there seems to be too general in comparison with the specific mentioning of 'thorns and thistles' here.

[149] Gregory of Nyssa, by contrast, says that Solomon's crown is the Church, which wreathes Christ's head with 'living stones'.

When it says, *Arise, look, daughters of Jerusalem*, it is the *daughters* of the heavenly *Jerusalem* who are intended, calling them to view their Lord bearing such a *crown*, He who for the Church's sake undertook great wonders. On the other hand it also refers to the earthly Jerusalem's daughters, to whom the Lord Himself turned and said, 'Daughters of Jerusalem, weep not for me' (Lk 23:28).

With which his mother crowned him. He calls Sion *his mother*, because Sion is translated 'mother'.[150]And those who *crowned* the Lord dwelt in her. For that reason, his crowning is said to have been *by his mother*.

On the day of his wedding, and the day of his happiness. Now, do not be surprised that he calls the day of His sufferings *the day of his happiness* and *the day of his marriage*. For the Lord Himself called that day and hour His glory, saying 'The hour has come, that the Son of Man be glorified' (Jn 12:23). He speaks of what is ours, as His; for that reason he took such a *crown*. On that day we were wedded and rejoiced—we who had existed in sadness for five thousand years because of our loss of Paradise,[151] and

---

[150] This may be an allusion to Gal 4:26 rather than an actual etymology, though Thomson, 'Song', points out that Procopius of Gaza (1636D), quoting Nilus, treats it as the latter.

[151] *Teaching of St. Gregory* § 670. See Thomson, 'Number Symbolism'. A standard patristic description of the six millennia, with the seventh millennium of rest, occupies *Teaching of St. Gregory* §667–671. Grigoris Arsharuni, in his *Meknut'iwn Ĕnderts'uatsots'* [Commentary on the Readings] (Venice, 1964); selections published in *Bazmavēp* (1935) 390–401, points out the parallel between man's creation on the sixth day and his salvation in the sixth millennium. For a French translation, see L. M. Froidevaux, *Grigoris Aršarouni. Commentaire du lectionnaire*, Bibliotheca Armeniaca Textus et Studia, 1 (Venice, 1975) Chapter 15. Interestingly, Narek counts the millennia as eight. The scheme of eight ages is also found later in Vanakan Vardapet's *Questions and Answers*, which describes them in the following manner:

And these are the heads of the ages: in the first, Enoch was translated; in the second, the Flood; in the third, the Tower was built; in the fourth, the good news was given to Abraham; in the fifth, Solomon built the Temple; in the

who had fallen from the glory which we had possessed together with the garment of light,[152] by the stripping away of which we were dishonored.

— CHAPTER FOUR —

The groom says
4.1 *Behold my Near One, my beautiful one, your eyes are doves.*

In other words, 'That beauty of yours has now come into being through my strange crowning. By it even you too were beautified, when I made the ugliness of your sin my own, together with my crown of thorns'. Lo, it is this beauty the purification of the font reveals, which became a 'new birth by the Holy Spirit' (Jn 3:5). By repeating this, he made it clear that they who are created anew have a more beautiful form and preserve it spotless;

---

sixth, Christ became incarnate of the Virgin; in the seventh age . . . , and at the start of the eighth will be the universal resurrection.

See also 6.7 below.

[152] Though *Teaching of St. Gregory* §280 mentions it only in passing, the motif of humanity's lost garment of light or glory recurs frequently throughout Armenian patristic literature. It also appears in at least one manuscript illumination miniature of Adam and Eve, where the Tree bears the inscription, 'I ate of the fruit and was stripped of the light' (oral communication of Y. Kutchukian). Chrysostom, *Homily* 15 on Genesis, says 'You see, while sin and disobedience had not yet come on the scene, they were clad in that glory from above which caused them no shame'; and in *Homily* 16, 'Their eyes were opened and they realized they were naked; because of the Fall they were stripped of grace from above' (John Chrysostom, *Homilies on Genesis 1-17*, 194–221). For the treatment of this idea in other traditions, see Sebastian P. Brock, 'The Robe of Glory: A Biblical Image in the Syriac Tradition' in *Spirituality and Clothing = The Way* 39 (1999) 247–259; Herbert R. Broderick, 'A Note on the Garments of Paradise', *Byzantion* 55 (1985) 250–254.

and it is much greater than the previous form which Adam had in his glory. As the blessed Gregory the Theologian says, it is a divine creation and greater than the previous one.[153] For that creation, although it was illumined and possessed a life without pain, without sadness, and with immortality, yet the temptation interrupted it—'If he keeps the command, then he will remain immortal'.

Now, however, to become even the son of God is a boon to which all people can attain. The divine Solomon, stupefied and amazed, portrayed this under the guise of what seems most desirable to us earthly creatures; he intends to make apparent our free gift of grace by this means. Nonetheless, even he was not adequate to reach ultimate knowledge, though he tries to describe it metaphorically.

But now, tell me, O Christ our Groom, among visible phenomena is there any fit metaphor for that beauty in which we have again been created? It seems to me that, rather, you wish to feed us milk, like children, and not solid food (1 Cor 3:2), because since we are still corporeal, being in this life, we cannot understand spiritual things.

Open your dove's eyes from your silence.

Lo, he testified to the statement that you are pure, and innocent like a *dove*. But no matter how much you are so, it is sealed off by *silence*, since one cannot express it, because you cannot hear. For your ears are vessels of clay and are not adequate to hear the 'unutterable things' (2 Cor 12:4).

---

[153] *Oration* 39. vii. In iii, enumerating the benefits of Baptism, Nazianzen refers to it as 'the Illumination of illuminations', like the Holy of Holies and the Song of songs.

*Your tresses are like the flocks of goats which appeared
from Gilead,*

In other words, you are beyond all passion—just as hair is dead—
lifeless, without desire, without pride, estranged from the world
and dead—as hair has no sensation [Nyssa 921C]. By the same
token, the *eyes* have vision, and do not turn aside to what is evil,
and are wholeheartedly for the good.[154]

> 4.2 *Your teeth like the flocks of shorn sheep which go
> up from washing;*

Because that which has been washed and relieved of the burden
of its wool is pure and pleasing [Nyssa 925B].

> *they have all borne twins, and there is none barren.*

In other words, 'the offspring of the desolate are more than those of
she who has a husband' (Gal 4:27). Now, these *teeth* having 'chewed'
purity, do not instruct only you, but they also *give birth to* others by
admonishing them thoroughly with words of doctrine, and rumi-
natively instructing them through a close exegesis of Scripture.

> 4.3 *Like a red thread are your lips, and your words are
> beautiful.*

First, the person whose *lips* are painted with blood is to be praised
for their redness [Nyssa 928C]. Then, the one whose *lips* speak
with the words of the Gospel and all spiritual sayings.

One should not omit to mention the *thread*, for there are
many things which are snared by this *thread*. Now, he says that the

---

[154] The translation of this paragraph is problematic. It is not clear whether the
commentator intends to say that the person addressed resembles both the hair
(dead to passions) and the eyes (alive to good), or whether, perhaps, there has
been a misreading of *ayts* (=goat) as *ach'k'* (=eyes).

words which arise from reddened *lips* are like a *thread*; they hook men, and draw them up towards God, in a good way.

> *Like the skin of a pomegranate are your cheeks, except for your silence.*[155]

A *pomegranate* has two natures: its appearance is unpleasant, while its unseen parts are appetizing and the occasion of much good health. Now the Bride of Christ; that is, the Church, has veiled her face with a virtuous way of life and an unsophisticated and homely manner [Nyssa 929B-C]. These are external, like *the pomegranate's skin*. Whereas laid up within her are hope and love and faith[156] towards God. By that hope she endures it all. Just as what is stored up within the pomegranate is much sought after for food, likewise the life of virtue is strenuous and is perfected with great effort, but the fruit of it is all glorious, and glorified. Concerning it the Prophet says, 'the king's daughter is all glorious within' (Ps 44:14).

Except your silence. How beautiful you are is muted, and is not revealed for now, for as long as you are enwrapped in the weakness of your flesh. As it says, 'What eye has not seen, neither has ear heard' (Is 64:4; 1 Cor 2:9).

> 4.4 *Your neck is like the tower of David, which is built in Talpiot;*

---

[155] The Greek word can be translated as 'veil' or as 'silence'. Narek uses the second meaning as the basis of his interpretation. With the addition of a single accent, the phrase 'apart from your silence' or 'except for your silence' becomes the imperative 'Open [them] from your silence'. (A vestigial remnant of the meaning 'veil' is contained in the citation from Nyssa 929 B-C.) Cf. 4.1 above and 6.6 below.

[156] An allusion to 1 Cor 13:13.

David built a famous tower; to its elegance he compares the Bride's neck.

a thousand shields hang from it, and all arrows of weaponry.

A *thousand* denotes multiplicity. As it says, 'The chariots of God are tens of thousands and a thousand are their drivers' (Ps 67:18) [Nyssa 936A].

The Apostle calls faith a *shield*, saying 'Take the shield of faith' (Eph 6:16), which hangs around the *neck*. Beautified with it, she is *like the tower of David*.

> 4.5 *Your two breasts are like two twin kids, which graze among the lilies.*

He mentions *two breasts*, because there are *two* natures in a human being: flesh and spirit [Nyssa 937B-C]. The body also has *two* eyes, and it has spirit and mind. They *graze* selectively, so that, avoiding the thorns, they may feed on *lilies*, that is, on spiritual food.

> 4.6 *Until the day breaks, and the shadows dissipate*

Who is *day* and light, if not the Holy Spirit, and even Christ Himself, who chases away the shadows from the mind. As it is said, 'From you Lord, is the fountain of life and in the light of your countenance do we see light' (Ps 35:10). By it the mind too is illuminated, and the heart as well, which lies between the *breasts* [Nyssa 936C-D], whose milk is collected and processed,[157] by agency of the spiritual way of life, to be given as food to others.

---

[157] The verb used (*matsanim*) is one indicating the making of yoghurt or curd.

Now, the Apostle, too, briefly explains this: the soul is the entire Church, and the graces which are distributed within it are the senses—members in the body, as it were (1 Cor 12:12-26). Those things this writer has enumerated one by one, calling them the *eye* and the *lip* and the *tooth* and the *cheek* and the *neck* and the *belly*. The *eye* is to be understood as the prophets who foresaw these graces; in other words, Solomon himself, and those like him.

The *neck*, upon which the head stands erect and by which everything alive above and below is joined together with all the senses—which was compared to *the tower of David which he built in Talpiot* for the prefecture of warriors—is the great Apostle Paul and those like him, upon whom Christ "stands". From them all life is distributed to the Church.

The *belly*, too, applies to our holy Illuminator, and John, and their like. The Lord bears witness to this: 'From their belly rivers shall pour out living water' (Jn 7:38); that is, the grace of the Spirit.

Likewise also the *teeth* with the *reddened lips* bringing up the words of Scripture from the *belly* and ruminating on them break them down into digestible pieces, making the unobvious things obvious, and offer them for people's understanding, illuminating the lesser members in the Church body.

By this, humanity is made complete, and becomes the Bride of Christ.

> *I went alone to the mountain of myrrh, and to the hill*
> *of frankincense.*

The blessed John mentions that this saying resembles what the Prophet says: 'I have trodden the wine press *alone*, and of the gentiles none was with me' (Is 63:3).[158] Now the *mountain of*

---

[158] The relevant passage in the Armenian text of John Chrysostom's *Commentary on Isaiah* (Venice: San Lazzaro, 1880; pp. 461–465) makes no illusion to the Song.

myrrh signifies the death which He suffered for us, having fought in single combat. *And the hill of frankincense* means that He trod the wine press on the Cross, united with God [Nyssa 944C].

> 4.7 *You are all beautiful, my Near One, and there is no spot in you.*

In other words, 'It is through My crucifixion and death that you have become so spotless and beautiful, and it is by the blood of Me, the Lamb who took away the sins of the world' (Jn 1:29,36). Too, whoever draws near to Him and partakes in His death,[159] receives His fragrance,[160] here compared to *frankincense* [Nyssa 940B].

> 4.8 *Come from Lebanon, bride, come from Lebanon, come and pass from the beginning of faith, from the peak of Sanir and Hermon, from the lions' den and from the mountains of leopards.*

That is, coming from the *mountain* enforested with sin to faith, being born *in the beginning* from Jordan—the font. The Jordan arises between these two mountains and spills forth. In it the Bride was washed and became beautiful, she who had dwelt with beasts, with *lions* and *leopards*, mighty and dominant and 'spotted' with idolatry, as it seems to me [Nyssa 944D-945A].

> 4.9 *You have heartened us, our sister bride, you have heartened us with one of your eyes, and with one chain of your neck.*

This the friends of the Groom, who are the angels, say to the beautiful one who is the Bride. *You have heartened us*; that is, 'You

---

[159] An allusion to Paul's statements in Rom 6:6; Gal 2:20, 5:24.
[160] An allusion to 2 Cor 2:15-16.

have given us soul and heart to see what we had not known; that is, the provident love which He has displayed towards humanity—birth through the font, adoption, and the kingdom as well—which He accomplished through the death on the Cross [Nyssa 948B]. With His *myrrh* you became a partaker in His death, and with His *frankincense*'s fragrance you will share in His glory. Now, through you, I have recognized Him, and His power, and His love towards humanity'.

Thus, the angels say to their *Sister*, who is the Church: '*with your* deficient *eye*,' (which is referred to as *one*) 'you, with your *one eye*, have surpassed us who are superior to you in our multitude of *eyes* and in our *neck*. We are mighty in two natures—that is in *eyes* and *neck*—yet through you do we see, and from you do we hear, being instructed in such unspeakable mystery and salvation'! This is what the Apostle is talking about when he says, 'Through the Church, the manifold wisdom of God shall be revealed to the principalities and powers which are in heaven' (Eph 3:10).

The intent of calling the Church *Sister* is to show our nature's pure relatedness to the angels. And the *chain of the neck*, shows that we have submitted to the yoke of Christ[161] with eager will [Nyssa 952C].

Thus, he said, 'At the call of the Groom you have *come from Lebanon*, and put on such grace. However, do not consider that coming to have been sufficient by itself; rather, *come* yet more and keep daily on the path; that is, on the way of virtue'. As the Prophet says, 'He shall go from strength to strength' (Ps 83:8). Gregory the Theologian also attests that one must be ever moving towards virtue, and agile.[162]

Therefore, he again repeats what he said at first, *Come from Lebanon*.

---

[161] An allusion to Mt 11:29-30.

[162] Thomson, 'Song', notes a general similarity to the second half of *Oration* 44.

4.10 *How beautiful have your breasts become, my sister my bride; they have become beautiful from wine, and the scent of your garments is better than any incense.*

Breasts are accustomed to give food to human beings who come to the earth through birth. By the same metaphor of the *breasts*, he presages the purity of the hearts of the saints who sprang up in the Church, for the heart is near the *breasts*.

But since he said earlier that *breasts* give milk, how does he now change it to *wine*, saying that *they are beautiful from wine*? One should thus understand the Apostle Paul's statement, 'Whoever drinks milk is ignorant of the word of righteousness' (Heb 5:13). Or the other one which says, 'Like children in Christ, I have fed you with milk and not with solid food' (1 Cor 3:2) [Nyssa 956A]. By this he indicates the feeding of the Church's 'childhood' with the milk which comes from the *breasts*. Now its perfection is fed with wine, for solid food and drink is for the mature (Heb 5:14). And as wine rejoices those who are replete with food, likewise the words of the Holy Spirit flowing from the hearts of the saints—that is, from their *breasts*—rejoice the hearers and grant them indescribable vitality and joy.[163]

The *scent of the garments*, which wafts like *incense*, is to be understood in the same way: those who hold fast to fragrant virtue and good works are causes of salvation not only for themselves, but also for those who draw near to them [Nyssa 957C]. They assist those who look to them, not only in their lifetime, but all the more after their death, even though much time may elapse.

---

[163] This verse is quoted in the sermon of Catholicos Yovhan Mandakuni (420?–490) reported in *The History of Ghazar P'arpets'i*, tr. Robert W. Thomson. Columbia University Program in Armenian Studies: Suren D. Fesjian Academic Publications 4 (Atlanta: Scholars Press, 1991) §100 (hereafter, Ghazar): 'Encourage the ignorant to suck the milk for nourishment; teach them to drink from the joyous cup for the sweet joy of their souls' salvation, from that milk and wine of which the wise Solomon, by the grace of the Holy Spirit, prophesied in the Song of Songs'.

> 4.11 *Your lips drop honey, my sister my bride, honey*
> *and milk are underneath your tongue, and the scent of*
> *your clothes is like the fragrance of frankincense.*

This requires no lengthy explanation. He calls sweet and appetizing doctrine *honey*, which is fed to humanity by those who are near to Christ and wedded to Him, and the hearts of the hearers are sweetened. As David says, 'Your words are sweeter to my taste than honey' (Ps 118:103). I forebear saying that for the Prophet what was bitter in the mouth before the eating, became sweet in the swallowing. For at the outset virtue is bitter, and afterwards it is sweet.

Milk and honey are under your tongue: *milk* is for the young, and *honey* for the mature [Nyssa 960C]. First of all, the *tongue* which gives these sweet foods, is to be understood as the blessed universal teacher John, and the Theologian likewise, and those who like them feed us sweet food.

Again he repeats himself, saying *and the scent of your garments like the fragrance of frankincense*. This is a fragrant sacrifice, which God smells as a sweet savor[164] [Nyssa 957A]—those who offer their will and thoughts and bodies to God as a living sacrifice (Rom 12:1).

> 4.12 *My sister my bride is an enclosed garden, an en-*
> *closed garden and a sealed spring*

See, although she is a *garden*, yet she needs to be *enclosed*, and although she is a *spring*, she needs to be *sealed*, so as neither to become food and drink for strange flocks nor to let fall her pearls before swine (Mt 7:6)—nor give them to strangers' ears.

---

[164] An allusion to 2 Cor 2:15, where Paul uses the Old Testament commonplace describing a sacrifice.

> 4.13-14 *Your emanation is a paradise of pomegranates*
> *with the fruits of its trees, a flower with fragrance, nard*
> *and saffron, calamus and cinnamon with all the trees of*
> *Lebanon, myrrh and spices with all foremost ointments,*

If I expound on this word by word, you my hearers will find it tedious, but since I have opened the door to those meanings which other *vardapet*s explore minutely, I shall summarize them. And I shall conclude with the Apostle's word which says, 'This is the fruit of the spirit; love, joy, peace' (Gal 5:22); and elsewhere, 'Compassion, mercy, faith, hope, love, meekness, humility, sweetness, brotherly love, unvengefulness, detachment, simplicity of mind and purity of soul, and other like things'.[165] Some of those to be implemented are austere, like *myrrh*, and some are sweet, like *ointment*. Some are delightful like *flowers*. Through these things, the Bride becomes God's *garden*.

Sweet *ointment* compounded of many substances, which was burned in the Mosaic tabernacle, was a veritable type of the myriad virtues that are in the saints, which God smells with greater delight than that erstwhile incense and than the evening and morning sacrifices.

The pomegranate tree, before its *pomegranates* are ripe, brings no enjoyment to those who eat; it is encased with thorns. So also is everyone who becomes God's garden and *paradise* in this life; first he must live with difficulty, with hunger and thirst and striving and exertion, and whatever other sufferings there are for virtue. Thus he constrains himself, and whatever trials come upon him involuntarily, whether caused by companions or by Satan, all of this he patiently and voluntarily bears for love of God. Afterwards, there will be appetizing fruit for God, like the *pomegranate*, which grows among thorns until it is ripe [Nyssa 969Bff]. In this way should one who will become Christ's Bride

---

[165] Here he adapts lists of virtues such as those found in Col 3:12, 1 Cor 13:13, Gal 5:23, and 1 Tm 6:11.

and His garden, live at first among the thorns, that is among the virtues; later there will be fruit for Christ the Groom.

Moreover, there will also be *flowers*, like *nard and saffron*, the one warm and the other sweet; thus, the warm one should ignite us with the love of Christ, and inflame the *fragrance* of virtue and all good works. They say concerning *saffron*, that it is intermediate, neither especially cool nor especially warm, but having instead a moderate power. By such a metaphor he teaches us that it is necessary for the garden of God to produce virtuous fruit, but one should avoid excess and keep to the mean, lest one stumble through lack of moderation [Nyssa 972A]. It is the same in faith: one should accept the Scriptures with firm faith, and not infer more than what is written, nor scrutinize the inscrutable, but consign all impossible, unlikely and unbelievable matters to the power of God, who in all things is able.

By the same token, if someone is in mourning over a sin which he has committed, he should not mourn excessively, lest he fall into despair and say, 'There is no salvation for me', and because of that either not turn from his sin or suffer the suffering of Judas, who hanged himself because there was no possibility of repentance: that was excessive mourning. But why should I recount these things individually? As the symbol of *saffron* instructs us, every manner of life and mode of behavior must remain within bounds, and not turn aside either to the right or to the left.

Calamus and cinnamon were cultivated by the Bride in the pomegranate orchard. We know *calamus* to be sweeter than all incense—so much so that it was commanded to mingle it with the incense which was to be burned to God on the altar [Nyssa 972D]. And they say that when *cinnamon* is introduced into a vat of briskly boiling water, it lowers the heat of the boiling water in it. Likewise if it enters into a hot bath, it instantly cools the house. There are other such things, which seem unbelievable to their hearers: they say that when a man is sleeping and *cinnamon* is nearby, whatever anyone asks the sleeper, he will answer; one has only to lay the *cin-*

namon on his mouth, and though he is asleep, he will be awake and answer the questions of the inquirers articulately and appropriately. He seems to be asleep, yet he is awake. Thus, this spice teaches us that the man who gives himself to God seems to be human, and yet is not human; for if thoughts of fornication trouble him, or of anger, or greed, or any other corporeal passion, he does not entertain them, but instead in his way of life he is like the angels, who are awake and never sleep, and are without passions and without needs. He is human, and not human, for a human is 'asleep', compared to the wisdom of angels [Nyssa 973A-C].

He compared to the Bride the fruit which is from the spiritual garden and *paradise*, as well as *myrrh and spices with all the foremost ointments. Myrrh* symbolizes the death of Christ, and His burial [Nyssa 976C], while *spices and the foremost precious ointments*, signify the unity of the godhead with the flesh, through which He suffered death.

He has shown that man was from the forest of sin like *a tree from Lebanon.* Having come *from Lebanon* and having become a fellow sufferer with Christ and partaken in His death, and having put sin to death, he became the fragrant Bride of Christ, united with Him in purity of life. As the Apostle says, 'We who were once baptized into Christ Jesus, were baptized into his death; we are buried with him in the baptism of death, so that as Christ rose from the dead with the glory of the Father, so also we might walk in newness of life. For as we were planted in the likeness of His death, so shall we also be partakers in His resurrection' (Rom 6:3-5). And he is redolent of divinity [Nyssa 977C]. As the divine Solomon said,

> 4.15 *a fountain of gardens, a well of living water and flowing from Lebanon.*

Herewith, he augments the Bride's beauty more than it was at first. Previously, he called the Bride a *garden*; then, a little farther on, *a fountain of gardens.* In other words, 'Not only did you become a garden, but having irrigated many others, you make them God's garden and paradise, to bring forth the fruit of righteousness' (Heb 12:1; James 3:18).

God Himself has been called a *well*; as He said through the Prophet, 'They have forsaken me, the fountain of living water' (Jer 2:13). Again, the Lord said to the Samaritan woman, 'If you knew the gifts of God, and who it is that says to you, "Give me to drink", you would have asked of him, and he would give you living water' (Jn 4:10). And again, 'Whoever believes in me, rivers of living water will flow from his belly' (Jn 7:38) [Nyssa 977C].

Now, just as those who share in His death partake in the fragrance of His divinity and are wedded to Him, so also do they who are wedded to Him become *wells of living water*, like Himself, even though they have come *from Lebanon*, that is from the forest of sin—for Lebanon is a forest. John the Evangelist explains this and what follows: 'This He said concerning the Spirit, which those who believed in Him were to receive' (Jn 7:39).

4.16 *Awake north, and come south,*

That is, go *north*, and come *south*. Satan and his works are called *north*. As the same Solomon says, 'The north wind is fierce' (Prv 27:16), for it is far from the warmth of the sun, and for that reason it is frigid. Likewise those who live far from the Sun of Righteousness are filled with satanic thoughts and are frozen in sin [Nyssa 984C]. They are not melted by the warmth of the sun; that is, they are not taught by the words of the sacred scriptures, which melt the ice of impenitence and sow contrition with the wind of the Holy Spirit, which is the *south*. He invokes the *south* wind; that is, the grace of the Holy Spirit, to come to the garden and chase away satanic works. For that reason he says, *awake north*—which means, go—*and come, south*; that is, the Holy Spirit and its warm wind, which chases away the winter.

blow upon my garden, and its spices will give forth fragrance.

This is the generous *blowing* of the Holy Spirit[166] on the *garden* of Christ, which has been called the Bride, whence various graces have blossomed among humankind. As the Apostle says, 'To one is given by the Spirit the word of wisdom, to another the word of knowledge according to the same Spirit, to another faith, to another working of miracles, to another discernment of the Spirit, to another prophecies' (1 Cor 12:8-10). Why should I list one by one the manifold graces which he has said are in the Church? He concludes, 'All this one and the same Spirit brings to success, and distributes each grace as He wills' (1 Cor 12:11).

This is what *Blow upon my garden, and my spices will give forth fragrance* means. The foremost *spices* were Paul and Peter and their ten companions, and our Holy Illuminator, and John Chrysostom and countless others like them [Nyssa 985A].

— CHAPTER FIVE —

The bride pleads that her groom may descend
5.1 *Let my Nephew come down into his garden, and let him eat the fruit of his trees.*

Seeing her great virtues, which she had learned by experience from the Groom and the angels, flourishing as in a paradise and in a *garden*, the Bride begs Him to *come down* and *eat*.

This indicates the regard of God towards those who do good. God is without lack, nonetheless He hungers and longs for our salvation. As He Himself said to His disciples, when they were

---

[166] Perhaps an allusion to Jn 3:8.

constraining him to eat bread, 'My food is to accomplish the will of Him who sent me' (Jn 4:34), which was our turning to Him and keeping His commandments [Nyssa 985C].

He Himself also said, 'I was hungry, and you gave Me to eat; I was thirsty, and you gave Me drink' (Mt 25:35). These words teach us humility; not to be proud of our virtuous way of life and to become careless, trusting in our good works, but to plead with broken heart and humble spirit[167] to receive the *fruit* of righteousness. He Himself commanded us to plead and say, 'Thy kingdom come' (Mt 6:10; Lk 11:2). The Groom sees this pleading, He who says through the Prophet, 'Before you call on me, I will hear you, and while you are speaking, I shall say Behold, I stand ready' (Is 65:24). Likewise the Groom, hearing the Bride's pleading, says, 'I have heard your prayer, and—

> *I have entered my garden, my sister my bride.*
> *I have gathered my myrrh with my spices,*
> *I have eaten my bread with my honey.*

He calls her *Sister*, and then *Bride*, for whoever does the will of God then verily becomes His *Bride*.

And *I have gathered my myrrh with my spices*. That is, 'The *fruit* of the death which I died for you I have gathered from you, my *garden*, and *my Bride*, fragrant *with spices* of virtue. I died, as indicated by the symbol of the *myrrh*, and by virtue of the love of the divinity united with my flesh, I am fragrant.

I have eaten my bread with my honey. Not only have you become food for Me, feeding Me with the *bread* of virtue, but you have been as sweet to Me "as *honey* with the honeycomb" (Ps 19:10), like the blessed teachers the Theologian and John, who speak as if from the mouth of God and say, "Feed Me with virtue."'

---

[167] An allusion to Ps 33:19.

He commanded Peter to feed on this same food, showing him the sheet in which were all living creatures; that is, telling him to present the gentiles to God as food, just like the Jews, without discrimination, and not to consider them unclean[168] [Nyssa 992A].

I have drunk my wine with my milk.

This He said to the sons of Zebedee: 'Are you able to drink the cup which I shall drink'? (Mt 20:22; Mk 10:38); that is, the death which He 'drank'; also, the *wine* that came through His blood.

In addition, He was given *milk*; that is, human childhood. By this drink, they who have drunk the cup of death became children in innocence, like sucklings. The Lord Himself said, 'If you do not return and become like children, you cannot enter the kingdom of God' (Mt 18:3).

Not to mention what the Lord drank and gave to the Disciples, saying, 'This is my blood; take, and drink' (Mt 26:27), and so on. That is:

Eat, my Near Ones, drink and be drunken, my brethren.

As the other Gospel writer says, 'If you do not eat the flesh of the Son of Man and drink His blood, you have no life in your selves' (Jn 6:53). Now, by His own drinking, and by then giving it to the Disciples, He showed that the Church and the Bride were to *drink* this very cup and become partakers in His death. Thus, the sacrament which we carry out recalls His death; by placing the awesome sacrifice on the altar before the Father, we hold up before the Father the death which He died for us, and through it we anticipate salvation for ourselves [Nyssa 989B-C].

---

[168] An allusion to Peter's vision in Acts 10.

Now, the blessed John says that He drank of His blood so that He might encourage them to drink, lest they say, 'How can we drink His blood'?[169] However, the real explanation is, 'My true *drink* is death and innocence; that is, *wine* and *milk*. You ought to drink it, and, as I have fed you with my blood, so you ought also to feed Me with your childlikeness and your death to everything that pertains to this life'. As the Apostle puts its, 'If anyone wants to become wise in this world, he will become a fool, so that he may be wise in that world' (1 Cor 3:18). And he shall feed Christ with his *wine* and with his *milk*, in order to take on himself His way of life. As the Apostle says again, 'Be emulators of me, as I am of Christ' (1 Cor 11:1). And in another place, 'Christ is in you, unless you be unworthy' (2 Cor 13:5). Gregory the Theologian also says, 'I understand Christ to be those who live according to Christ'.[170]

Now, having said *drink and be drunken*, he adds

5.2 *I sleep, and my heart remains awake.*[171]

In other words, this drinking is not the drunkenness which brings numbing sleep, like the wine which is from the vine; rather, 'As I was *awake* in the grave in terms of my divinity, and *asleep* in terms of my flesh's death, so likewise they who drink this drink, awaken with Me, with the Lord's own immortality'. This is what it means when it says, 'He shall live forever' (Jn 6:51, 58). Albeit having a human nature they "sleep", yet bearing the grace of the Spirit within themselves, they are awake.

---

[169] *Homily* 82 On Matthew (82.1).

[170] Thomson, 'Song', points to the introduction of *Oration* 21.

[171] The verse is also used in *Physiologus*: 'As in the Blessing of blessings it said, "I sleep, and my heart is awake". Although His flesh slept, yet His godhead was awaks, as always at the Father's right, wakeful and unsleeping.' (Gohar Muradyan, *Physiologus*, 89.)

Now, if it were not thus, how, with this weak flesh, could the apostles have suffered so many torments and the martyrs so much tribulation—as also did the ascetic fathers? Especially our Illuminator—whose spiritual wakefulness ten men, hanging him upside down on a gibbet for seven days and beating him, were not able to numb by means of such bitter tortures. Rather, elevating his mind wakefully towards God in those days he laid before God compassionate intercessions for the salvation of our country.[172] A beating with a single stick is sufficient to bring numbing sleep to our minds, but the blessed one—maintaining his mind undistracted amid those boundless tortures and his tongue constant in requests to God—could not but resemble the *wakeful heart* of Christ and the *sleep* of His flesh; by putting to sleep the natural passions, he was a partaker in Christ's death with wakeful mind.[173] This is what it means when it says, *drink and be drunken, my brethren*, for 'having drunk suffering, I slept according to the flesh, while My heart remained awake according to My divinity. Likewise, you are to resemble me by this *drinking* of my death.'

> The Bride senses the Groom's knocking at the door
> The voice of my Nephew, he knocks at the door.

Observe well, how wakeful a mind[174] they receive who drink that cup and wine in this slumbrous life, according to the Gospel exhortation, 'Let your belt be girt about your waist, and your lamps lit, and be like people who expect their Lord, when He may return from a wedding, so that when He comes and knocks,

---

[172] Agathangelos §74–99.

[173] Gregory of Narek was fond of recalling the meaning of his name in Greek, and of applying that meaning to the activities of other saints named Gregory as well, such as Saint Gregory the Illuminator.

[174] He is making another play on the meaning of the name Gregory as 'wakeful'.

they may open to him at once. Blessed is that servant, whom
His Lord shall find awake when He come' (Lk 12:36-38) [Nyssa
996C, 997B]. The saints who were wedded to Christ the Groom
were like this, standing at watch[175] and hearing the voice of their
Nephew Christ, who *knocked at the door*, calling them to enter into
the kingdom of heaven. The Groom, who is Christ, says when
He knocks at the door,

> *Open to me, my Sister, my Near One, my dove, my perfect one.*
> *For my head is filled with dew, and my hair with the fine rain*
> *of night.*

Briefly, now, this is the interpretation. *Open to me my Sister, my*
Near One, my dove, my perfect one. With these words he foretells
the illumination of the Bride through baptism: 'through the birth
of the Spirit and the drinking of the mystical blood, you have
become *my Sister* and *my Near One,* and you have been justified
by the Spirit, taking on the nature of a *dove,* and you have become
perfect. For you have become God's child, and whoever is worthy
to become God's child is perfect in everything, for what higher
glory is there than this on earth or in heaven?'

Nonetheless, if we do not preserve that grace and utilize it
and the glory which we have been given, we shall be like our forefather Adam, who, having received illumination and life without
need or pain or death, and Paradise as well, lost them again by
not keeping them or utilizing them. He teaches us, too, not to
become careless about our being perfected through grace, but to
be solicitous of it, 'as though we had not received it' (1 Cor 4:7).
For the giving of perfection is His prerogative, and the preserv-
ing of it is up to us, as the blessed Teacher says. Concerning this

---

[175] Perhaps an allusion to Gregory the Theologian's *Oration* 45, popular in the
Armenian tradition. It begins with the quotation from Hab 2:1, 'I shall stand at
my watch. . . .'

he says, 'Open the door of the road which leads to life, and do not presume that you will rest and sleep and have an easy life by means of your perfection'![176] As the Apostle says, 'If anyone considers himself to know something, he has not yet understood as it is right to understand' (Gal 6:3). And again, 'I do not consider myself to have attained. But there is one thing; that, having forgotten what is behind, I press forward—I run carefully after the call of God in Christ Jesus' (Phil 3:14).

Now, *open to Me* your entrance, *for my head is filled with dew, and my hair with the fine rain of night*. It is as if He is displaying, at the Second Coming, the wounds which He received for our sake. But there, He displays them in order to rebuke us, who are found ungrateful for His benefits, whereas here He displays them in order to exhort us. He reminds the Bride of the sweat which He suffered for fear of death in that night—as it says in the Gospel, 'Sweat flowed from Him in great drops' (Lk 22:44). He says, It is through My sweat that you have put on that innocence of a dove and that perfection, and have become my Sister and Bride; by My sweat on that night, I removed the sweat of the curse (Gn 3:19), and being wounded with you I endured with sweat. Now, preserve that which you have received; that is, the innocence of a dove and that perfection, and do not lose it again, for there will be no second Cross, and no second death for your sake.

The bride says this
5.3 *I have taken off my robe; how shall I put it on? I*
have washed my feet; how shall I dirty them?

That is, *having taken off the robe* of punishment for my transgressions[177] through those great favors of yours, and your sweat for

---

[176] *Homily* 55 on Matthew stresses this idea, although there are no direct verbal parallels.

[177] See above, n. 152.

my sake, *how shall I put it on* again? [Nyssa 1004D]. Perish the thought! And how could I, who have been dressed in light and been given the authority to direct myself toward heaven and to join the ranks of the angels, *dirty* the *feet* which You have *washed* through baptism like the feet of the blessed apostles [Nyssa 1008B], and bound up from the poison of the biting serpent,[178] by walking in the ways of sin—fornication or murder or fraud or the like?!

> 5.4 *My Nephew put his hand through the hole, and my belly was moved for him.*

Look here: even though someone may be enlightened through the Spirit like Paul or Peter, and attempt to become a seer of the mystery of Christ, he will still, instead of the whole person, see only the *hand*, and that through a narrow and small place, as *through a hole*. Thus the Apostle says, 'Now we see as in a mirror, in likeness, but then face to face. Now I understand a little of much, but then I shall know even as He knew me' (1 Cor 13:12) [Nyssa 1012A]. He is saying, 'Whatever grace the Groom has given me, and whatever He has promised to give, and whatever He has borne for me, and whatever grace has come to us through His death, and whatever other such immeasurable and unspeakable gifts He has here shown to the saints, compared to what He will show us and give us knowledge of in the life to come, these are like a person seeing only the *hand through* a *hole*, or like a drop of water compared to the water of the sea, or like a lamp compared to the sun, or like a babe in its mother's womb compared to an old man'.

Note, too, that even at this fleeting, tiny glimpse her *belly was moved*; as it said, *my belly was moved for him*. In the same way Paul,

---

[178] The expression that baptism secures one from the biting serpent is also found in Gregory Nazianzen, *Oration* 40.19.

too, was dazzled by a small glimpse, and it blinded his eyes. The same was true of John the Apostle in his vision, and true of Ezekiel as well—and his was merely a vision of angels! As Daniel, too, said, 'Lord, my belly was moved within me at your appearing', and so on (Dn 10:16; 2 Cor 12:4) [Nyssa 1012B]. Just as feeble eyes cannot behold the sun, by the same token human nature cannot behold the divine things nor comprehend them, so long as one is in this life. For which reason, it was by taking Paul out of the body and leading him to the third heaven that He there showed him things which cannot be spoken of. And when he returned to earth, he could not relate with his corporeal mind and lips the ineffable things which he had seen and heard. Instead he said 'I heard unutterable things, which it is not right for a man to speak' (2 Cor 12:4); that is to say, the corporeal tongue cannot render the mystery of the incorporeal.

Finally, if anyone should say that *the hand* of the Nephew which was put *through the hole*, is the Son, because He is called the Father's 'right hand',[179] and that *the hole* is to be construed as the flesh which He joined with His divinity, this is not far removed from the true meaning.[180] For as the days of the Temple were a small *hole*, so also was our nature united with the divinity *a hole*. Nonetheless, I prefer the prior explanation; consonant with Scripture, especially with the prophets, it can be extended to many applications.

[179] The interpretation that Christ is the Father's right hand is particularly apparent in exegesis of the Psalms. The commentary of Vardan the Great (1200?–1271) on Ps 44:4 says succinctly, 'Your right hand and arm, Father, is Your Son, Your Only-begotten; and the light of Your countenance is Your Holy Spirit'. *Meknut'yun Saghmosats' Dawt'i* [Commentary on the Psalms of David] (Astrakhan, 1797) 153.

[180] Thomson, 'Song', points out Origen's use of *hole* as a symbol of the Incarnation.

5.5 I arose to open for my Nephew. My hands dripped myrrh, and my myrrh-covered fingers were upon the handles of the lock.

When I saw *the hand* stretched out through the *hole*—that is, certain mysteries revealed by God through a narrow aperture—the eyes of my spirit were opened. I saw as much as it is possible for corporeal eyes to see, and my spirit awakened from the stupor of sin. I rose up from the enchantment of earthly passions, laying aside those lusts, and I made myself die to sin, dead with the One who died, the Immortal One who died for me. Dying, as the Apostle says, 'with Him by baptism into death, whereby also we have also risen with Him by the operation of faith in God', and so on (Col 2:12).

Now it is clear that first it is needful to die, and to 'put to death the members of the flesh' (Col 3:5), as the same Apostle affirms, and then there will be an entering of God and the divine mysteries into a person. This is what he means by saying, *I opened for my Nephew* [Nyssa 1016C].

My hands dripped myrrh, likewise also *my fingers were upon the handles of the lock*. The *myrrh* foretells death, and the *hands* are agents of work. Now, the hand of the Nephew Christ reaches for the hand of the Bride—that is, of the faithful—and their *hands*, the *hands* of the Bride, equally draw near to the hand of the Groom through being cleansed of sin and by dying with Him. This is as the Lord Himself succinctly said, 'If anyone comes to me, and does not hate his entire family, and even his own soul, he cannot be my disciple' (Lk 14:26). Again, 'Strait is the gate and narrow is the way which leads to life' (Mt 7:14) [Nyssa 1024C-D].

Now, obviously, that road is followed with difficulty and by dying; yet for the person in whom the love of the Groom finds place, the difficult seems easy through hope in Him. Rejoicing over this the great Apostle Paul encourages us saying, 'The sufferings of this time are not worthy to be compared with the glory to come, which is to be manifested in us' (Rom 8:18).

You observe this at present: many kings and queens have led their lives as they pleased, but on their last day they went to their death and left the world repenting, and in advance of the day of judgment they are tormented by conscience at their evils and by fear of the Judge. By the same token, however, many kings and rich men have despised this world, and at the final day of their summoning, they have departed the world joyfully, going with the hope of what lay before them, rejoicing with unspeakable joy at the bargain they had made; for they had exchanged earth for heaven, and before the day of recompense it was as if they had already here received their reward, and were in a state of rejoicing as well. They bless God ceaselessly, who allowed them to recognize the futility of this vain life, and to seek out life eternal.

Now, it is Christ who is called the *Groom* and *Nephew*, as I have often said. He is called the *Groom*, because He loved humanity as a groom loves his bride. The Apostle affirms this, saying, 'I shall betrothe you to one husband, to set you before Christ as a chaste virgin' (2 Cor 11:2). And this same Christ is called the *Nephew*, because both Jews and gentiles are descended from Adam; for this reason they are called brethren. Since Christ is from among the Jews, the Church also—that is, the newly believing gentile peoples of Christ—calls Christ *Nephew*. And the gentiles are called *Bride* and *Sister* and *garden*. A bride ought to preserve her purity and love for her groom, the one man to whom she is betrothed, and if she preserves it not, and loves another, she has defiled the bed of her groom, and has become estranged from him. So also the faithful who have been joined to Christ through baptism and have become partakers in His flesh and blood, but thereafter separate themselves from Him through love of this world and partake of various delusory desires—fornication, murder, pride, greed, vainglory, hatred, jealousy, and such like evil things—have dissolved the love of Christ their Groom and the vow which they made to one another, and have been wedded to Satan, the teacher of evil. They will rightfully receive unfailing torment. If, however, they return to Him, the Lord is a lover of humanity even under those circumstances, for He is merciful, and He does not desire the death of the sinner (Ez 18:32). For that very reason He even took on flesh and died a despised death. In like manner should the *Sister* have pity, and the *garden* bring forth fruit for its Cultivator, and not become food for strangers.

But let us grasp the words, in order:

> 5.6 *I opened to my Nephew; my Nephew had gone,*
> *and my soul went out with his word.*

See how, as she *opened*, He *had gone*. This means that once I had lifted the eyes of my mind to the meaning of Scripture, to behold the inexaminable depths of the knowledge of His grace, once I had opened my heart to embrace that fleeting glimpse, and to examine and become informed of and comprehend the depths of His knowledge, what eluded my weak mind's grasp so awed me that for desire of it I would have forgotten that knowledge which I had received when *I opened*.

For that reason she says, *my Nephew had gone*; it is as if no sooner was He seen than He at once withdrew, swift as the lightning. *And my soul went out with his word*; that is, 'having obtained a small glimmering of his words my soul left me and pursued His words'. To put it another way, I recognized him, and I was united to his love, and I was ebullient with His commandments. And thinking that I had attained something, I recognized myself to be all the more distant from attainment; seeing the true Sun, I recognized by His light how distant I am from knowledge.

I brought to mind that which this same divine Solomon said in another place: 'Whoever increases knowledge, increases pain' (Qo 1:18). By saying this, he does not discourage one from gaining knowledge of Holy Writ, lest one's pain increase; rather, he exhorts one to grow yet more in knowledge, and by that amount of knowledge to understand that the knowledge of what eludes one is knowledge unfathomable. For as a drunkard but thirsts the more, no matter how much he drinks, so also is the person who yearns after the meaning of the divinely inspired Scriptures: no matter how much he learns, he desires to learn yet more, knowing that he will never uncover the full understanding of the sacred Scriptures. Once his desire for its meaning has been kindled, it becomes a kind of hurt in his spirit, for by means of a little understanding he recognizes the boundlessness of what eludes him, and the desire for that knowledge infects him like a pain, albeit that pain and solicitude increase his healing discoveries [Nyssa 1028A-B].

> *I sought him, and I found him not; I called him, and he did*
> *not answer me.*

This attests to what I have said, that in comparison with what eluded her, it seemed as though 'I have not seen, nor have I so much as heard the voice of the One whom I glimpsed and to whom I *opened*'.

> 5.7 *The watchmen who were going about the city found*
> *me; they struck and wounded me, the guardians of the*
> *ramparts took from me my garments.*

Now, the *guardians of the ramparts* are to be understood as the ministering spirits, the angels. The Apostle Paul declares, 'Are they not all spirits under obligation, who are sent for the service of those who are to inherit salvation?' (Heb 1:14). And the psalm-singer Moses says, 'He set the boundaries of the heathen according to the number of the angels of God' (Dt 32:8).[181] So the angels are guardians of unbelieving mortals, according to their

---

[181] *Teaching of Saint Gregory* §297,321. See also *Eghishē, Questions et réponses sur la Genèse*, trans. S. Kogian (Vienna, 1928) 9–10.

provinces and cities; while for the faithful, every soul has its own angel. This is all the more true for the saints; as the Prophet says, 'Armies of the Lord's angels are around those who fear Him, and they preserve them' (Ps 33:7).

Now, if the angels are guardians, to *strike* and *wound* and *rob* is an activity, not of theirs, but of thieving spirits. So it is obvious that *they struck and wounded me* and *took my garments* means, 'I could not attain to and search out the mysteries of God; nonetheless I had hope that in my quest I might at least learn from *the guardians of the ramparts*, from the saints or from the angels. Concerning themselves, they attested that they suffer the same disabilities. Then I despaired when I heard that they experienced the very same failure of wisdom, and it was as difficult for me as if they had *wounded me*, and *taken my garments*, for the *garment* of my expectation was stripped from me. Nonetheless, although they had dashed my hopes in this precious quest, I yet persisted in my search because of the great longing and desire and thirst of my soul, and the love which joined me to the Nephew. Not accepting the prospect they offered, I laid them under oath and said,

> 5.8 *I charge you, daughters of Jerusalem, by the powers and the forces of the field, that you find my Nephew, tell him that 'I am overwhelmed by your love.'*

See how incomprehensible and insupportable is the Church's love for God! The ranks of confessors bear witness to this, those who for the sake of Christ undertook such sufferings as are beyond the capacity of flesh to sustain. While Christ, seeing the warm zeal of such love on their part, caused them to go on living amid the pain of their sufferings, according to their desire—as is also the case for sinners in eternal torment.

He did this for three reasons. First, because the saints would have liked, had it been possible, to have died for love of Him not once, but ten thousand times; nay, daily, as they said in so many words. Thus Saint Gregory said to Trdat, 'I have requested Him to make me endure it'.[182] Likewise, in his prayers he begged God to make him endure it. Now, since the desire of the just is acceptable to Him, He grants them endurance.

Second, so that He may make the heathen understand the saints' passionate love for Him, and create among the former a zealous desire to burn with that kind of love. Thus Hadrian, witnessing the bitter plight of the saints, adjured them saying, 'Tell me truly, what reward do you expect, that you bear such torments? It must be extremely great'! Because of that, he too believed in Christ, and was martyred with them.[183]

Third, so that the saints, surviving such dangers, may know that life is from God, and that He is Lord of life and of death.

I have charged you, daughters of Jerusalem, by the powers and forces of the field. This I have once demonstrated—that she calls this world a *field* [Nyssa 1041C], and *adjures* them by that whence the world's *force and power* comes—whereby it is established, and by which it is preserved in unshakeability; that is, by Christ.

If they *find the Nephew, tell him that* the Bride is *overwhelmed by His love.* Now, to the soul which possesses it, the questing for love is blissful. As Paul himself boasts, 'Neither angels nor principalities . . .' and so forth, 'is able to separate us from the love of Christ' (Rom 8:38-39). Behold, this is love! which has praise in heaven and on earth, now and in the day of Christ—not the distorted love either of goods or of authority or of beauty or of other such things, which in this world brings disrepute and in the world to come, eternal torment.

---

[182] Agathangelos §102. The request for endurance is found in Gregory's prayers, reported in §86, 87, 90, 98.

[183] 'The Martyrdom of Adrianos', in *Vkayk' ew Vkayabanut'iwnk'* [Martyrs and Martyrologies] (Venice, 1874) 29.

> *The daughters of Jerusalem and the guardians of the ramparts*
> *ask the Bride*

Having taken an oath, they ask the Bride about the form which He took from us, for they have not seen Him. As I wrote earlier, they have come to experience it through us—and they are still learning.[184]

> 5.9 *What is your Nephew more than other Nephews,*
> *o beautiful among women? What is your Nephew, that*
> *you do thus charge us?*
> *The Bride describes the Nephew:*
> *My Nephew is white and red, one among ten thousand.*

By this she denotes the body and blood of our humanity, which He took from the Holy Virgin; *white and red* because He took on mortal existence from the Virgin, with flesh and blood. Nonetheless, the Virgin did not conceive by means of a man's seed, nor is this a corrupted generation. Rather, it was a conception by means of the Holy Spirit, and a birth from the Virgin who remained the same Virgin after that birth. He came through 'locked doors' (Jn 20:19) in a way not comparable with other births. Thus, she says *one among ten thousand,* for there were no pangs at His birth, and neither pain nor sadness. Rather, as the angel had announced joy and rejoicing to the Virgin, His birth was correspondingly replete with happiness [Nyssa 1052C-1053C].

> 5.11 *His head is of finest gold.*

As that *finest gold* is purer and more valuable than other gold, so also is our *Head,* Christ, purer than all the pure things which are

---

[184] The idea that the angels learn of the incarnate Christ from humanity will be repeated below in the commentary on v. 17.

in heaven or on earth. As the Prophet said, 'He committed no sin, and there was found no guile in his mouth' (Is 53:9). The Lord Himself said, 'Which of you will rebuke me for sin'? (Jn 8:46). He became moreover the purifier of all sin, Who was 'tempted in all ways like as we, yet without sin' (Heb 4:15), as the Apostle says [Nyssa 1056A-B].

His locks are curly, black as the raven.

In a scriptural context, these are not ordinarily to be praised, but are ignoble. Nonetheless, stooping to our level, she describes His goodliness, for deep black hair is extremely beautiful for youths. He is also 'fairer to look upon than all the children of men' (Ps 44:3), as Solomon's father said presciently.

Now, do not be surprised that the Bride describes the beauty of the Nephew under the guise of gold and jewels and other earthly delights. For the Apostle says, 'The invisible things of Him from the beginning of the world, are understood to be seen through the creatures' (Rom 1:20) [Nyssa 1049B].

5.12 *His eyes are like doves upon abundance of waters, washed with milk, resting upon the abundance of the waters.*

In other words, He is innocent. The Lord praised the *dove* for being thus (Mt 10:16). That is how His eyes are: He does not possess an array of maleficent, perverse, deceptive glances like those of human beings, but straight, true and piercing ones [Nyssa 1057D]. They see what is carried within a person, and are not erring, deceived by appearances, as the Evangelist John said (Jn 7:24). Rather, they see even before creation; the Prophet Jeremiah said, 'Before you were created, I know you' (Jer 1:5).

Washed with milk, for the appearance of milk is not like that of water or other things in nature, which show in themselves that which they are not. Instead, it displays only its own nature, and it cannot show anything else in itself like other liquids do [Nyssa 1060B].

But what does it mean, *resting upon the abundance of waters*? Water reflects and mirrors the sun; in the same way, He appears in those who refine and purify themselves from the grime of sin, and to those observing, He seems to be *resting upon* them. 'And he shall be like a tree planted by the rivers of water, bringing forth fruit that does not wither' (Ps 1:4) [Nyssa 1061A], and bearing fruit endlessly.

> 5.13 *His jaws,*[185] *like dishes of incense, emit a fragrance of processed ointments.*

This indicates the meticulous, deeply ruminated words of the teaching of *vardapet*s. They are guides of the Church, who by the continual, unwearied motion of their *jaws* sweeten the minds and thoughts of humanity with sweet, *processed ointments* [Nyssa 1065B]. The things collected in pure hearts, as in *a dish*, they spread out before people, neither obscuring the incomprehensible things in great profundity, nor making the mysteries of God too plainly obvious. Instead, they dispense the knowledge of Scripture at an intermediate level of instruction, so that it may neither be despised as something negligible, by being too easily acquired, nor cause despair among those who desire to learn, by its unintelligibility. Rather, with a modest effort, they are able to garner the words of Scripture into their hearts' store. As animals which graze and ruminate regurgitate their food, so also do *vardapet*s bring up again the words of the Holy Spirit gathered in their hearts. Regurgitating and ruminating on them, chewing them fine by

---

[185] The word *tsnōtk'* indicates the whole maxillary region of the face; Gregory chooses to interpret it as meaning *jaw*, and uses that understanding as a springboard for his elaboration on the importance of verbal teaching.

the unwearying motion of their *jaws*, they dispense from their mouth the enlightenment of the sacred Scriptures, like *processed ointment*, into the minds of humanity.

> *His lips are lilies; they pour out myrrh in abundance.*

Now see this praise repeated: as the *jaws* become *dishes*, proffering the delectable, unalloyed chalice to the spirits of the hearers of the Word, by the same token the lips become *lilies*. They *pour our myrrh in abundance*, for they advise us to die to the flesh and to put to death the members of the body (Col 3:5), not by any partial mortification,[186] but fully; that is, by a complete death—mortifying the thoughts of the mind, so as not to think on things earthly but on things heavenly; mortifying the belly by restricting its intake of foods; mortifying the eyes by gazing not with lascivious appetite, but on legitimate beauty and on the face of the longed-for Groom, Christ, to whom we have been verily wedded [Nyssa 1065D].

Following this same line of thinking, you will understand that all the members, and all the senses, by whose mortification we shall receive true life, are admonished by the *lilified lips* of the saints.

> 5.14 *His hands are turned gold, filled with gems of Tarsus.*

See how she articulates the praise of each individual member one by one. As *turned* vessels are altogether refined and pure of anything vulgar or ugly, so are the Nephew's *hands*, like *gold*, pure of sin. [Nyssa 1069A-B]

---

[186] This is the only recorded occurrence of the word *sakawamerut'iwn*. Gregory of Narek is well known for his creation of new words in the context of his poetry, but instances of such creativity are less frequent in his prose.

Not only does it lay hold of its work, like a human hand, but it is *filled with gems of Tarsus*. As Ezekiel put it, 'Their wings are filled with eyes'[187] (Ezek 10:12). Now, if all the members of the angels, God's servants, are eyes, and they are filled with vision, how much more is this true of Christ, God's Incarnate Word, who, although He took on our nature from the Virgin, yet every member, united with His divine nature, was an eye, and had vision. Our Illuminator Gregory says, 'God is utterly Ear; He is utterly Eye; He is utterly Word'.[188] He is not like us, whose individual members have individual functions—the eye cannot hear, nor the ear see, nor the mouth walk, nor the foot speak, nor can they perform any other member's function.[189]

Although He joined with our nature in the flesh, yet together with it He maintains the whole of His divinity's omnipotence and all-seeingness.

> *His belly is like a tablet of ivory set with jewels, with jewels*
> *of sapphire.*

She shows that the divine *belly* is not like ours, a mere receptacle for food and drink, but although He was fed by our food, yet was his *a tablet of ivory set with jewels, with jewels of sapphire*, that is, a vessel of divine teaching and scripture. Thus, whoever believes in Him receives a divine *belly*, and 'rivers of living water shall flow from his belly' (Jn 7:38). Then, however much that divine *belly* may be subject to the passions of the flesh, it remains a receptacle, as it were, *a tablet*, for His divine wisdom, which is incorruptible, as they say that *ivory* is [Nyssa 1073A-1076B].

---

[187] The Armenian word *akn* can mean 'gem', 'spring', or 'eye'. That range of meaning makes this interpretation possible.

[188] *Teaching of St. Gregory* §309 describes God as absolute Sight and absolute Word, among other things. Absolute hearing is not included there.

[189] An allusion to 1 Cor 12:14-26.

5.15 *His legs are pillars of marble set upon golden bases.*

See how accurately the divine Solomon describes the incarnation of Christ! In the Bride's words, he signifies the perfect humanity of the Nephew, completely mingled with His divinity. Let the vile Nestorius be ashamed, that undoer of the churches, participant with the Jews and sharer in the ideology of the Muslims![190] Desiring to substantiate the divine incarnation, indistinguishable and united, Solomon symbolically expresses the commingled divinity, member by member and sense by sense. Beginning from the head he goes on through all the members, thereby leaving the vile Nestorius at a loss for words. What else could the *pillars of marble with golden bases* be, but the incorruptible, pure, impassible power of the godhead, united with the flesh!

His stature is like Lebanon, choice as the cedars.

What does this signify? Having declared the divine in flesh as one Person, how can He be compared to the multitude of the *cedars* of *Lebanon*—cedars whose multiplicity is proverbial: 'The just shall flourish like palm trees, they will be as many as the cedars of Lebanon' (Ps 91:13). He is obviously announcing to both the rational and the insensate [alike] that although He was confined in flesh by virtue of that union, yet His power and stature is taller than the *cedars* of *Lebanon*, and more plenteous. He is not saying that His power and stature is only that great, but because He took upon Him what is ours, one should use metaphors taken from what pertains to us. By the same token, the Prophet says, 'He shall sit on the throne of David, and His kingdom shall succeed'

---

[190] See R.W. Thomson, 'Muhammad and the Origin of Islam in Armenian Literary Tradition', in D. Kouymjian, ed., *Armenian Studies In Memoriam Haïg Berbérian* (Lisbon: Calouste Gulbenkian, 1986) 829–858.

(Is 9:7). As Gabriel also said to the Virgin, 'The Lord God shall give to Him the throne of His father David, and He shall rule over the house of Jacob forever' (Lk 1:32-33). In condescension to us, He who was King of every land deigned to be called king merely of Jacob's house.

> 5.16 *His throat is full of sweetness,*

By *sweetness*, she signifies the divine *throat*'s utterance, full of *sweetness*; raising His voice He called out therewith, 'Come to me all you who labor and are heavy laden, and I will give you rest' (Mt 11:28), and again, 'I have not come to call the righteous, but sinners' (Mt 9:13, Mk 2:17, Lk 5:32). There are other such *sweet* calls to sinners and the wicked: as He said to the fornicating woman, 'Your sins are forgiven you' (Lk 7:48), and to the other fornicatress, 'Nor do I condemn you; go, after this sin no more' (Jn 8:10-11).

> *and he is altogether desirable.*

Behold, she says *altogether desirable*; that is, He is above every desire—in Him every desire ceases, for there is found no further desire to desire.[191] In line with this, the Lord said, 'Many prophets and kings desired to see what you see, and did not see it, and to hear what you hear, and did not hear it' (Mt 13:17). Elsewhere, the Lord said to the disciples, 'The day will come when you will desire to see one of the days of the Son of Man, and you shall not be able to see it' (Lk 17:22). The tax collector Zaccheus desired to see Him and, having spiritually seen God concealed in flesh, he stripped off his status, and his possessions, recognizing that he desired only the Lord.[192] The apostles, having seen the *altogether desirable* One aright, left everything—wife and children, father and mother and

---

[191] A similar remark is made by Gregory Nazianzen in *Oration* 21.1.
[192] An allusion to Lk 19:1-10.

goods, and so on—and followed Him (Mt 19:2-7,28), for they recognized with certainty that among all the things we desire to see, only He is true. Even Herod 'had for a long time desired to see' the Lord (Lk 23:8), but the eyes of his spirit, blinded by sin, darkened the sight of his corporeal eyes, which induced him to denigrate the very thing he had desired. This happens now, too, among those who are unworthy to see the wonders of His deeds; they do not see aright, for their guiding mind has been blinded.

> *That is my Nephew, and that is my Near One, O daughters*
> *of Jerusalem.*

Insofar as she was able, she showed Him to the *daughters of Jerusalem*, He who is beyond words and metaphors, seeing His beauty to be greater than any of the children of humankind.

> *The daughters of Jerusalem ask where her Nephew has gone*
> 5.17 *Where has your Nephew gone, O beautiful among*
> *women? Where has your Nephew gone? We too will*
> *seek him with you.*

Here he calls the angels, dwellers in the heavenly Jerusalem, *daughters of Jerusalem*. Now observe well, that the One who is invisible to them they desire to see in the flesh. He was seen by us in the flesh, having been among us. Through us they came to learn of His descent from heaven and His incarnation, and they still continue to learn. As the Apostle affirms, 'So now it will be revealed to the powers which are in heaven, through the Church' (Eph 3:10); hearing from us of His salvific incarnation, they will become knowledgeable of it, and being astounded with a boundless wonder at the measureless love which He has towards us, and at His incomprehensible humility, uniting their voices with ours they will bless Him and join in our celebration, as the *vardapets* explain.

Moreover, they call the Bride *beautiful among women* because of the *beautiful* way of life which the Church has received through the coming of Christ, of which we hold up the Bride as an example. Similarly, it says *women*, because bridehood is properly for women.

— CHAPTER SIX —

6.1 *My Nephew has gone down into his garden.*

The faithful who have been wedded to Christ she calls a *garden*. In another place the father of this same Solomon calls them a *vineyard* (Ps 79: 9,16), and Isaiah does likewise (Is 5:3-7), while the Nephew Himself, Christ, says in the Gospel, 'I am the Vine, and you are the branches' (Jn 15:5).

> *My Nephew has gone down to his garden, among the fields*[193]
> *of incense, to shepherd his flock in the meadow and to gather*
> *among*[194] *the lilies.*

What is called a *garden* is also called a *meadow*; the *Nephew* also calls Himself a *Shepherd*, saying 'I am the good shepherd' (Jn 10:11). He came to *shepherd* and to pasture the sheep, that they might no longer be shepherded by avaricious shepherds. As He says through Ezekiel the Prophet, 'They have eaten the good

---

[193] The 1840 edition preserves the reading of the Zohrab text, 'i tashts khnkots'' (among the basins of incense), while the 1789 edition reads 'i dashts khnkots'' (among the fields of incense).

[194] In the commentary which follows, Grigor seems to be reading *i mēj* (among) as *i mēnj* (from us); perhaps the text was corrupted. Neither *i mēj* nor *i mēnj* is attested in either the Zohrab Armenian text or the LXX.

pasture first themselves, and drunk the clear water first themselves, and they have left the trampled, leftover food and the
water muddied by hooves, for the flock' (Ezek 34:17-19), and,
'They slaughtered the fat ones among them, and did not care for
the wounded' (Ezek 34:3-4), as well as other like statements in
which He protests, through the prophets, against the wickedness
of the shepherds.

Through the same Prophet, He declares that He Himself is
become a *shepherd* (Ezek 34:11-16) who skillfully pastures and
tends the sheep and does not allow a thief to take them. Feeding us with virtue and justice, He *gathers from us lilies*; that is, the
'flowers' of faith in the Word, and sanctity [Nyssa 1093A-B]. In
these, Christ the Groom rejoices.

> 6.2 *I am my Nephew's and he is mine, who shepherds*
> *among the lilies.*

With these words the Bride expresses the warm love which she
has towards her Nephew, and she does not desire to be parted
from his pastoring and go after a flock to a strange pasture; as
the Nephew Himself, Christ, said, 'My sheep hear my voice, and I
know them and they follow me' (Jn 10:27); 'They will not follow a
stranger, but rather flee from him' (Jn 10:5). For the flock, having
received visionary eyes, follow the shepherd Who feeds them *lilies*.
He first gives as food His body and blood, and afterwards ineffable benefits: here in this world the savor of the understanding
of Scripture, which is sweeter to the taste of the saints than honey
to the mouth (Ps 118:103), and yonder, in the next world, that
which is beyond understanding. As the Theologian describes it,
'His teaching, and our learning'.[195] This He spoke of as 'to drink
it new with you in the kingdom of the Father' (Mt 26:29).

---

[195] *Oration* 40.46.

> *The groom says to the bride*
> 6.3 *You are beautiful like fragrance, my Near One, you*
> *are beautiful as Jerusalem, recounted as a wonder.*
> 6.4 *Turn your eyes from me, for they have roused me,*

Here you see the uncontained praise of the Bride by the Groom. The Bride has recognized the Groom, and has described with praise each of the incarnate Word's senses. With inexpressible wonder she has depicted, insofar as was possible, the object of her desire by means of our own visible and corruptible images. She has acquainted them, to the extent that they desired to learn, with His beauty, which is beyond our nature and beyond visible and corruptible things, as well as with the warmth of her insatiable love towards Him. Seeing this, with His divine mouth Christ the Groom blesses the faith of the Bride, and the beauty into which, in her every member and sense, she has been transformed through the font. For it came about exactly as the Theologian said: 'Gazing upon God, to become God'.[196] This shows that those who look to God and draw near to Him, acquire God's beauty, just as a wick, by approaching the lamp, is transformed into its very light.[197]

Now, as the Bride has denoted the beauty of her Groom and Nephew, the Groom indicates that the Bride has become, or taken on, the same semblance. He says, *You are beautiful, my Near One, like fragrance*. You see, the Bride, by being *Near* to the Groom, Christ, has by virtue of that become *beautiful like fragrance*. For just as whoever draws near to a fragrant thing also smells sweet, so likewise whoever draws near to God, is theified.

---

[196] Thomson, 'Song', references *Oration* 38. The same idea is present in Basil *On the Holy Spirit* IX.23. See n. 229 below.

[197] Narek's *Ban* 93.17 uses the same image. Thomson, 'Song', notes that it has a parallel in the Armenian version of Basil's *Hexaemeron* III.7 (Venice 1830) p. 57; however, that parallel is not present in the Greek of Basil.

You are beautiful as Jerusalem; for she has become the abode of the beautiful Groom, like the heavens and the heavenly Jerusalem.

Recounted as a wonder: that is, you have been *recounted* as a marvel, so that the very angels will be amazed, seeing your transformation from the sinful blackness which you had before you approached Me, into the marvelous beauty of purity whereat they *wonder*. The Lord Himself marveled thus at the faith of the centurion and said, 'I have never found such faith, no not in Israel' (Mt 8:10/Lk 7:9).

Turn your eyes from me, for they have roused me. 'This signifies the clarity and accuracy of *your eyes'* gaze at Me, whereby you comprehended the beauty of My incarnation; that I came into being through a weak and earthly nature. This was not comprehended by the angels but you comprehended it and saw Me with sight that exceeded nature. Those eyes *roused me. Turn your eyes from me* to search out the beauty of My unattainable nature, lest by seeing too much and by lingering in your examination, the eyes of your mind be dazzled and blinded as were the bodily eyes of Paul by looking at the fierce light.' For just as peering at the sun renders the eyes of the viewer defective, so also does excessive attachment to the depths of the knowledge of God cause bedazzlement to the mind's eyes. For the extent of God's Being in insight and power and wonderworking no one can attain to; it is unattainable even to the angels, let alone to humanity.

Now Christ the Groom says, *turn your eyes from me, for they have roused me* with fear and wonder. With wonder, by virtue of their sharp vision, and with fear, lest you be blinded by too much looking. Moses, too, turned his face when he had seen a little, and did not dare to look.[198] Elijah likewise covered his face with

---

[198] An allusion to Ex 3:6.

his leather cloak when he saw only the back; as it were, a mere echo of the Voice.[199]

> *your tresses like shorn flocks which have appeared from Gilead;*
>   *6.5 your teeth like shorn flocks which come up from*
>   *the washing.*

Her *tresses* approach the Groom's tresses, blackened for our sake when He took ours upon Him, and 'He who knew no sin became sin for us, that we through Him might become righteousness' (2 Cor 5:21). We were justified, whitened through baptism and *the washing* of the font, flocking *from Gilead* with a multitude of believers wedded to Christ. By the same token, *teeth* chewing on the Word of life are *like shorn flocks which come up from the washing* of the spiritual water, which washes us cleaner than clean sheep.

> *All of them bear twins, and there are no barren ones*
>   *among them.*

This washing of the faithful flocks Isaiah attested to earlier; 'Rejoice, O barren one, who have not given birth; call out and cry aloud, you who have not been in labor; for the sons of the barren woman are more than those of the married woman' (Is 54:1). Hereby, he predicts the fruitfulness, in upright living, of the multitude of believing gentiles. Just so, at one point, the same Prophet Isaiah, crying out from the Lord's mouth asks in wonder, 'Who are these, who come flying like the clouds, and who come to me like a flock of doves with their chicks?' (Is 60:8).

> *Your lips are like a red thread, and your words are beautiful.*

---

[199] An allusion to 1 K 19, esp. v. 13.

6.6 *Your cheeks are like the rind of a pomegranate,*
from your silence.[200]

He repeats again what He said previously in praise of the Bride
drawing near to the Groom: her eyes draw near to the divine eyes,
her hair to His luminous hair, her head to Christ the Head, her
lips to the Lips which poured forth life. Thus her *lips* were *reddened*
with the blood of Christ [Nyssa 1105D], and they speak as He
taught her to speak: to pray for her enemies, and to bless those
who persecute her (Mt 5:44), and the like.

And as the *pomegranate* by the ruddiness of its *rind* silently
causes one to anticipate the sweet nourishment stored up within
for the health of the sick and for those who desire it, so also do
God's chosen ones, by giving a small, visible manifestation of
good works, silently tell of the boundless store of virtue and piety
within their heart and mind; for whatever a person seeks out
with wisdom is apparent on his face[201] [Nyssa 1108A-B]. This is
what *from your silence* means. However beautiful you are, however
filled and adorned with various senses, you remain *silent*, and it
cannot be told until the day when all deep things will come to
the surface, and all invisible things will be seen, and the silent
things be heard, because the Groom Himself will display them
at the awesome Judgment of angels and men.

Now, by enumerating these few things, he implies the multitude of saints who, in this era of six thousand years, have been refined and purified from sin though trials and various tribulations
which they have endured at the hands of Satan and of satanic
humans, and have become *queens and concubines and princesses*
of the Groom Christ.

---

[200] Cf. note to 4.3 above; compare 6.6 below.
[201] Perhaps an echo of Prv 15:13.

Commensurate with their individual efforts and exertions they have been designated as—and have become—*queens and concubines and princesses*. As he actually specifies,

> 6.7 *Sixty queens and eighty concubines and princesses without number;*

By this, he expresses the multitude of those who in the eighth millennium will be glorified with Christ, and rejoice at rest with Him. Inasmuch as they labored with Him during their time, in the six millennia, they are also to rejoice with Him, as our Holy Illuminator says.[202]

The number *sixty* can have two applications, because sixty can be divided into six tens or five twelves.[203] Here, it is five twelves: these indicate those who by their five senses were chosen from among the twelve tribes of Israel during this six thousand year time span. Because of their status as firstborn, these are called *queens*, for they were pleasing to God before the gentiles were. As it says in the Revelation of the Evangelist John, counting every tribe individually, there were twelve thousand from each tribe (Rv 7:4-8).

The *eighty concubines* and the *princesses without number* are those who were pleasing to God from among the gentiles. By using this number, he is not setting a numerical limit on the saints, but rather he expresses this—whether in units or in tens—to show that through Christ's coming the justified ones among the gentiles have become more numberless than the Jews.

And secondly, by means of the *sixty* he alludes to the six thousand year age, and to those who during it—by dint of much sweat and labor—have been tried like silver in the crucible (Zec 13:9) and, as I said previously, have received the title of *queenship* because

---

[202] See above, n. 151.
[203] 6 x 10 and 12 x 5 both equal 60.

they have become more dear to God. Even here in this world they were glorified by human beings, and there in the world to come, they are to be yet more glorified. Such were the Holy Mother of God, and John the Baptist, and the Protomartyr, and the apostles, and our Illuminator Gregory, and the universal teacher John, and that proponent of the Trinity, the Theologian.

The *eighty concubines* are junior to the above in productivity but greater than the princesses. Those *eighty concubines* will be crowned in the eighth millennium.[204] And those who by their various modes of life and their penitence have found reconciliation and will attain the kingdom in the eighth millennium, are called *princesses*. They have no number, for those who are saved through repentance are innumerable. Thus he calls the martyrs *concubines*, and the hermits and penitents, those poor in the flesh, he calls *princesses*, together with those who at the hour of their departure from this world find forgiveness of sin through tears and repentance and attain the kingdom through communion in the body and blood of Christ. The Holy Illuminator, too, considers the penitent and the confessors to be one class together with those who repent at the hour of their death. He includes the martyrs and the hermits and the *vardapets* and so on, and he assigns no number to them.[205] Now, take whichever of the two interpretations pleases you—or both of them—for the meaning of Scripture is interpreted in many ways.

> 6.8 *My dove, my perfect one is unique, only daughter*
> *of her mother, the chosen one of her parent.*

You see, although the *queens* and *concubines* and *princesses* are various in terms of their names and glories, nonetheless in terms of

---

[204] Cf. 3.11 and n. 151, above.

[205] *Discourses, Homily* 13, 169–170. There, Saint Gregory lists the classifications of those who are remembered in the Eucharist.

the font and of their tearful confession they are *one*, being *doves* of the *Mother* Church, being *only children* also *of their parent*, the Holy Spirit. For this reason he says, *my dove, my perfect one is unique, the only daughter of her mother* the Church, *the chosen one of her parent* the Holy Spirit, through the birth of the font. For the Holy Spirit brings forth through baptism, and the Church nourishes by means of the body and blood of Christ. Basil attests to the same, saying, 'Likewise also your true Mother, the Church, has called the multitude of her obedient children who do her will; I mean, you faithful people'. And he says further, 'Being faithful children of a loving Father and a faithful Mother; that is of God and of the Church, maintain unshaken love towards your Father. Regarding the congregation of the saints, who are the treasures of your Mother, the Church, rejoice delighting in hope, so that the grace which illuminated them may make you, too, worthy to attain to "the portion of the lot of the inheritance of the saints in light" (Col 1:12). Continuing onward, he refers to 'Stephen, holy son of holy Mother Church, and boast of Her whole assembly'.[206]

Note how he called the Church *Mother* both of faith, and of Stephen, as well as of the other holy apostles and prophets and martyrs, and of all the faithful. For although the saints are not equal in glory, yet they are equal as offspring of the holy Church, and from this Church they are translated into the One Church in the heavenly Jerusalem. Thus, one ought to love the Church more than one's physical parents, because of her greater birthing. For as the spirit is greater than the flesh, so also is the Mother of the spirit greater than the mother of the flesh.

Now, as those who are estranged from their mother's milk and from her nourishment die, so also those who are estranged from the Church and her breasts—that nourishment by means of

---

[206] The editor of the Armenian text (Venice 1840) refers to the *Eulogy on Saint Stephen*, *Oration* 41 of Basil of Seleucia; PG 85:461-473. Thomson, 'Song', notes that no such quotation appears there.

Scripture which is the Church's *breasts*—and do not enter into [the Church] with desire and longing and are not fed in her with Scripture, cannot live, but die an eternal death. Seeing such people, the Prophet bemoaned them saying, 'Sinners have been estranged from their mother, they have been deceived from the womb and have spoken falsehood' (Ps 57:4); that is, they have held in odium the confession and the oath to love their Father God and their Mother Church which they swore at their birth of the font, and have become estranged. Whomever Satan has found outside their Mother, who is the Church, he takes captive, like a slave trader who steals children whom he finds far from their parents.

Moreover, the prayers which one should make in the Church, before its altar, where the Holy Trinity dwells, they offer among the rabble and in the public squares and in unsanctified places, and the honor of the Church they hand over to vulgar folk and to the streets. For these transgressions they will find not mercy but condemnation, they who denigrate the Church and enact their worship outside of her! Many words and mournful lamentations should be devoted to those who do these things, and on another occasion these should be made explicit, for there is no small damage caused by these people.[207]

But we shall continue to expound on what lies before us.

> *The daughters saw her and praised her; the queens also*
> *blessed her.*

Daughters and *queens* saw the Bride and blessed her. Here it is the gatherings of the angels which he calls *daughters* and *queens*, 'The assembly of the firstborn, written in heaven' (Heb 12:23).

---

[207] This alludes to the T'ondrakites, of affiliation with whom Gregory of Narek's own family had been accused. See Garsoïan, *Paulician Heresy* and other works referred to above, n. 43.

See to what glory we humans have attained! The angels, who are immortal and honored with brilliant glory, and are enspirited with a surpassing nature, and are near to God, call humanity *blessed*. And rightly so, for God is with human beings,[208] and moreover our nature has been made god, and has been united with God, the God of the angels. In awe and trembling the angels praise our divinized nature and bow down to it and regard it with trembling. For 'no one has ever seen God' (Jn 1:18, 1 Jn 4:12), and our nature, which was united with God, is by virtue of that union also invisible to the angels.

And again, the angels, who are incorporeal, are called 'servants of God' (Ps 103:4 / Heb 1:7), while humans, who are made of dust, are offspring of the Holy Spirit and hold the rank of sons,[209] and feed on His body and blood. Receiving through us that to which they did not even dare to approach and were not able to see, the angels actually need us, and they are jealous of the immeasurable gift which has been given to us by the Groom. As the Lord says in the Gospel parable, in the words of the elder son, 'How many years is it that I have served you, and have never transgressed your command? You have never given me a goat that I might make merry with my friends, but for him, who ate up your living with harlots, you have killed the fatted ox' (Lk 15:30)—that is, the Son of God slain in the flesh which He took from us.

In addition, they, who were superior to us, have even become our servants. As the Apostle says, 'Are they not all ministering spirits, who are sent to serve those who are to inherit salvation?' (Heb 1:14).

Now, when *the daughters and queens* are blessing the Bride, they say,

---

[208] An allusion to the name 'Emmanuel' (Mt 1:23; Is 7:14).

[209] This recurrent New Testament terminology appears in many places, among them Jn 1:12, Rom 8:14, 2 Cor 76:18, Gal 4:5-6, Phil 2:15, Heb 12:7-8, 1 Jn 3:2.

> 6.9 *Who is she who has appeared beautiful as the*
> *morning, choice as the moon, as the sun, recounted*
> *as a wonder?*

Truly, it is *a wonder* for someone of an earthly nature to become like *the morning* and like *the moon* and like *the sun, recounted* for the angels' *wonder*. The Lord attests to this, too, saying, 'Then the righteous shall shine forth like the sun in the kingdom of Heaven' (Mt 13:43). The righteous shall shine forth even more than the sun, but since there is not on earth anything brighter than they, the righteous are perforce praised through this simile.[210]

> *The groom says to the bride*
> 6.10 *I went down to look at the garden of walnuts,*
> *to look at the fruit of the watercourses, to see whether*
> *the cypress has blossomed, the vine has blossomed, the*
> *pomegranate has blossomed.*

This is worth investigating; He has called the Bride a *walnut garden*, but then He sought to see what other plants—*the vine, the cypress* and *the pomegranate*—were producing, and not the garden.

Now, it seems to me that here the *walnut garden* means the earth, and the people living in it he calls *walnuts*—for the walnut is composed of two natures, one being the shell, which has a woody nature, and one being the fatness within it. The soul, too, encased by the flesh, is 'fat' with power, provided that they

---

[210] Similarly, Chrysostom says in his *Homily* 14 on Genesis, 'When [Jesus] had clarified all that for them, he then said, "Good people will be as brilliant as the sun in the kingdom of their Father"—not for the reason that good people will have only that kind of brilliance, but to show that they will have much greater brilliance; he mentioned that kind because it is impossible to find a stronger image than that from among visible things.' St John Chrysostom, *Homilies on Genesis 1-17*, translated Robert C. Hill, The Fathers of the Church 74 (Washington, DC: The Catholic University of America Press, 1999) 182.

join together in righteousness and are not working against one another. As the Apostle says, 'The flesh desires in opposition to the spirit, and the spirit in opposition to the flesh, and since they are in opposition to one another, you cannot do what you would' (Gal 5:17).

So if those which are opposite to one another are found to be in agreement, by drinking in the *watercourses* of the Spirit *the fruit* will flourish, and with fitting beauty in appearance they will grow tall, like *the cypress*, and the flesh will be as incorruptible as the spirit; *the vine* will bring forth such wine that the cluster may be trodden for the cup of the heavenly Groom and become food for the Heavenly Sovereign, just as *the pomegranate* is for kings.

As for the descent which he mentions—*I went down to the walnut garden*—that indicates the incarnate descent of the Word of God, who in due time descended to earth, to those who had been 'cultivated' by the Law and the prophets, in order to make them display to perfection, by their flourishing harvest, the genus of salvation's fruit. For the former had preached the coming of the Saviour that was the *blossom*. And at the time indicated, God's Only Begotten came, to gather in the *fruit* of the vineyard through His incarnation, as is explained in the Gospel parable.[211]

The bride says to the groom
6.11 *There shall I give you my breasts. My soul did not know; it made me as the chariot of Aminadab.*

When the Bride heard the *descent* of the Groom and His quest for the *blossoms*, she responded, 'Not only have I flowered with noble *blossoms*, but I shall feed you what you seek from humanity, as your divinity pleases, feed you without depletion from

---

[211] There are several parables having to do with seeking fruit at the appointed time, but the one intended seems to be that recounted in Mt 21:33-41, Mk 12:1-10, Lk 20:9-17.

my breasts, feed you with the purity of my holy heart which is in proximity to my breasts'.

My soul did not know; that is, as the milk from the invisible *breasts* becomes immaculate food for children, so do thoughts warmed by an immaculate love, together with a person's unknowing, become 'food' for God, who seeks nothing from humanity but a pure heart wherewith 'they may see God' (Mt 5:8), and wherein He may rest. As the Prophet says, 'Where shall I rest, if not in the meek and the humble of heart, and those who tremble at my words' (Is 66:2). And like *the chariot,* they will be the resting place of the Groom with supreme glory.

> *The daughters and the queens say to the bride*
> 6.12 *Return, return Somnite,*[212] *return, return, and we*
> *will look on you.*

See the angels' wonder at the transformation of human nature from evil to good. *We will look* shows the astonished vision of the angels; we who were a breed apart from angelic ways have now surpassed the angels in angelic vision. For they, having an impassive nature, unblemished and effortless, have been bested by us; with our earthy, passion-filled and frail nature, we have surpassed them in power, conquering our lusts and passions and the needs of our nature. Rightfully do they wonder, and seek the sight of this.

The Groom causes the angels, whom He calls *daughters and queens,* to look with even greater wonder, by saying to them:

---

[212] *Somnite* is used for *Shunamite* in the Armenian text of 3 Kings 1:3. The Zohrab text of the Song of Songs has *ogoghomats'i* in 6:12, and *odoghomats'i* in 7:1. Later editions regularized these to *somnats'i.* On *odoghomats'i,* see Euringer, 273 (for a full reference, cf. n. 97, above).

— CHAPTER SEVEN —

The groom says to the daughters and to the queens
7.1 What do you see in the Somnite who has come like
the troops of armies?

That is, what can you see of *the Somnite's* beauty, who through the
fruits of her good works has multiplied *like the troops of armies?*
Nonetheless, I will make it known to you. And then he gives
indications of it, descriptively.

He calls the Bride a *Sidonite* because of their greater evil; for
they have been more assiduous in idolatry and in every wickedness, like the Sidonites.[213]

How your walking has become more beautiful with shoes,
daughter of Nadab.

Observe that the Groom first called the Bride a *Sidonite*, as the
angels also had previously called her a *Sidonite*. But here he names
her *daughter of Nadab*, showing that those who were the offspring
and *daughters* of defiled ancestors[214] became the offspring, *daughter* and Bride of Christ, so they no longer have bare feet suscep-
tible to the bites of the serpent, but having been reinforced *with*

---

[213] The antecedent of the pronoun 'they' is unclear, making the sentence difficult. Sidon appears in the New Testament as a point of comparison for the
even greater wickedness of Chorazin and Beth Saida (Mt 11:21-22; Lk 10:13-14).
Gregory Nazianzen speaks of the 'abomination of the Sidonians' in *Oration* 40.42.
The identification of *Somnite* with *Sidonite* is truly strange.

[214] Thomson, 'Song', suggests that this may refer to the story of Nadab and
Aibhu, Aaron's sons, who presented unauthorized fire before the Lord and were
struck down for their insolence (Nm 26:61). However, they had no offspring, and
Aaron their father was not accounted defiled. A more apposite reference would
be to Nadab, son of Jeroboam: 1 K 15:26 says that he 'did what was evil in the
Lord's sight and followed the example of his father'.

shoes of righteousness, they are impervious to the venom of the biting Serpent.

Moreover, they have been washed of sin 'with water and spirit' (Jn 3:5) by the Saviour, as were the feet of the apostles, who also received authority 'to tread on serpents and scorpions and all the power of the enemy' (Lk 10:19). For that reason they have increased in beauty, for they have 'shod their feet with the preparation of the gospel of peace' (Eph 6:15), as the Apostle says.

> *The fit of your pillows*[215] *resembles beads fashioned by the hand of a craftsman.*

Now, as Her feet were strengthened against the biter, and were *beautified* by such *shoes*, so also has her head, which had fallen level with the ground from the heights of Paradise, been raised[216] from destruction, by means of a *pillow* like *fashioned beads*.

The brain's intelligence resides in a person's head. Now, it is obvious that as a *pillow* lifts and rests the head; so also does knowledge of Scripture and understanding of God's commandments raise and rest the head, for thereon does all the turbulent rocking of storm-tossed thought come to rest, leaning thereon as on a *pillow*. The *pillows* do not allow one to be vainly drawn into the pitching waves of idle speculations. It is for this reason that he said, *the fit of your pillows resembles beads fashioned by the hands of a craftsman.*

The *fashioned bead* gathers into itself the diverse range of the beauties of pearls. In the same way, the knowledge of Scripture—*fashioned* by the prophetic books, the Law, the apostles,

---

[215] The word *bardz* has a range of meanings, including 'thigh, pediment, base, status, place at table, or pillow'. That range of meanings makes Gregory's interpretation possible, and unique to Armenian.

[216] The operative play on words here features the word *bardz* ('pillow') and the verb *bardzranam* ('to rise' or, in the participle, 'being raised').

the *vardapets*, the martyrs' heroic exhibitions, and the struggles of ascetics, and by the self-same Gospel's injunctions and good news—like a *pillow* placed beneath the cranium, does not allow it to drop to the ground.

The 'pillowless' head of the schismatics dropped to the 'ground' of errant knowledge. Being unable to *fashion* an understanding of Holy Scripture, they divided Christ's incarnation into two natures, and they understood the words of Scripture in a variety of divergent ways: such were Arius and Macedonius, and the vile Nestorius, destroyer and devastator of the world, and a myriad other heretics. Concerning behavior and food and all the created beings of heaven and earth, angels and human beings, and the Second Coming and the awesome Judgment and the everlasting Gehenna, they also invented erroneous tenets and taught them to others.

Now, too, there are many who impart such erroneous teaching. They do this because of two things. One, because they have not examined Scripture, but have instead considered their own wisdom sufficient for investigating knowledge. So did the ancient philosophers; with all their wisdom they were unable to tear themselves away from idolatry, and through wisdom to recognize God (1 Cor 1:20-21). Hence the Apostle complains that if one had wanted to investigate wisely, it would have been possible to discover the Creator by means of the creatures (Rom 1:19-21); that through understanding the impermanent, feeble and changeable nature of the creatures, one could realize that there is Another, their Creator: it was for this very reason that God conferred on us the advantage of wisdom.

The second reason is that because, through sin, people are far from the protection of the Spirit's wings, a profane, contentious spirit has infiltrated and teaches his own understandings and makes them 'rest' therein, deserted by the spirit of rectitude. The saints' heads come to 'rest' on no such *pillow* as this, but on the one which is made and *fashioned* by the hands of that *skillful craftsman*, the Holy Spirit.

7.2 *Your navel is a turned goblet, not lacking mixed wine.*

The navel likewise contains the same meaning. *Turned* and shaped *goblets* are desirable in and of themselves, and they spur the minds of drinkers, and more especially those of stewards, to create in them *mixtures of wines.* Likewise also the *navel,* made true and pure of sin, becomes the receptacle of the Spirit's grace, and of the unadulterated wine,[217] and of the sweet drink of the words of the Old and New Testaments *mixed* together. The sight of the latter's beauty incites one to drink deeply even before the hearing of it—the hearing of what has been purified and refined, gathered in the *navel.*

Your belly is like a heap of wheat ringed with lilies.

Our Holy Illuminator recounts, often and minutely, singular praise concerning the *belly* and other beautified senses.[218] Such things are actually the earthen vessels of spiritual treasure: as the Apostle says, 'We hold this treasure in clay vessels' (2 Cor 4:7).

If this is so, why is it that such valuable treasure is placed in earthen vessels? Paul himself explains it: 'That the superiority of the power should be God's and not ours' (2 Cor 4:7b). For the power of God appears all the greater in a weak vessel's bearing the weighty and unbearable.

This is to be seen even among the creatures; the heavens and the earth, having been placed upon a weak foundation remain firm, and maintain everything unshakable.

---

[217] This is perhaps an allusion to the wine of the Armenian eucharistic chalice, which is not diluted with water.

[218] *Discourses Homily* 20, pp. 220–225, describes at length the proper functioning of the sanctified senses and bodily parts. This is a recurrent theme in Saint Gregory's work; a similar descriptive list, minus the description of the belly, can be found in *Homily* 11 (pp. 139–140). It is also to be found in Gregory Nazianzen, *Oration* 40. 38–40.

The frail nature of the *Theotokos*, too, became the vessel and bearer of the unbearable nature of God's Word, combined with the flesh which derived from her.

In the same way, weak human beings, having received the graces of the Spirit in their *bellies*, piled one upon the other *like a heap of wheat*, have with the 'teeth' of teaching[219] ground them into bread to feed the hungry and those who long for such spiritual food.

And *ringed with lilies*: by their marvellous color, like lilies, they invite the angels to *look on* them. As it was said previously by *the daughters and queens*, 'Return, and we will look on you'.

7.3 *Your two breasts like two twin fawns of a gazelle.*

As the Theologian says there are two modalities in the human being—soul and mind.[220] Both are perpetually attached to the heart, where the *breasts* are also located. Because of this, he refers to as *breasts* those things which reside near them. As the *breasts* are vessels of milk and give life to infants, so also are the mind and the spirit alert, illumined and sharp-sighted as a *gazelle*; seeing the distant divine things as they do those things near at hand, they unerringly show the way, for themselves, and also for others who follow them, and they preserve them from the snares of hunters. Too, they feed those who, in terms of sin, have become like children, in the same way as *breasts* feed children.

7.4 *Your eyes like the pool of Esebon by the gates of many daughters.*

[219] The word for teaching, *vardapetut'iwn*, connects this comment with earlier ones on the nature and importance of *vardapets*. See also n. 19, above.

[220] Gregory may be referring to *Epistle 51, To Cledonius* (First Epistle against Apollinaris), where the Theologian says of Christ, 'If He has a soul, and is yet without a mind, how is He man?' Translation from A Select Library of Nicene and Post-Nicene Fathers, 2nd series, 7 (Grand Rapids; Eerdmans, 1978) 440b.

That land is very far away in terms of distance, and no one gives any information concerning it. But I imagine that that land is high, and at its foot it has a great lake opposite it. By the same metaphor, the *eyes* of the Bride, the Church, enlarged by the greatness of the Spirit, look unwaveringly towards *the gates* of heaven, where the *daughters* of the multitude of the angels are encamped, turning neither to the right hand nor to the left. They await the King of Heaven, watching avidly so that they may be worthy to enter through those *gates*, where the *daughters* of that city abide.

> *Your nostrils like the tower of Lebanon situated towards Damascus.*

As *the tower of Lebanon* is properly *situated towards Damascus*, so also do your *nostrils*, properly *situated*, desire to scent the sweet, savory fragrance of the oil of purification which comes from the supernal *Damascus*, that is from the City of Heaven.

Not to mention that Paul first received the precious knowledge of the Trinity there, on the approach to *Damascus*, and from Anania the Damascene he received the cure for his eyes' blindness, through the laying on of the latter's hands (Acts 9:17). He smelled that intoxicating, thrilling fragrance, and caused all the gentiles to smell it as well. Their *nostrils* having once smelled that fragrance, they were not sated but were enraptured as though inebriated with good wine. Imbuing the casing of the brain with satisfying, angelic slumber, it brought rest also to those exhausted by sin.

> 7.5 *The tresses of your head like purple, like a king with his crown on his head, at the race course.*

Purple is the proper prerogative of kings. A king alone has authority to adorn himself with purple. So also those *heads* which

have the *hair* and the form and the glory of the heavenly Bridegroom are resplendent with purity as if with *purple* raiment, or
like *a crown* on the head of a king among his troops, *at the race
course.*

Now, one might ask, of what kind are the *crowns* granted
to martyrs, such as those which have appeared for many of the
saints like the Forty Martyrs of Sebastia[221] and the companions
of Ghewond[222] and many others.

A crown is placed *on the heads* of kings because the most honorable of all the sensory organs of a human being is the head.
In it is stored the brain, whence intelligent thought arises, and
[the head] is the beginning of life. In it are also the eyes which
see the light, and it is the location of the palate, and of the nose,
and of the ears' hearing; the mouth, too, which preserves vitality
through food and drink and through words reveals to listeners
the understanding and wisdom of the heart. One *crowns* it, so that
the brain may teach to the soul and to the understanding, the
works and words and virtues and devotion and love and mercy
which are pleasing to God, and whatever other intentions and
activities may be like them.

Now by ringing the head with a *crown* one wreathes it as the
cause and advisor of all good. By crowning the head, one causes
the whole person to appear as if wreathed with munificence.

---

[221] This group of military martyrs, known in Armenian as the Forty Youths.
They died in 316 by being exposed in freezing water. Popular throughout the
East, their forty-domed shrine stood in Sebastia (now called Sivas, in modern
Turkey) until the Mongol invasions. After its destruction, the name 'Forty
Martyrs' remained attached to the Armenian cemetery in Sebastia. T'orgom
Gushakian, *Surbk' ew Tōnk'* [Saints and Feasts] (Jerusalem: St. James Press,
1939) 77–79.

[222] He was martyred in Persia in the fifth century. The story is found in Elishē,
History of Vardan and the Armenian War, Chapter 8, trans. Robert W. Thomson.
Harvard Armenian Texts and Studies 5 (Cambridge: Harvard University Press,
1982) [hereafter, Elishē] ; and in Ghazar, §57.

A crown set on the head signifies the ineffable illumination and power of God clothing the *head*, the intermediary of so many good thoughts and helpful studies. As the same Solomon says elsewhere, 'You will receive a crown of grace for your head' (Prv 1:9). He refers to as *grace* the divine power's clothing of the head, which is adorned as with *a crown*. By means of corporeal things, he is giving an image of the invisible glory, and by means of illusory and vain things he is giving an image of the invisible things which are truly to be desired.

Therefore, blessed are they who are worthy of the unfading *crown* and are wedded to Christ, for they will share His *crown* in the endless kingdom of Christ.

> 7.6 *How beautiful and delightful you have become;*
> 7.7 *love to your delicacy!*

Look precisely at the praises listed for all the Bride's senses; see how, having listed them one by one and praised them, he summarizes them again, by saying *how beautiful and delightful you have become.* The real beauty of a human being is to cause all one's senses to serve God, and to divinize them by drawing near to God, by participating in the divine works, in order to become worthy of hearing such words from Christ the Bridegroom: *you have become beautiful and delightful to me.*

What immeasurable bliss! by the mouth of God to be professed *beautiful and delightful* to Him whom all the saints, apostles and prophets desired, the martyrs and ascetics, and the *vardapets* of the Church with all her clergy. Becoming the Daughter and Bride of God, they forgot their people and their fathers' house (Ps 44:11); becoming strangers to the world and whatever is in this world, they became *delightful* through their virtuous ways of life, and were loved by the Groom, who said, *love to your delicacy;* that is, 'I love your great *delicacy* just as bodily bridegrooms love their physically delicate brides'.

> *Your stature has become like a palm tree's,*
> *and your breasts like clusters of grapes.*

'You have become as dear to my sight as the height of *a palm tree,* *and your breasts* are appetizing to me as to children'. Building on this he adds,

> 7.8 *I said, I will go up the palm tree, I will lay hold of*
> *its height,*

See here the immeasurable love of God towards the saints and the just; He is as pleased to rest upon the saints as to sit on the cherub throne. And this is a proof to you: He descended to the patriarch Jacob and, grappling with him lovingly as peer with peer, he contended with him as if to lay him low, and taking hold of his sinew he immobilized it.[223] He said through Isaiah the Prophet, 'Where shall I rest, if not in the meek and humble, and those who tremble at my word?' (Is 66:2). So does He dote upon and yearn for the saints, as for those immeasurably dear.

Seeing the delightful stature of the Bride like that of a *palm tree,* the One who 'bowed the heavens and came down' (Ps 17:10), and *laid hold* of our nature for the sake of the indescribable love which He had for us, said *I will go up, I will lay hold of its height.*

> *and your breasts will be like clusters of the vine,*
> *and the fragrance of your nostrils like apples,*
> 7.9 *and your throat like noble wine.*

A *cluster* of grapes first rejoices the eyes with the sight of it before it is eaten. Likewise, the words of grace which flow from the heart's

---

[223] Gn 32:22-31.

breasts cheer first the ears and then the heart of those who have an appetite for the Word.

And the fragrance of your nostrils like apples; that is, the *fragrance* of the holy way of life, which reaches out to great and small like the fragrance of *apples*. The Heavenly Bridegroom smells this more than those 'shadowy'[224] sacrifices and gifts which were referred to as 'a sweet savor to the Lord' (Ex 29:18 et al). For it was not the odor of cooked flesh which was a sweet savor to God, but it was the purity of those making the offering which rejoiced Him, and was a sweet savor to God, as was the case with Abel's sacrifice.[225]

And your throat like good wine. As wine makes those who drink it happy, so also does the song of those who are holy and spotless, and the words of their *throats*, make the Heavenly Bridegroom happier than do the sung doxologies of angels. For the latter praise Him by virtue of their potency and passionlessness, which makes their song not surprising; whereas it is most marvelous that a human being, who is made of earth, and suffers passions and needs, should resemble those who are without passion and without need, taking on the *throat* of the seraphs and singing what they sing. How could this fail to make the Groom happy?

The *daughters and queens* were astonished at the marvelous beauty and appearance of the Somnite—that is, the Bride—and said to her, 'Return, return, O Somnite, that we may see your new and exquisite appearance'. Taking up this call of the angels—that is, the call of the *daughters and queens*—the Groom responded and said, 'What do you see in the Somnite? You cannot see how desirable she is except through me, who am able to reveal publicly the concealed virtues of humanity'. Then, recounting one by one

---

[224] Following Col 2:17, it was usual for the Fathers to refer to Old Testament types as 'shadows' of corresponding realities in the New Testament or in the future world.

[225] The story of Abel's sacrifice is found in Gn 4:2-4, and is referred to in Heb 11:4 and 12:24.

the marvels of her senses, He made known to them the beauty of the Bride. In a similar way,

> *the Bride says this in the presence of the daughters and queens*
> *Going with my Nephew in uprightness, sufficed with my lips*
> *and my teeth*

This means, 'I have become marvelous to you because, renouncing the worldly, sin-loving, serpent-induced deceptions of my forebear I have followed my Nephew in an *upright* way of life. He put on what is mine, and with what is mine, He overcame, and showed me the upright way; having first done it Himself, He then instructed me.' As the evangelist Luke says in his second book, 'Jesus began to do, and then to teach' (Acts 1:1). For this reason He became man: so that He should first do all which He taught in words, and teach meekness and humility by deeds. As the Lord Himself said, 'Learn from me, for I am meek and lowly in heart, and you will find rest for your souls' (Mt 11:29).

In the same way, He would teach benevolence; to the one who struck His divine face He responded benevolently, 'If I have spoken anything evil, bear witness concerning the evil. But if good, why do you strike me?' (Jn 18:23). And when they called Him a demoniac, He did not respond with abuse, but benevolently said, 'There is no devil in me' (Jn 8:49).

The One who prayed for his crucifiers, 'Father, forgive them, for they know not what they do' (Lk 23:34), taught tolerance in the same manner. Likewise he demonstrated the completion of his work through a donkey, and epitomized his humble life by riding on an ass (Mt 21:5-7, Jn 12:14-15).

He did the same at the wedding: changing the water into wine (Jn 2:1-11); he shared in the joy of those who rejoiced, and offered them a gift. In mourning, too, he demonstrated the extent of his sadness by weeping, and taught us to mourn with our bretheren in their sadness (Jn 11:33-35). And by making up the amount of food with the barley loaves and the fish, and seating the people on the grass (Mt 14: 19-20, Mk 6:39-42, Lk 9:14-17, Jn 6:10-11), he showed us how to satisfy our modest, brute needs. And everything else, too, which it is needful to learn, he has first borne in himself and demonstrated to us that same path.

For this reason the Bride says, *Following my Nephew in uprightness*. In other words, 'I have *followed* Him in all the *upright* things which he did on earth, and I have imitated him'. As the chosen vessel (Acts 9:15) Paul says, 'Be imitators of me, as I am of Christ' (1 Cor 11:1).

By what was the Bride empowered to be a fellow traveler on Christ's way? By the awesome mystery of Communion—by the body and the blood of Christ which He gave to us for strength. 'He made us bold to drink with our lips and break with our teeth that on which you the angels, you *sisters and queens*, did not dare to gaze; we were allowed to break with our teeth Him of whom no bone was broken on the Cross, as the Prophet had predicted aforetime (Ps 33:21). In our easily incinerated flesh we are not consumed by the uncontainable and flaming fire, whereas you angels are not able to look upon it—nor do you dare to. I have become the container for the Uncontainable, like the *Theotokos*, who received Him into Her womb and was not burned, and like her archetype the burning bush.'[226]

Thus does the Bride boast before the angels; as it were, boasting in the unspeakable gift of the Groom. Going on she adds,

7.10 *I am my Nephew's, and His returning is to me.*

That is, having been joined to Him through this food, I am His and He is mine. As the Lord Himself said in the Gospel, 'Whoever eats my body and drinks my blood will live in Me and I in him'

---

[226] Ex 3:1-6.

(Jn 6:56). And again, 'As you, Father, are in me, and I in You, so that they also may be in Us' (Jn 17:21), and 'I in them, and You in Me' (Jn 17:23).

His returning is to me; over and above this unity, she also says that He is coming again to take us to Himself (Jn 14:3), and to rank us in His glory, and to gird Himself and serve us, as He Himself said (Lk 12:37).

> 7.11 *Come, my Nephew, let us go out into the fields, let us rest in the villages.*
> 7.12 *Let us go out early into the vineyard, let us see if the vine has blossomed, the cypress has budded, the pomegranates have blossomed.*

Here you see the unity of the Bride with the Groom. Previously, the Groom said *I descended to the orchard of walnuts to see if it had blossomed* with those very fruits which the Bride now mentioned. That indicated the coming of Christ to earth to see if the seeds which the prophets had sown, had *blossomed*. These came to fruition with His coming.

Now the Bride, united with the Groom, desires to partake in His viewing of the productive fruits and flowers. Previously, the Groom said *I descended*, that is, 'I came down from heaven' (Jn 6:38,41), whereas here the Bride says, *Let us go*, for, being on earth, she loves to go about with Him who 'appeared on the earth and went about with human beings' (Lv 26:12). As He said, 'I have other sheep who are not of this fold, and I must bring them hither as well, and they will hear my voice and they will become one flock and one shepherd' (Jn 10:16). He actually did go about with the Bride—that is, with the apostles—not only throughout Judea, but also among the gentiles, where were the Samaritan and the Syro-Phoenician woman and many others.

After the Ascension, too, He went about with the apostles and with their disciples, and with the *vardapet*s and with the martyrs, to preach and to see the *blossom* and the fruit of the word of faith. His dominical promise bears witness to this: 'I am with you always, until the end of the world' (Mt 28:20).

Now, the apostles did not attain to the end of the world; thus, it is clear that until now He still goes about with all the faithful to see the *blossoms* and to rejoice in the production of fruits. Mark the compassion of both the Groom and the Bride towards the faithful: she does not wait for an order, as did the prophets of old, but having received the same love as the Groom's, she begs to go about in search of the wandering and in quest of the lost. Many of the apostles and *vardapets* dedicated themselves to the work of cultivating this compassion, as did our Illuminator, who, leaving his wife and children, came voluntarily to Trdat, and besought God for the conversion of all humanity. There are various pleading requests in his prayers, which this is not the time to repeat.[227]

She mentions *the vine and cypress and pomegranate*, for some of those who have turned to faith and became wedded to Christ bear fruit, but not through knowledge. Such were the centurion and Cornelius, and even Paul himself, who was 'blameless in terms of the Law's righteousness' (Phil 3:6). The latter are clusters of grapes, and *pomegranates*, but are not complete in their knowledge of God. While some are without fruit, like Onesimus,[228] and like the *cypress*.

> 7.13 *The mandrakes have given forth their scent, at our gates are all fruits, the new with the old; what my mother gave me will be laid up for you, my Nephew.*

The mandrakes have given forth their scent. Thanks to the attestations with which I have instructed you, the phrase before us has

---

[227] For Gregory the Illuminator's prayers of intercession, see Agathangelos §94–98.

[228] This may be an allusion to Phlm 11, where Paul tells Philemon that Onesimus has been 'hitherto useless to you'.

no need of further interpretation. Nonetheless, in brief it means this; they give thanks for the *fruits* of faith in those who, through the preaching of the apostles and the numberless *vardapet*s after them, became pleasing to God through a panoply of virtues—some through the blood of their witness, some by the prowess of their ascetic life, some through celibacy, some through their oversight as prelates and priests, some through poverty and sickness, some through wealth, by making their goods available to all. As well as all those who in a similar fashion have been united by love of God, faith, hope, charity, humility, holiness, fraternal love, benevolence, tolerance, long-suffering, lack of attachment to goods, and disregard of earthly things, desire for heavenly things, fear of Gehenna and desire for the King and the Kingdom.

All of this that she said—*the mandrakes have given forth their scent, at our gates are all fruits, the new with the old; what my mother gave to me will be laid up for you, my Nephew*—these are the apostles' and prelates' words of praise for the faithful in Christ, whom they offer to him as 'a people prepared (Lk 1:17)', now and on the great day of Judgment. They too will say the words of the Prophet, 'Behold I and the children whom God has given me' (Is 8:17-18, Heb 2:13). Whoever gives an account of the people without shame, and offers them to God, is like this statement of hers, *I have kept it for you my Nephew. The new with the old*—from among contemporaries and from among the ancients.

But when she says, *what my mother gave me*, the *mother* is the catholic Church, and the Holy Spirit, who gave birth through the font, and Christ who nourished us with His blood.

— CHAPTER EIGHT —

8.1 *Who will cause you, my Nephew, to suckle at my breasts?*

It is as if to the saints, because of their unquenchable desire, attainment of God's glory becomes incredible, even taking into account their efforts and striving, and the longing of their heart. It is because of the saints' spiritual humility, that they do not feel they have the right to open their hearts' *breasts* to Him. As the Apostle Paul said, 'I do not consider myself to have attained' (Phil 3:12-13).

The other saints were the same. Knowing that the destruction of our forebear, and even more so that of Satan, came about through arrogance and pride, they have struggled for spiritual humility, to consider themselves more lowly than all, and to be oblivious of their own labors, and to account themselves unworthy of God's service. They have been instructed by the Lord who said, 'When you have done all which is commanded, you should say, "We are useless servants; we have done what we were obliged to do"' (Lk 17:10). That is to say, a servant who does not go beyond what is required in his service, is useless. Thus they schooled themselves to remain humble, and to count themselves unworthy of His grace. As the Apostle said, 'I am the least of all the apostles' (1 Cor 15:9, Eph 3:8).

This is likewise an activity of all the saints and those filled with the Spirit—however much rectitude one may achieve, or however much love for God one may demonstrate, with humble mind one should not consider that he is cognizant of God, but should consider himself as one of the unworthy. It is for this reason that she says *Who will cause you to suckle at my breasts*—that is, to accept the love of my heart towards you.

Then she adds,

> *Finding you outside, I shall kiss you, and you will not despise me.*

What does this mean? Is your love something *to be despised*? No, this wild love is worth boasting of, and displaying in public.

Anyone who has tasted of that Love, has become inebriated with love of it and has *despised* wife and children and goods and possessions and authority and glory, nay and even his very self. Made perfect through death and blood and poverty, they have *kissed* Christ and been kissed by Him. This is a love proud and beatific, praised both by angels and by human beings.

> 8.2 *Taking you, I shall lead you to the house of my*
> *mother, and to the chamber of her who bore me.*

She said, *finding you outside, I shall kiss you,* and then *taking you I shall lead you to the house of my mother and to the chamber of her who bore me.* The Apostle interprets this saying, 'Whose house we ourselves are' (Heb 3:6), having become the abode of the Holy Spirit and of our Mother's Father. Clearly, as Basil says, 'Wherever the Holy Spirit is, there the Father and the Son are recognized to reside'.[229] As He says through the Prophet, 'I shall dwell in them, and walk among them'.[230] Now, the Bride has become the *chamber* and *house* of the Groom. The way to that *house* is humility, and whoever is not humble drives the Holy Spirit away, and does not give Him rest, as Basil says.[231]

> *Then, having brought you to the chamber,*
> *I shall make you drink spiced wine, the juice of pomegranates.*

[229] See note to 6.8. The editor of the Armenian text (Venice 1840) refers to Basil of Seleucia's *Eulogy of Saint Stephen*; Thomson, 'Song', notes that this quotation is not to be found there. The idea that the Spirit, the Father and the Son are inseparable is, however, the recurrent theme of Basil of Caesarea's *On the Holy Spirit*, especially XI.27 and XVI.37. For a recent translation, see Basil the Great, *On the Holy Spirit*. Popular Patristic Series (Crestwood, New York: St Vladimir's Seminary Press, 1980.)

[230] This quotation represents the combination of Lev 26:12 and Ez 37:27 as given in 2 Cor 6:16.

[231] See n. 228, above. Basil of Caesarea's *On the Holy Spirit*, 61 speaks of the kinds of people who drive the Holy Spirit away.

This is what it means. She said, *Who will cause you to suckle at my breasts?* Now, having found Him *outside* and having been made worthy of a *kiss*, and then having taken the Groom into *the chamber* and into *the house* of the soul and into the heart, and having become the abode of the Trinity, she promises to have Him drink the *wine* of happiness and the *juice of pomegranates*. These are the heart's consciousness of the mysteries of God's goodnesses, unintelligible to sinners, whereby God is fed and by which drink He is nourished, for this is the 'food of God'.

She adds, 'Not only did I become the dwelling of God, or of the Groom, but by Him was I overshadowed and protected'. As she continues,

> 8.3 *His left hand was under my head, and his right hand embraced me.*

By this she expresses His ineffable protection and solicitude on behalf of the Bride, who is the Church.

> 8.4 *I adjure you, daughters of Jerusalem, by the powers and the forces of the field, that you arouse and awaken love while He pleases.*

This I am explaining for the second time. Having noted the manifold grace there is for us, and the incomprehensible gifts, she *adjures* the angels with an oath to glorify and praise with her God's love towards us and to *arouse* it. For she does not consider herself alone sufficient to bless God's benefits in such a way that Love will be yet more *awakened* through our praise and glorification of Him.

One of ten lepers returned to the Lord and gave such thanks, with a great voice of praise, for his physical healing that he received spiritual illumination and eternal life as well (Lk 17:11-19). Whereas the nine who proved ungrateful to their Benefactor were deprived of one of the more perfect gifts, as well as of commendation by His divine mouth.

Now, the Bride is not ungrateful for God's incomprehensible favors, and for such great gifts. She *arouses* the Groom's love by giving thanks to Him herself, and calling upon the angels to share in our thanksgiving for those gifts which He desired to give us, and which our forebear was not worthy to receive. That is what *arouse Love while He pleases* means: He sought thanks from the nine and did not find in them what His will sought.

> *The daughters and queens say*
> 8.5 *Who is this, who goes up whitened, leaning on her Nephew?*

The angels marvel at the purity and luminosity of our disgraced and sullied nature, which has encountered such unfathomable grace. Having been united with her Nephew Christ and *leaning on* Him, [our nature] ascends where the hosts of angels dwell. She has become the traveling companion of Christ who, taking us by the hand, has led us into the place of the fallen angels, with the result that the ones whom Satan could not bear to see in Paradise, he should see occupying his own place in glory.[232]

> *The groom says to the bride*
> *I shall awaken you under the apple tree;*
> *there did my mother bear you, there did she who bore*
> *you travail.*

First, it is appropriate to look at the nature of *apple trees*, and then to understand the *awakening* which takes place under one. The apple is a healthy food, and especially appetizing to the ill. It is

---

[232] See n. 131, above.

fit even for kings, and it tickles the palate of those who smell it with a medley of different scents.

Saint Gregory our Illuminator says this too. He likens to an *apple* the words of the Law and the prophets,[233] given to us by the Holy Spirit; first, on Mount Sinai through the agency of Moses, and then at various times He caused it to grow through the prophets. Birds, by sitting on their eggs for an extended time, transmit life to them through their warmth at the Creator's command. In the same way our nature, having been placed beneath the Law and the prophetic messages for an extended time, was incubated by God the Father, and by the Son, who is referred to as our Groom and Nephew, and was given birth to by the *Mother* of All, who is His begetter by nature and ours through grace.

He uses the word *travail; travail* is indicative of a *mother*. Therefore it is Christ's Father and ours to whom he referred as *mother*. The Father, however, was *in travail* in His messages through the Law and the prophets, and *gave birth to* His children through water and the Spirit (Jn 3:5) as brothers of Christ. So our Mother is One—the Father Begetter, the omnipotent God.

Christ was born first. By His baptism and through the font and by the coming of the Holy Spirit, He opened the heavens closed by Adam, and bestowed on us the same birth of the Holy Spirit. He was called Son of Man, and made us sons of God. As the blessed teacher John says, 'absolutely do not doubt that you are God's son'.[234] For it was even more impossible for the Son of God to become Son of Man, than for the son of man to become the son of God.

Now when the Bride adjures them to *awaken the love* of the Groom, she is responding to that love long since *awakened*, which

---

[233] *Teaching of St. Gregory* §347 compares the Law to the apple of Eden; the Law was a life-bringing fruit, given to counteract the deadly effects of the fruit eaten in Eden.

[234] *Homily 2 on Matthew*, §3.

Adam rebuffed by his transgression. Yet according to His for-bearing mercy and according to His creatorly love, He did not forsake us, but taking pity on us again, through the Law and the prophets, as through an instructor, He cared for us, and *travailed*, and brought us to birth again, 'Not by corruptible seed', as the Apostle Peter says, 'but by the incorruptible, living and eternal word of God' (1 Pt 1:23).

Thus he says, *under the apple tree shall I awaken you; there did my mother bear you, there did she travail who bore you.* That is to say, His love was *awake* towards us, and to benefit from it required only willingness on our part. So, 'Because of the Spirit's influence and by that new birth from My Father, you have come to know the great love for you of Him "Who did not spare His own Son, but gave Him up for the sake of us all"' (Rom 8:32), as the Apostle said.

Now,

> 8.6 *Set me as a seal upon your heart, and like a ring on your arm,*

That is, preserve and *seal your heart* and *your arm* with *Me*, so that you do not fall once you have arisen, and do not forget the bene-fits which I have conferred you through My incarnation, when I made you the son of My Begetter. Do not give *your heart* again to Satan's councils, nor stretch out your hand and *arm* to him,

> *for love is strong as death, and jealousy is fierce as hell.*

In other words, *death* is *fierce* for those to whom it comes; so also is *jealousy* powerful *as hell*. In the same way, those who have been loved by Me with such love and in return for that love relinquish My love and love the adversary—that is, the sin and wickedness and love of this world—*Jealousy*, the Lord's sadness and wrath, will attack him *like death*, and as a result he will undergo incur-able sufferings.

If women beloved by their husbands requite their husbands' love by offering their love to an adulterous lover, not only do they extinguish their husbands' love, but, above and beyond that, they call down upon themselves a hatred which is greater than all hatreds, and become estranged from their husbands; many even meet a wrathful death at their husbands' hands. As this same Solomon says, 'The sadness of her husband is filled with jealousy, and it will not abide until the day of wrath' (Prv 6:34). How much more, then, will the wrath of our Groom and God and Saviour be *strong as death and hell* against us, who are wedded to God, when we display hatred towards Him for His assiduous love, and against Satan who, like an adulterer, steals away our sacred marriage with Christ and usurps it. Having fallen in with all his vile councils and deeds, we open our souls wide to him. For this reason we rightly find that immortal *death* is our recompense, and bottomless *hell*.

So what mouth can adequately praise the one who, having recognized such love, realizes both how to exalt God and how to maintain His love and not spoil it with sin. And on the other hand, what mouth can adequately bemoan those who have become estranged from such love through sin and have become denizens of a deathless hell!

Concerning this he adds,

> *Its wings are wings of flaming fire,*[235]
> 8.7 *and many waters cannot quench love, and rivers will not deter it.*

This is obvious in physical love, too; wherever holy love resides, be it parental or marital or whatever, *rivers* cannot *deter it*, neither

---

[235] The last part of this verse is quoted in Ghazar's 'Meghadrut'iwn Stakhōs Abeghayits' [Accusation of Slanderous Monks], which follows the main body of his *History*. There (§187) the verse is part of an explanation of the opposition between love and mercy.

can sword nor fire nor death. How many have been betrayed to fire and water and the sword, and to famine, for their children's sake, and likewise for the sake of their lords! In the same way, love towards God, too, cannot be sapped from human beings; it overcomes fire and water and bonds and flayings and imprisonment and wife and children; all of these the saints—the apostles and prophets and martyrs and ascetics—overcame by means of it, intoxicated with the love of Christ.

> *If a man give all his living for his love, they will despise him with contempt.*

This is to be understood in this way: love of God is not like love of human beings, particularly love of sin which, the more it increases, the more one is *despised* and treated *with contempt* by people. By contrast, love towards God is worthy of limitless praise and exaltation. Thus David boasts, 'I have loved you, O Lord my strength' (Ps 17:2), and 'My heart fainted, and my flesh; God of my heart, God my portion forever' (Ps 72:26); that is, You are my portion, and when I remember You, my heart faints—and 'My heart will rejoice in the living God' (Ps 83:3). You will find many other such delightful words of his, replete with the warm love of God. Paul has innumerable words in the same vein, as do the other apostles, and innumerable *vardapets* and saints of God, too. Warmed by that love they overcame the world[236] with all its wants and temptations.

> 8.8 *Our sister is little, and she has no breasts; what shall we do for our sister, on the day when it will be manifest to her?*

---

[236] An allusion to 1 Jn 5:4-5.

8.9 *If she be a wall, we shall build upon her towers of silver. And if she be a gate, we shall build for her cedar panels.*

This statement is to be understood in this way: it is said by the angelic powers concerning the Bride, who is the new Church which is from the gentiles (Acts 15:19). She is called *sister* because of her having come from the same Creator and creation; *little sister* because of our less honorable nature, for we are earthy. Even though the other, fiery nature; that is, the spirit, was yoked with our body, yet we are less than the angels. The Prophet testifies, 'You have made him a little lower than Your angels, but with greater glory and honor have You crowned him' (Ps 8:5), and so on.

God glorified humanity with such honor that Satan, conceiving jealousy against them, wished to snatch it from them. For that very reason he fell from heaven, and from his own glory. Now, the angels are bewildered at how our weak nature has attained to both the sight and the knowledge of the unbearable, divine mysteries and glory.

As I have written many times, it is the storehouses of the heart and mind which he refers to as *breasts*. And the angels are puzzled, knowing that our nature cannot bear that immaterial cargo. Thus he says, *What shall we do for our sister on the day when it will be manifest to her?*; that is, when it is told to the *small* and *breastless* and witless nature of humanity that God has taken on earthly nature—in the belly and in the womb at that—and has been born of a virgin womb, as are we ourselves, albeit the Virgin remains a virgin—and He has been nourished with milk. It would take too long to enumerate all that God bore, taking upon Himself everything humans bear except for sin.[237] He submitted to being spat upon and slapped and beaten with a whip and mocked with

---

[237] An allusion to Heb 4:15.

robes and crowned with thorns and struck about His divine head
with a reed, and being nailed to a cross naked with criminals and
being fed with gall and vinegar. And God died and was pierced
with a spear by the soldier and was wrapped and buried and so
on. How could a *small* and *breastless* creature, upon hearing such
a tale, believe and accept it?

This may be applied to the *Theotokos* as well, hearing from the
angel, 'You will conceive' (Lk 1:31), and accepting it and bearing
Him in her womb, and so on. Truly, this is puzzling, 'a stumbling
block to the Jews and foolishness to the gentiles' (1 Cor 1:23) as
the great Apostle says. But one can only submit to the Spirit of
God, 'Who does great things and unsearchable, and marvelous
works without number' (Jb 5:9).

Not all people were able to believe concerning that, for there
was no place found in them for the Holy Spirit, who would have
shown them the impossible things as possible.[238] So it is that the
angels, who are dubious about our *small* and *breastless* nature, go
on to say, *if she be a wall, we shall build upon her silver towers. And
if she be a gate, we will create for her cedar panels.*

Now in the prologue to this book I said that there is no prophetic consistency in meaning, because this has been translated
through many languages: from Hebrew to Hellenic, and from
Hellenic to Greek[239] and Syriac, and then to Armenian. But the
gist is this: 'had she not been a human being and a living creature
created by the Creator of all, and had she been *a wall*, we could
have added to her, and we would have made the addition of
very *silver*, building a *tower*. If she had been a *gate*, we could have
created for her *cedar panels* and augmented her diminutiveness,

---

[238] An allusion to Mt 19:26, Mk 10:27.

[239] This puzzling sentence reads, 'yebrayets'wots'n i hellenats'i, ew i
hellenats'woyn i yoyn, ew yasori. ew apa i hay' [From Hebrew to Hellenic, and
from Hellenic to Greek, and to Syriac, and then to Armenian]. One suspects that
an incorporated gloss may be the source of the confusion.

so that the mass of the *wall*, or the entryway of the gate, would have become sturdier'.

Hearing this, the Bride makes bold to answer the doubting angels. As it is actually written,

The bride dares to say
8.10 *I am a wall, and my breasts are like a tower;*

That is, 'Don't be overly concerned about my weak nature, for through the power of the Almighty, I who am *small* am greater and more solid than *a wall*, and though I am breastless, *my breasts are like a tower*. For He who created heaven and earth and our nature and yours from nothing, has made me great and has made my *breasts* greater than yours. So what you cannot hear and bear and endure, my weak nature, having been made more capable than yours, has heard and borne and believed'.

Then she goes on to say,

I was in his eyes like discovered peace.

'I was lost like the piece of money and the sheep which are mentioned in the Gospel parable by my Groom (Lk 15:4-10), and I aroused war and upset between the heavenly and earthly beings because of our rebellion. Now through the Groom's Cross I have become *in His eyes* true *peace*, and have been *discovered* from my lost state'.

Again adding to his allegory, the divine Solomon says,

8.11 *Solomon had a vineyard in Beghmawon*

Beghmawon is a fertile land in Judea. By it he indicates the earth, and the human race which is in it. *Solomon* stands for Christ, who 'became our peace' (Eph 2:14), for the name Solomon is translated 'Peace'. The *vineyard* is the faithful: David the Prophet and Isaiah and the Lord Himself in the Gospel call them a vineyard.[240]

Moreover,

> *He gave his vineyard to husbandmen;*
> *each man he says shall bring of his fruit a thousand pieces*
> *of silver.*

This does not need many words of interpretation. But blessed are they who give the *fruit* in due season when the heavenly *Solomon* demands it,[241] whether it be personal *fruit*, or the *fruit* of those to whom a people has been entrusted. For whether they possess much or little grace or people or goods, spiritual and physical leaders must give account to the heavenly King *Solomon*—this includes bishops and priests, kings and princes, and other functionaries, whether physical or spiritual.

By the same token, the layman and the soldier must give account of wife and children and servants. For if he attends only to his own needs for service and sympathy and loyalty and taxes and percentages and so on, and does not exert himself to care solicitously for their spiritual and physical needs as well, he will be punished by Christ. And if he sees any faulty sin in anyone, he ought to heal it with love and tears, and apply remedies with compassion as he would to his own self, not tyrannically and with a haughty mind, inflated with the authority which he holds, whether it be spiritual or physical, whether it be over his family or his servants.

Through the prophets, the heavenly *Solomon* blames anyone who takes the fleece and milks the milk, and slaughters the fat ones, and does not take them to fertile places of pasture. This applies to anyone who does not take care of his comrade and his

---

[240] Cf. 6:1 above.
[241] An allusion to Mt 21:33-41.

servants and his brother as he does his own self, by teaching them holiness and charitable ways and humility and assiduousness in prayer, diligence in fasting and in going to the house of God and in instruction, visiting the sick and the imprisoned, going out to receive guests and to send them off, honoring the churches with gifts and offerings and vessels, and marking the dominical feasts with wakeful praises, with lighting of lamps, and gifts. In the same manner also teaching them to observe the memorials of the saints, and to honor priests as servants of God and leaders of the people of Christ, and not to serve kings and masters superficially, but from the heart, and other such principles of Christian life, which we cannot enumerate here.

God, who is referred to as *Solomon*, requires of spiritual and physical leaders, that they do what is appropriate to each, and give instruction humbly: it is for this reason that they rule us. Spiritual leaders ought to battle Satan together with us. Physical leaders ought even to spill their own blood on our behalf and to war against enemies, and to liberate us from enemies either by paying tribute or by slaying them.

In addition, they ought to judge righteously, with unceasing impartiality, as God's servants, and to consider every man's house as if it were their own. Thus King Trdat the Great, even while he was still a pagan, wrote to his country, 'As a landowner who tends his own property, so ought we to tend this land of Armenia'.[242] Thus could a pagan take such care for the prosperity of the land and for the salvation of its people that, to achieve that end, he would torture the saints in order to turn them from Christianity to the worship of idols, saying, 'The gods require it of us, and all our service to them is of no account if we are not diligent concerning this'.[243] Of Saint Gregory Trdat said, 'For fear of the gods I did not

---

[242] Agathangelos §130,136.

[243] This, too, would seem to be from Agathangelos, but I have found no counterpart to it there.

remember his great and faithful service'.[244] The Persian king also wrote to Vardan and his companions in the same vein.[245] And there were many others who did so as well, even though they had no apprehension of hell and torment and judgment.

Now, as for us, who are in a state of understanding and have believed in Christ and await His coming, and who know certainly that we have to give account of all that, as also of our personal thoughts, words and deeds, how much more should we have a care lest we stand ashamed on the terrible day before the heavenly *King Solomon*, when He requires *fruit* of His *vineyard*! They who render their *fruit* plenteously are blessed a myriad times, but woe ten thousand thousand times to those who have no *fruit* to offer up!

Now, Solomon began this disquisition with the allegory of our forefather's creation in Paradise and his fall from glory, and his resumption of glory through the coming of Christ, and the marriage to the latter of the gentiles and their encountering various and diverse graces, which we have arranged and set in this book. Now, he brings it to a conclusion with an allegory of the Bride, called the *vineyard*, and His Second Coming, and His demanding of *fruit* from the righteous, who were previously referred to as the Bride. This illustrates His exceeding love towards humankind, in that not only are we wedded and united to Christ the Groom, but we are also His food; as fit grapes in His *vineyard*, we have been laded onto serving dishes for Christ the King.

He gave his vineyard to husbandmen. The husbandmen are those whom I mentioned. To repeat, every individual is His *husbandman*.

---

[244] Agathangelos §68.

[245] Elishē, Chapter 2, gives the text of the Letter of Mihrnersēh to the Armenians, in which the Persian king outlines his obligation to 'give an account' of the Armenians before God.

Every man shall bring of his fruit a thousand pieces of silver. Now, he called it a *vineyard*, and said its fruit is *silver*; how could this be consistent? unless, as is obvious, we have to do with an allegory—which, in fact, the whole book of the Song of Songs is. So, it is the multivarious and perfect fruits of the just that he refers to as *thousands*. And he calls them *silver* because like choice silver is tried in the furnace, so also are the saints tried like *silver* here on earth and 'purified and refined sevenfold of earth' (Ps 11:7/6).

8.12 *My vineyard is before me;*

This was not so while humanity was on earth, and was below heaven, separated from it as by a curtain; rather, it is *mine*, and for me, and *before me* always. The Apostle also attests to this, saying, 'Now we see as with a mirror, in semblance, but then face to face' (1 Cor 13:12). Many other such things were also said by the saints to reassure us of this.

thousands for Solomon, and two hundred for those who keep its fruit.

Here you see the measureless love of God for humankind, concerning which the Theologian also says, 'God rejoices at nothing so much as at humanity's uprightness and salvation'.[246] That is, God does not enjoy anything so much as He does a just and holy human being. For that reason He made the heaven and the earth, and whatever is in the earth, and for that reason He Himself became human, and all the rest of it.

Now, *thousands for Solomon* He says of Himself: 'It is a greater gift and joy for Me to find an upright and fruitful human being than it is for the human being himself. The difference is as great

---

[246] *Oration* 39.20.

as that between a *thousand* and *two hundred*; *a thousand* for me, and *two hundred* for the one who has *two* natures, spirit and flesh, united in one. They are perfect to Me, Who am perfect in My godhead and My humanity'.

Perfect man was likewise perfect God, in order to transform us perfectly. For ten and one hundred and one thousand are perfect numbers. One is perfected in ten, and not before, and if one repeats the pattern, ten is the same; ten tens make a hundred, and no more. Likewise, ten hundreds make a *thousand*.[247]

Next he mentions giving wages to the *husbandmen*: not only those who *keep* themselves, but those who in their leadership capacity, whether spiritual or physical, *keep* and are true cultivators of the *vineyard*, receive wages from the Lord Jesus Christ.

The bride says
8.13 *You who sit in the garden, others hearken to you;*
make your voice audible to me.

The Groom called the Bride a *vineyard*, and others had already called her a *garden*. Repeating this same thing now, the Bride calls herself the *garden* of the Groom who requires *fruit* from the *vineyard*. What she says means this: 'You are my strength, and by your help and empowerment do I give *fruit*. Only *make audible to me Your voice* which said in the Gospel, "Come to me all you who labor and are burdened, and I will give you rest"' (Mt 11:29).

The Bride pleads, 'Only *make your voice audible to me* so that without erring I may follow after You, the Shepherd who said "My sheep hear my voice, and they follow me, and they will not go after a stranger, but will flee from him, for they do not recognize

---

[247] In addition to making a general, arithmetical statement, it may be that Gregory is describing a four-columned computation table, where the units are written in the first column, the tens in the second, and so on. Thus, 'the *ones* come to an end at ten, and not before'.

his voice"' (Jn 10:3-5). She asks that she may keep close to the *voice* of the Desired and Wished for One. Following Him without erring, she will give Him the *thousands of silver* and the *fruit* of the *vineyard*, and the produce of the *garden*.

'*Others hearken to you.* It is as if they are all awaiting You. You are the expectation of all—of heaven and earth, and all that has been created in them. This is what *others hearken to you* means. *Make your voice audible to me*, too, as it is to the angels who are nearer than we, and are illuminated by Your light; they are illuminated by You in the same way that we are illuminated by the sensible and comprehensible sun'.

> 8.14 *Fly, my Nephew, and be like the roe or like the young hart upon the mountains of spices.*

See the addition to the requests of the Bride, to hasten Him to her help. She is like the Psalmist Prophet, who said, 'Hasten to help me' (Ps 39:15), and 'Do not delay' (Ps 39:18; 69:6). And again, 'My heart fainted' (Ps 72:26), 'Hear me speedily',[248] and 'Make haste to help me Lord, of my salvation' (Ps 37:23), and others of similar nature.

Saying *Fly, and be like a roe or a young hart*, she begs Him to arrive swiftly, as in David's requests, like *a roe* and *a young hart*, who are sharp eyed and swift in coming. It also brings in something concerning the Second Coming, when the Groom will require *fruit* of all; then there will be a cry in the middle of the night, 'Behold the Bridegroom comes, go forth to meet Him' (Mt 25:6) who sees every thought and deed.

As in the imperfect metaphor of the *roe* and the *hart*, He lives on the *mountain* heights: that is, in people who, in this world, are like *mountains* in virtue, and through their virtuous way of life are

---

[248] This phrase occurs in Ps 68:18; 101:3; 137:3; 142:7.

fragrant like *mountains of spices*. There in the next world, they will *fly* up to the heavenly *mountain* with the Groom.

As the Theologian says, He will go in swiftly, after the fashion of the allegorist's words here: *Fly, my Nephew*. For *fly* means the same thing as *run swiftly*. Now, having said that He will enter in *swiftly*, he adds that some—those wedded to the Groom—will enter in with Him, while others will remain outside, prevented, 'having wasted in preparation the time when they should have been entering. Afterwards many will weep, having learned too late the penalty for sloth, when there is no more possibility of entering into the wedding chamber. They will wish many times over for that which they wickedly closed to themselves'. [249]

In another parable, they are likened to the people whom the good Father would have caused to rejoice at the Groom's good fortune, but who hesitated to come to the wedding—one for the sake of his newly wedded wife or for the sake of a yoke of oxen obtained with difficulty—thus forfeiting the greater things for the lesser (Lk 14:16-24).

Now the Theologian says, as Solomon had already written, that when the Groom *flies* or *goes swiftly* to heaven—when the One who judges sinners and invites the just, comes—taking those who are worthy to go with Him, He will enter *swiftly* like one who *flies*, and the door will be closed to sinners. 'For the time that they should have spent preparing to go, they wasted instead on useless things, worrying about the things of this world—yokes of oxen and wife and children and fields and other things which are preoccupations of the world. Later, they will weep tears in vain, having learned too late and understood their loss when it was no longer possible to mend it'.

Adding to this he says, 'For none of the scornful enters in, nor the lazy, nor the unclean, not even if one has been able to sneak

---

[249] The extended metaphor of the wedding feast and the exclusion therefrom of the foolish virgins has a parallel in Nazianzen's *Oration* 40.46.

by, here in this life, without a wedding garment, being deceived by vain hopes'.[250] He means that in this life we deceive ourselves with vain hopes, one person talking about such-and-such, and another about thus-and-so: 'For Christians there is no hell', or, 'God is merciful, who became human for our sake and suffered and died on our behalf; how could He forget His compassion, and send us to eternal fire or cast us out of the wedding chamber?' This is what it means, to 'be deceived by vain hope'.

And he goes on, 'When we shall be inside, then the Groom will recognize those whom He will teach; those souls who have gone to be near Him will be with Him—as it seems to me, He will teach them the most perfect and purest things'.[251]

Now grasp what the Theologian is saying here: everything which was said or taught to us by the Scripture, the Law and the prophets, and the Gospel—that is, Christ and the apostles and the *vardapets*—those who spoke plainly, and those who spoke in parables, were all imperfect and indirect compared to the teaching which is to come, the most perfect and the most pure things which the Groom, as *Vardapet*, will teach to the perfect in glory as perfect as the angels, and to the pure in a purity as perfect as the seraphs and cherubs.

The same Gregory the Theologian, in another place, interprets the Lord's saying, 'I shall not drink of the fruit of the vine until I drink it new with you in the kingdom of my Father' (Mt 26:29), as referring to the perfect teaching which is His to teach and ours to learn.[252]

---

[250] The editor of the Armenian text (Venice 1840) refers to *On the Baptism of Christ* and *On Pascha*. The quotation is to be found in *Oration* 40.46. The phrase about recognizing loss 'when it is impossible to mend it' is found earlier, in §24.

[251] *Oration* 40.46. The idea that the righteous will be taught in heaven seems to hark back to prophecies like that in Micah 4:2.

[252] *Oration* 40.46.

Now, it is the highest and greatest of mysteries that Solomon has allegorized by means of the Song of Songs: the entirety of Christ's coming and His death, together with His sufferings, and the resurrection and the Second Coming and the wedding of the gentiles to Christ the Groom and the illumination of the Church, and the outpouring of the Spirit's grace in prophecy and mission and teaching and martyrdom and virginity and priesthood and the ascetic life and ways of penance, and the hope of sinners and the dead, thanks to the sacrifice of Christ. Yet, in comparison with what the saints are going to learn in their state of renewal and perfection through the Groom's love, these things which were said by Solomon pale—as does everything else concerning all these miracles of God which have happened and which are going to happen, everything that has been related by the ancients and by people of more modern times, no matter how capable of speaking and teaching the Lord Jesus has made them.

Let us conclude these words of interpretation on the Song of Songs, by saying that both we who have interpreted these words and you who study them will participate in the things of which the Theologian has just reminded us, through our Lord Jesus Christ Himself, to whom be glory forever and to the eternity of eternities.

Again, ever more praise to our Lord Jesus Christ, the Giver of grace, together with the Father and the Holy Spirit, to the eternity of eternities.

Amen.

— COLOPHON —

In the Armenian date 426 (= AD 977) and in the Armenian kingdoms, I, the priest Gregory of Narek, son of Bishop Khosrov of Andzewats'ik', was constrained by the pious and Christ-crowned ruler Gurgēn, son of King Abusahl Hamazasp, to interpret the awesome words of Solomon and to explicate the deep, hidden things in them. These are enjoyable to hear, because he speaks about a groom and bride, as well as about breasts and red lips, beautiful cheeks and ravishing eyes, and about a sister and a nephew and maidens, and all the other like things that have to do with falling in love and throbbing hearts, the conjunctual union of generative love. Hearing this, people with uncomprehending minds have understood it in various terms. Consequently the ruler, out of concern for this, sent to me once, and then twice. At that point, I did not dare to demur, for I recognized that his directive was pleasing to God, and at his instruction, I explicated the Song of Songs.

Though it was through fear of disobedience, lest the royal dictate remain unfulfilled, that I took upon me a work greater than myself, it was nonetheless great audacity on my part, and worthy of criticism by all, and I might well have anticipated reproof from God as well. Yet, holding before me the royal order, I hope to be exonerated by both God and man. For it is Christ's own commandment to 'be obedient to kings as to God'.[253] God considers that whoever is obedient, is obedient to Him, and whoever is found to be disobedient, God accounts that also as disobedience

---

[253] See n. 105, above.

to Him. So I beg you, studious readers, do not heap blame on me because I have undertaken a work which was greater than my worth, for considering who was making the request, I could not well hang back. Rather, hoping in the One Holy Spirit, I reflected that He would not ignore requests made to Him. I began to seek with prayer and tears the help of Him who, looking upon my unworthiness, and upon the zealous desire of the one who had given the commission, opened my mouth to make these brief remarks,

to the glory of Christ.

Amen.

Selected Bibliography
Works in Western Languages

Bundy, David. 'Gregory of Narek as a Reader of Genesis: The Case of the *Book of Prayers*'. *Saint Nersess Theological Review* 2/2 (July 1997) 181–197.

Cowe, Peter S. 'The Impact of Time and Place on Grigor Narekaći's Theology, Spirituality and Poetics'. *Le Muséon* 108 (1995) 85–102.

Euringer, Sebastian. 'Ein unkanonischer Text des Hohenliedes (Cnt 8 15-20) in der armenischen Bibel'. *Zeitschrift für alttestamentliche Wissenschaft* 33 (1913) 272–294.

———. 'Das Nomen gentilicum der Braut im armenischen Hoheliede'. *Handēs Amsoɥrya* 41 (1927). Cols. 617–624.

Grigor Narekats'i, *Matean Oghbergut'ean*, introduction by James R. Russell. Delmar, New York: Caravan Books 1981.

Grigor Narekats'i. 'Le lettre dogmatique'. *Bazmavēp* 51 (1983) 59–64, 113–119.

Heyer, Fredrich. 'Die Glaubensaussagen der Elegien des heiligen Gregor von Narek'. In *Unser ganzes leben Christus unserm Gott Überantworten: Studien zur ostkirchlichen Spiritualität*, ed. Peter Hauptman. C. F. von Lilienfeld, 65 Geburtstag; Kirchen im Osten 17. Göttingen: Vandenhoeck & Ruprecht 1982. Pp. 183–202.

————. 'Biblische Bezüge in den 95 Elegien des Gregor von Nareg'. in *Armenia and the Bible*, ed. C. Burchard. University of Pennsylvania Armenian Texts and Studies 12. Atlanta: Scholars Press, 1993. Pp. 87–96.

Ghazinyan, A. 'The nature of Gregory of Narek's Book of Lamentation'. *Essays in Honour of Archbishop Norayr Bogharian. Revue des Études arméniennes* 18/1. Paris: 1984. Pp. 109–124.

van Lint, T. 'Grigor Narekats'i's Tagh Yarut'ean. The Throne Vision of Ezekiel in Armenian Art and Literature I'. in *Apocryphes arméniens: transmission — traduction — création — iconographie. Actes du colloque international sur la littérature apocryphe en langue arménienne* (Genève, 18–20 septembre 1997), ed. V. Calzolari Bouvier, J-D. Kaestli and B. Outtier. Lausanne: 1999. Pp. 105–127.

Mahé, J.-P. 'Echoes mythologiques et poesie dans l'oeuvre de Grigor Narekatsi'. *Revue des études arméniennes* 17 (1983) 249–278.

Mercerian, Jean. 'La vierge Marie dans la littérature médiévale de l'Arménie: Grégoire de Narek et Nerses de Lampron'. *Al-Machriq* 48 (1954) 346–379.

Mistrih, V. 'Commentario sul cantico dei cantici di Gregorio di Narek'. *Studia Orientalia Christiana Collectanea* 12 (1967) 465–534; 13 (1968/69) 199–261.

Müller, F. 'Bemerkung über Grigor Narekatsi'. *Wiener Zeitschrift für die Kunde des Morgenländes* 8 (1894) 208–210.

Papazian, Michael B. 'Faces of God in Medieval Monasticism and Theology: Anselm of Canterbury and Gregory of Narek'. *Outreach* (January–February 2004) 31–35.

Russell, James R. 'The Song of Christ's Ascension (Tagh Hambarjman) of St. Gregory of Narek'. *St. Nersess Theological Review* 2:2 (1997) 113–130.

————. 'Armenian Spirituality: Liturgical Mysticism and Chapter 33 of the Book of Lamentation of St. Grigor Narekac'i'. *Revue des études arméniennes* 26 (1996–1997) 427–439.

——. 'Grigor Narekats'i'. in *Studies in Classical Armenian Literature*, ed. J. Greppin. Delmar: 1994. Pp. 128–151.

——. 'Two Notes on Biblical Tradition and Native Epic in the "Book of Lamentations" of Grigor Narekac'i'. *Revue des études arméniennes* 22 (1990/1991) 133–145.

——. 'A poem of Grigor Narekac'i'. *Revue des études arméniennes* 19 (1985) 435–439.

Sarkissian, Chahan. 'La signification spirituelle du Commentaire de saint Grégoire de Narek sur le Cantique des cantiques'. *Saint Grégoire de Narek. Théologien et Mystique: Colloque international tenu à l'Institut Pontifical Oriental 20-22 janvier 2005* Edd. Jean-Pierre Mahé and Boghos Levon Zekiyan. Orientalia Christiana Analecta 275. Rome: Pontificio Istituto Orientale, 2006. 245–254.

St. Grigor Narekatsi; Speaking with God from the Depths of the Heart, introduction and translation by Thomas J. Samuelian. Armenia: Vem Press, 2002.

Terian, Abraham. 'Saint Gregory of Narek on the Human Nature'. *Saint Grégoire de Narek Théologien et Mystique: Colloque international tenu à l'Institut Pontifical Oriental, 20-22 janvier 2005*. Edd. Jean-Pierre Mahé and Boghos Levon Zekiyan. Orientalia Christiana Analecta 275. Rome: Pontificio Istituto Orientale, 2006, 99–111.

Thomson, Robert W. 'Grigor of Narek's Commentary on the Song of Songs'. *Journal of Theological Studies* 34 (1983) 453–496; repr. in Thomson, Robert W. *Studies in Armenian Literature and Christianity*. London: Variorum, 1994. Article 18.

Zekiyan, Boghos Levon. 'Le dinamiche dell'amore nella mistica e nella percezione metafisica di San Gregorio di Narek'. *Per una metafisica dell'amore*. Quaderni di Studi Ecumenici 10. Venice: Istituto di Studi Ecumenici, 2005. 21–42.

Index of Biblical Quotations

Lightning Source UK Ltd.
Milton Keynes UK
UKHW010641270421
382706UK00001B/92